The
Sovereignty
SOLUTION

The Sovereignty SOLUTION

A Commonsense Approach to Global Security

Anna Simons, Joe McGraw,
and Duane Lauchengco

NAVAL INSTITUTE PRESS

Annapolis, Maryland

Naval Institute Press
291 Wood Road
Annapolis, MD 21402

Library of Congress Cataloging-in-Publication Data
Simons, Anna.
  The sovereignty solution : a commonsense approach to global security / Anna Simons,
Joe McGraw, and Duane Lauchengco.
     p. cm.
  Includes bibliographical references and index.
  ISBN 978-1-61251-050-7 (hbk. : alk. paper) 1. Military policy—United States. 2.
National security—United States. 3. Sovereignty. 4. Political culture—United States. 5.
United States—Foreign relations—21st century. 6. United States—Strategic aspects. 7.
World politics—21st century—Forecasting. I. McGraw, Joe. II. Lauchengco, Duane. III.
Title.
  UA23.S5226 2011
  355'.033573--dc23

                                                                    2011025671

♾ This paper meets the requirements of ANSI/NISO z39.48-1992 (Permanence of Paper).

Printed in the United States of America

19 18 17 16 15 14 13 12 11   9 8 7 6 5 4 3 2 1
First printing

Contents

Preface

This manuscript grows out of a summerlong seminar held at the Naval Postgraduate School in 2006. One aim of the seminar was to take a small group of military officers, present them with a difficult problem, and have them help develop a paper every bit as good as anything a Washington think tank might produce. Another goal was to help demonstrate to the Department of Defense how cost-effective it can be for DOD to look within more often rather than turn to think tanks that, often, deliver little more than conventional inside-the-Beltway thinking. A third was to showcase what officers with significant operational experience are capable of when challenged to chew over something no one yet has the answer for.

I was lucky. Mr. Andrew W. Marshall, the director of the Office of Net Assessment, often described as the Pentagon's internal think tank, not only agreed to sponsor a pilot seminar of this sort and thereby give field grade military officers an opportunity to think at the grand strategic level—something no one usually asks them to do—but I had a surfeit of talent to choose from.

There was some method to how I went about picking the participants because I needed a spread in terms of military specialty, operational background, and experience. In the end, seminar participants were three Army Special Forces officers (more commonly referred to as Green Berets), two Army Civil Affairs officers, a Navy SEAL, a commander of one of the Air Force's special operations weather detachments, a former armor turned Psychological Operations officer, a military intelligence officer, and an A-10 pilot who recently served as an instructor at the Air Force's version of Top Gun. Represented in this mix was a lot of time spent in conflict zones like Kosovo, Iraq, Afghanistan, and the Philippines. We had all regions of the United States represented, spanned the Judeo-Christian gamut, and were politically diverse. Essentially, we were an American microcosm.

I am sure that no matter which ten students I had tapped in my department, which is Irregular Warfare and Special Operations–oriented, we would have produced something new and interesting. Having said that, though, not everyone (even in our small group) could participate as fully as he or she might have initially anticipated. Life intruded: childbirth, serious illness, other family complications, and imminent deployment to combat zones. In addition, everyone was involved in other classes and had other projects.

Which brings me to Joseph McGraw, Don Redd, and Duane Lauchengco: They helped develop major portions of what follows; and Joe and Duane are now willing to promote something that represents true "out-of-the-box" thinking. Could this jeopardize their careers? It certainly should not; but so prophesied one of their other professors who himself is a retired Special Forces colonel and doesn't like this strategy. Nor was he the only faculty member rattled by an early, abbreviated version of our argument published in the spring 2007 issue of *The American Interest*. What we were arguing for, my colleagues said, was too direct.

But not everyone objected. We received, and continue to receive, strong encouragement from all manner of serving officers recently returned from Afghanistan, Iraq, the Philippines, and elsewhere.

That support, already, should say something—since *they*, the men and women tasked by Washington to protect the rest of us, may be the individuals most anxious for the United States to adopt a more prudent, feasible national security strategy. Not only do individuals like my coauthors have a better sense than most about what is or is not possible at the pointiest end of the policymaking spear, but they also recognize how easy it is to criticize current ways of doing business. In fact, all the officers I teach know how to engage in blistering critiques. Yet, they also know criticism fixes nothing. It is not a remedy. I shouldn't speak for all, but I think I can speak for most of the hundreds I have taught over the past decade: the United States needs to change *something* in order to effect a significant shift in what the military is sent abroad to accomplish.

Although the three of us who have written this book believe we outline the shift the United States *should* make, we are also supremely realistic. Even if this is not the solution we think it is—even if, as a thought exercise, it only serves to spark debate—that in and of itself will mark a decisive improvement. The country desperately needs a serious debate that goes beyond the usual platitudes and bromides.

⅄   ⅄   ⅄

Two final notes: What began as a forty-minute briefing and then grew into a concept paper could easily be developed into a manuscript twice this long. I have collected stacks of news clippings, strategies, and studies several feet deep, all published since the summer of 2006. We cite many of these here and doubtless could have kept digging for more. However, this is largely a conceptual argument, and it projects more than it reflects. Our purpose is not to analyze and indict recent policy or re-analyze the roots of American foreign policy. Many scholars have already done that. We draw on their research to support our arguments, but our purpose is to push the discussion forward. For that reason, too, we have not written this in the style of a normal policy document targeted exclusively at readers in Washington.

Instead, we have written it to be read by Americans who care about the future, not all of whom reside inside the Beltway.

For those inside the Beltway, meanwhile, as well as for others curious about how we would tackle objections to our argument(s), please see our extensive notes. In the notes we highlight where we agree or disagree with others' arguments, elaborate on some of our ideas, and present additional corroborating evidence.

Finally, the usual disclaimer: the views expressed in this book do not represent those of the U.S. Army, the U.S. Navy, the Department of Defense, or any office of the U.S. Government.

—*Anna Simons*
January 2011

magine the United States by fall 2012. The country will be in the midst of its next presidential election. For months we Americans will have been subjected to nothing but negative ads. Flyers will arrive in the mail daily and callers will interrupt citizens nightly, reminding us it is our duty to reject the other party's candidates. Pundits will fan all sorts of flames, treating the election as a verdict on the Obama administration, and once again we will be divided into red and blue, CNN versus Fox, Left versus Right. Doubts first raised during the 2004 Bush–Kerry presidential election will be revisited and re-stoked, with each party accusing the other of being too weak on terror, but for radically different sets of reasons.

Even during the 2008 presidential election season one could occasionally hear news talk show hosts ask guests which party might benefit more if there were a terrorist incident before the election—a topic that would have been altogether unthinkable a decade ago.

Remember the 2000 presidential election? The country divided itself without any overriding national security concerns. Yet, by 2004 (three years after 9/11), security was considered *the* major issue, and voters split into two ferociously partisan camps. In 2008 the who-can-you-trust issue resurfaced in the Democratic primaries, as Hillary Clinton and Barack Obama volleyed this question back and forth through a series of television commercials, though perhaps most telling was vice-presidential candidate Joe Biden's prediction just before the election: "It will not be six months before the world tests Barack Obama like they did John Kennedy . . . we're gonna have an international crisis, a generated crisis, to test the mettle of this guy."

For decades, disagreements over how best to achieve security have been used by each party to mobilize its base. One consequence? The subject has become so routinely spun and counter-spun that it is hard for anyone to gauge how safe Washington has (or hasn't) made us.

But—what if terrorists *were* to strike? Say they derailed a fast train between Boston and New York: 90 dead. Or hit the Mall of America: 180 dead. Or set off a series of car bombs in San Francisco: 250 dead. Add in the detonation of a low-yield nuclear device in a midwestern city: 10,000 dead.

Chicago is burning, America. What *do* we do?

In the immediate aftermath, here is what some would do: first responders would respond magnificently—we know that. Communities from across the country would flood Chicago with help—we know that, too. At the same time, millions of Americans from all walks of life would demand immediate retaliation, regard-

1

less of whether we know who or where the culprits hailed from. Not only would the entire country be on edge—more with rage than fear—with flags unfurled and patriotism invoked, but images of 9/11 would be replayed. And the networks would visit, and revisit, and re-revisit that September morning. This time, though, unlike that day in 2001, there would be no end to the finger pointing.

Large numbers of Americans would cast about for whom to blame, and they would not just look abroad. For those on the political Right, the enemy would include the progressives who have weakened our defenses, refused to authorize decisive action against terrorist regimes, leaked national secrets to the liberal media, and fought tooth and nail to prevent the interrogation of captured terrorists and enemy combatants. For the Left, the enemy would be found in conservative circles: those who pursued a false war for false pretenses, made up intelligence in order to attack Iraq, and thereby alienated our global allies and countless millions in the process, essentially guaranteeing us future reprisals.

In such a vitriolic atmosphere, what should our national response be? Given our current national strategy, what *should* Americans expect? What should the rest of the world expect?

Who knows? This is not meant to be a facetious answer. But the truth right now is that there is no coherent plan that addresses questions like: *If* terrorists were to strike Chicago tomorrow, what would we do? When Chicago is burning whom would we target? *How* would we respond? There is nothing in place and no strategy on the horizon to either reassure the American public or warn the world: attack us, and this is what you can expect.

Truth be told, most contemporary national security strategies ignore the possibility of another calamitous attack on U.S. soil. Nor is there a contemporary strategy that examines the state of our social fabric in light of our foreign policy or our foreign policy in light of what we might all agree America should stand for. This means that the policies we do have will not only prove useless at the most crucial hour—right after impact—but worse, without offering clear guidance either to government agencies or to citizens about what we Americans should expect from government, too many of us will be left questioning whether the government has any usefulness at all.

The potential for such doubts poses a real danger. For all the attention that is accorded the need to better secure America's physical infrastructure, no one considers our latent domestic divides as a potential national security vulnerability. Yet, what better way is there for adversaries to do lasting harm to the United States than to cause us internal ruptures?

That represents one glaring hole in strategic thinking.

A second is that the United States, at this moment, is the world's most militarily powerful country—indeed, history's most powerful country. Yet, we have somehow permitted non-state actors and groups like al Qaeda to become such scourges that they increasingly determine how we wage war, not to mention how we conduct foreign policy. Leading strategists contend that we have little choice but to overhaul our military if we hope to overcome asymmetric foes in the future. But, this begs the obvious question: why should we allow others to dictate terms of *our* engagement at all?

Surely the United States has the wherewithal to turn the strategic tables on non-state actors and their state sponsors, and to wage the kind of war we want.

Don't we?

▲ ▲ ▲

Examine the range of national security strategies that ricochet around Washington: virtually none takes America's strengths as its starting point. None begins with what the United States *could* do if only we had the gumption, or what we might *have* to do should our adversaries gain more of an upper hand than they currently possess.

Examine much of what is said in policy circles: few national security strategies offer much beyond laundry lists with a lot of generic "shoulds." For instance, the United States should "work more closely with allies." But work more closely with allies to do what *specifically*? *How* specifically? With what resources? To what strategic ends?

The aim of this book is to go beyond the usual bromides. This is not another variation on a think-tank theme. What *The Sovereignty Solution* instead proposes is a strategy based on accepting certain realities about us *as* Americans—and making something *of* these. For instance, we Americans laud transparency, consistency, and dependability. We also favor the decisive application of overwhelming force. Why shouldn't we have a national security policy that builds on this foundation?

Most Americans subscribe to the principle "to each his own." Yet, we have never had a national security strategy built on the quid pro quo that says "respect our sovereignty and we will respect yours" to other countries.

Why not?

If we coauthors had to boil down our argument to an elevator speech it would probably go something like this: No more anti-American violence. Achievable, we believe, by adopting a "live and let live" philosophy with a powerful kicker: "don't violate U.S. sovereignty, or else."

Under the rubric to be outlined in these pages, the United States would put every foreign leader on notice: "if you want to be treated as the head of a sovereign state we now hold you accountable and responsible for anyone who carries your passport and/or makes use of your population to kill or injure us."

Indeed, all of the principles the Sovereignty Solution draws on should be comfortingly familiar to Americans, though how we reassemble them does represent a shift from the paradigm that those raised during or after the Cold War are used to. There are also strands to our argument—like the need for a less divisible America—that will benefit the United States regardless of whether the strategy presented in these pages strikes readers as acceptable in full. At the very least, the United States should develop several of the capabilities we describe simply so that the country can better withstand a strategic shock or weather a prolonged crisis no matter who is in political power in Washington.

⋏   ⋏   ⋏

Here is how our argument unfolds: In chapter 1 we review what strategy consisted of in the twentieth century and what makes the twenty-first century so very different. In chapter 2 we consider what makes the United States itself different, as well as what the differences among us mean for national security. We will argue that we are becoming increasingly divisible, creating a vulnerability clever adversaries can exploit.

Chapter 3 introduces sovereignty as a frame of reference for global order. We will explain what strengthening state responsibility would entail, what it would do for the United States, and what the United States would have to do in order to make it work. We will continue this discussion in chapter 4 as we describe the ways in which reinvigorating sovereignty would change how international relations are conceived and conducted. One of our recurrent themes will be that putting teeth back into accountability and responsibility would advantage the United States in myriad ways, including military ways, but only if we Americans acknowledge certain realities about twenty-first-century warfare.

In chapter 5 we will present arguments for why the United States needs to return to Declarations of War, why it is important that Americans reconsider Just War Theory, and how such a reassessment would lead to a different set of metrics for defining who should and should not be considered a combatant in future conflict. How exactly the United States might mature the American vision of war segues us directly into chapter 6, where we revisit issues of national identity and cohesiveness.

We will make the case in chapter 7 that, while a more indivisible America will certainly advantage us, the "don't tread on me—to each his own" foundation on which sovereignty rests liberates every country to set its own course with no more browbeating by the U.S. government. We will explore just how liberal an approach this really is and what a true respect for others' cultures means. Specifically, we will talk about foreign aid and assistance, and education and training. Chapter 8 broadens this discussion by reviewing sovereignty's implications for alliances and multilateral agreements. Similarly, chapter 9 considers the implications of this strategy for the application of military force.

We will offer final thoughts in a conclusion where we will also remind readers what this strategy is not. For instance, we will reiterate that reinvigorating sovereignty is not neo-isolationist and that what we are really arguing for is the application of a single golden rule, equally applicable inside and outside states, but one that does not rely on values the United States mistakenly presumes to be universal. One way to summarize such a golden rule is "nobody should do unto others what they would not want done to them," with the qualifier that in a Sovereignty Rules world the United States would not be the least bit vengeful.

Chapter 1

Global Insecurity Today

Pick any potential set of problems or open Pandora's box just a crack and, unfortunately, all sorts of catastrophes suggest themselves. There are one-thousand and one ways in which the United States can be blindsided. We humans are diabolically clever. There are also billions of us. These days it takes only a few to do significant damage. Try, then, to identify potential sources of trouble. They come in too many shapes and sizes. While it seems a stretch to suggest that U.S. security might be threatened by a butterfly flapping its wings in the Amazon, the assassination of an archduke did cause a world war once upon a time, and an overnight coup in a country like Pakistan could not only do irreversible damage to stability in South Asia—which might *feel* a world away—but if the Pakistani military lost control over even one or two nuclear weapons, Chicago could wind up as much a target as Calcutta.

That is one problem. A second is that if no one can divine what types of threats the government should most worry about, how does it properly and prudently allocate resources? The U.S. treasury is not bottomless. Yet, without some sort of plan the president and his advisors could well feel pressured to *have to* lash out in the aftermath of a truly bad event.

Talk to those who study and hope to help shape Grand Strategy one day, and many will tell you it is always preferable to be able to act with malice aforethought, and clear intent. For instance, in the wake of an attack on Chicago, or anywhere, Washington should want to immediately reassert U.S. primacy and compensate for whatever vulnerabilities had just been exposed. But at the same time, Washington would be smart to use this "occasion" to reset not just America's, but other countries' agendas. Perhaps the United States would want to make specific demands on allies (or adversaries) in order to cause *them* to have to readjust in ways that then restore our preeminence. Or, alternatively, the United States might make a dramatic move to transform a region vital to U.S. national interests.[1]

According to those steeped in Grand Strategy, grand strategists not only need to ask discomfiting questions ahead of time, but should try to figure out what opportunities to seize in order to turn something disadvantageous into an advantage. Their aim? To move the United States that much closer to securing its long-term goal of continued prosperity, which itself is a perpetually moving target given the dynamic world in which we live: "a grand strategy is not simply a reaction to a threat. It is a pro-active posture, designed to seize the initiative and shape the international environment to the state's advantage."[2]

For instance, say Chicago really was burning after the detonation of a low-yield nuclear device. Without question, grand strategists would want government to douse the fires, aid the victims, monitor levels of irradiation, and do everything else most of us would want it to do, including identify and target the perpetrators. But why not also do something dramatic about weapons of mass destruction (WMD) in light of the horrors the world just witnessed? Maybe the United States should demand a worldwide ban on all nuclear weapons and proof of compliance. Or, maybe the United States would be better served by targeting rogue proliferators.

According to students and practitioners of Grand Strategy, it is critically important not only to stay poised to snatch opportunity from the jaws of seeming defeat, but to contemplate what, in advance, might seem to be politically unacceptable courses of action. Not only do times change, but—through disaster, the thinking goes—times *can* be changed. "You never want a serious crisis to go to waste. . . . What I mean by that is that it's an opportunity to do things you could not do before."[3]

Often people associate Grand Strategy with chess. If, for instance, it looks like country X will be a rival in the near future, better for the United States to check country X's ambitions now and best to do it indirectly. Grand strategists might then suggest things the United States could be doing already to affect country Y with whom country X has critical trade ties. The aim with such maneuvers is to think several moves ahead and position oneself accordingly.[4]

The business world offers grand strategists additional lessons. Some of the takeaways from business are as follows: try to affect how the other side spends money. Make your adversaries think you are going to do something you are not planning to do. Reinforce their fears.[5] According to conventional wisdom this is how the United States won the Cold War; we strategically misled the former Soviet Union via our defense spending and encouraged the Soviets to misallocate their resources in some areas while we blatantly outspent them in others.

Those who think in terms of Grand Strategy clearly believe that to be good at Grand Strategy means to be wily. The watchwords are "Be clever." Think in terms of second- and third-order effects.

But, unfortunately, thinking you are smarter than your adversary and thus can outsmart him does not always deliver success. Expedience, expense, efficiency, and effectiveness can all be hard to gauge, particularly when they start to bleed into one another, which they invariably do. It is easy for an idea to seem clever. One now-classic example is the Iran-Contra affair—the 1980s episode in which arms were sold to Iranian revolutionaries in order to free Americans seized in Lebanon, while the proceeds from the arms sales went "to anti-Sandinista rebels in Nicaragua to circumvent a ban on funding for them imposed by Congress." Who could have thought up such a cockamamie scheme? "[CIA director William] Casey must have felt like the master of a magnificent game, *until it all went wrong.*"[6]

To this day there are many in Washington who believe the most prudent thing the United States can do to save American lives and dollars abroad is to work through proxies to include proxy heads of state. But, how wise does "using" others ever turn out to be? Often the United States forgets that people we regard as our patsies have their own reasons to work with us and are using us as much as we use them.[7] This may be especially true when it comes to foreign leaders. "This is the U.S. commitment trap. Committed to the survival of allies but lacking the leverage to discipline recalcitrant regime leaders, America creates a strategic vulnerability that even weak client states can exploit. The commitment trap reduces America's credibility as a reform advocate. It binds the United States so that America cannot walk away from allies without eroding its credibility. Curiously, this trap isn't sealed abroad but at home."[8]

For a vivid example take Ngo Dinh Diem, the president of South Vietnam (1955–63): "At first Diem demonstrated a heartening degree of courage and understanding, but gradually, like most of our allies in the underdeveloped world" he slipped out of our control.[9] One could add a host of other names to such a list: the Shah (Iran), Mobutu Sese Seko (Zaire), and Ferdinand Marcos (the Philippines).[10]

In hindsight, it is easy to conclude that the United States has periodically erred. But perhaps given the specter of mutually assured destruction, such transgressions should be forgiven. After all, checkmating the Soviet Union was clearly American policymakers' paramount concern during the Cold War. Or, as former National Security advisor Zbigniew Brzezinski is said to have put it as recently as 1998, "What is most important in the history of the world? The Taliban or the collapse of the Soviet Empire? Some stirred-up Muslims or the liberation of Central Europe and the end of the Cold War?"[11]

Clearly neither Brzezinski nor his advisors envisioned what blowback from a bunch of seemingly unsophisticated Afghans and Arabs might amount to more than a decade after the CIA first started arming the mujahidin in Afghanistan.[12] However, to have been asserting this still in 1998—only three years prior to 9/11 and five years after the first attack on the World Trade Center towers—points to the very real dangers whenever individuals believe they have taken all relevant second- and third-order effects into account.

Numerous Cold Warriors remain convinced that the United States faced a far greater menace from the Soviet Union than we do today from al Qaeda and other Islamist groups. And maybe they are correct. However, prudence suggests that we might want to suspend that judgment, at least until the Islamist threat is well and truly behind us. In fact, recent history suggests that whenever policymakers believe they are capable of (a) taking into account all second- and third-order effects worthy of consideration, or (b) playing various games of multidimensional global chess against multiple opponents at once, they tend to reveal how much they *don't* know. At the same time, even when policymakers *are* cross-culturally astute and recognize that people who seem technologically unsophisticated can still be formidable foes, it is not clear that banking on others to do our fighting for us is ever worth the risk.

Consider Israel: Israel went out of its way to help support Hamas when Hamas was in its infancy, in order to create competition for Fatah and the PLO. Looking back now, would Israelis consider this a wise decision?[13] Beyond what should be the obvious lesson—the enemy of your enemy won't necessarily remain your friend—looms Mary Shelley's Frankenstein allegory: be midwife to forces you can't control and at some point you'll be sorry.[14]

Or, consider just one other example of what seemed like a smart move at the time: It wasn't long after World War II when Washington policymakers "imagined the United States with a little hourglass full of oil, rapidly running out. Estimating that the country had enough oil to go it alone for just two years in a protracted war with the Soviet Union, they began to pursue a deliberate strategy of importing oil from Middle Eastern countries to make our oil supplies last longer and to flood Middle Eastern kingdoms with cash to keep the Soviets at bay."[15]

Who, at the time, foresaw where *this* might lead?

The Grand Strategic Imperative—"Align Ends, Ways, and Means"

The approach we offer in this book does not require that Washington play chess with other countries or use proxies to try to achieve our grand strategic ends for us. In fact, by taking a commonsense approach to the Grand Strategic imperative, "align ends, ways, and means," the United States would eschew all such gamesmanship or sleight of hand.

According to the Grand Strategic imperative, "align ends, ways, and means," a country and its policymakers should relate ends to means, intentions to capabilities, and objectives to resources.[16] Translate this into everyday language and it tells policymakers, don't overspend, don't oversell, don't overreach, and constantly reassess. Or, as John Lewis Gaddis has put it more recently, "grand strategy is the calculated relationship of means to large ends. It's about how one uses whatever one has to get to wherever it is one wants to go."[17] Or, as Jeremi Suri intones, "Grand strategy is the wisdom to make power serve useful purposes."[18]

Some who write about strategy emphasize constraints: "Strategy is the art of connecting aspirations with prudent plans and finite resources."[19] Or, they warn, "fundamentally, strategy is about setting priorities and making choices between competing alternatives under conditions of limited resources."[20] Political ends and military means have to match.[21] Citing Bernard Brodie, Richard Betts describes the essence of the challenge this way: "The question that matters in strategy is: Will the idea work?"[22]

What, meanwhile, helps to determine whether an idea might work? For starters, it behooves anyone thinking about devising strategy to remember President Eisenhower's admonition from the start of the Cold War: "we must not destroy what we are attempting to defend."[23] What Eisenhower meant when he said this was that the means should never overpower the ends and that the United States should never permit security to trump liberty. Yes, the instruments of power should always be readjusted to take advantage of new technologies, but not if these subvert the larger purpose, which is to preserve the American way of life.

The "American way of life"—that, too, is something everyone pays homage to, but few actually define. In Eisenhower's day the American way of life was probably best described as "freedom of choice for individuals, democratic procedures for government, and private enterprise for the economy";[24] no different—really— from what distinguishes the American way of life today.[25] In fact, this continuity between what mattered to Eisenhower and what constitutes the American way of life more than fifty years later should be telling on at least two counts. First, it suggests that certain core values still hold. Second, we Americans would not be who or where we are today if these values had not already proven their worth.

Of course, one glaring difference between Eisenhower's era and ours lies in who and what we Americans are defending our freedoms, procedures, and enterprise from. Eisenhower's foes were first the Nazis, then the Soviets. Today, if you visit any American war college or the Naval Postgraduate School in Monterey, California, military officers from Eastern Europe sit side by side with American officers—*that* is how much the world has changed. During the Cold War all Americans in uniform understood that the United States faced a singular superpowerful adversary. Since then, though, who is our rival? For every three officers who suspect China, at least three shake their heads "no." Indeed, some worry that the more talk there is of China posing a threat, the more self-fulfilling a prophecy this will become—all of which underscores the larger point: when it comes to whom or what most threatens our national existence, there is no consensus.

For the first time in recorded history, the world's dominant power lacks a clearly identifiable competitor. Greece had Persia, Rome had Carthage, Spain had England, and England had France and then Germany (twice). Just glancing back over the sweep of military history, it is clear that dominant countries, including the United States during the Cold War, have always known who to monitor and what to pay attention to. Rivalry—not paranoia—has helped contour strategy.[26] At the moment, with no clear singular rival, the United States is left with no choice but to try to hedge its bets.

This represents Major Challenge #1: Who and what to focus on—states or non-state actors? Near peer competitors or superempowered individuals?[27]

Major Challenge #2 is that the non-peer adversaries we do have—self-ascribed Islamists—are much more familiar with us and with how America works than we are with them. Actually, this challenge is likely to be true of any adversary from this point forward. In some ways, others' familiarity with us is the ultimate proof of our success as a country: the United States has become so dominant that it has led others to study us far more than we study them. But also, because we are so eager for people to adopt our practices, buy our goods, and to like (if not admire) us, we Americans endlessly self-promote. That is not a criticism. For sound ideological reasons we are happy to make ourselves understood and we are as close to having rendered this society an open book as any that has ever existed.

Unfortunately, however, this openness leads to Major Challenge #3: we are riddled with soft targets. Israelis may be accustomed to reporting any unattended package in any public space, but we are not. No doubt we Americans could change our behavior fairly rapidly in the wake of a string of subway bombings or mall attacks, but it would still be easy for a small number of dedicated terrorists to have a paralyzing effect—as did the Beltway snipers John Allen Muhammad and John Lee Malvo in the Washington, DC, area in 2002. Worse, as Bruce Hoffman points out, "terrorism surfaces spasmodically, and this is why it affects us so profoundly psychologically; it is not a continual threat."[28] Our guard goes up; our guard goes down. Only nine years prior to Washington, DC, snipers Muhammad and Malvo turning their car into a shooting platform, Mir Aimal Kasi shot five employees in a somewhat similar fashion outside CIA headquarters in Langley, Virginia.

Despite the now-common argument that no country can wage war against a tactic—which is what many, but not all terrorism experts claim terrorism to be—such an objection actually masks an uglier truth about the challenges involved in combating those who willfully seek to shock us. Watch footage of the Palestinian attack on Israeli athletes at the 1972 Munich Olympics; it is amazing how bumbling and amateurish the terrorists look.[29] Terrorists have grown exponentially more sophisticated since television first captured their efforts live over three decades ago. "Back then" terrorism as theater was a clear work in progress. Today we sit much closer to the other end of the learning curve. Or, as Martin Van Creveld notes of Israel's counterterrorism efforts: "seldom have so many, fighting so few, achieved so little at such cost."[30] What provokes him to make this comment are the "hidden" costs Israelis pay to field armies of private security guards, in addition to state-run military, intelligence, and police services.

Among terrorist tactics, suicide bombers represent the ultimate precision-guided weapons, as useful for targeting key individuals (whether the prime minister of India or the Northern Alliance's most promising leader in Afghanistan) as turning randomness itself into a terror multiplier. Worse, the potential number and range of targets they can strike remain endless. By fall 2010 more than 1,400 people had blown themselves up in Iraq alone (with hundreds more setting themselves off in Afghanistan, Pakistan, and Somalia), acts that suggest how unlikely we are to ever put this genie back in the bottle.[31] More sobering still is that, in the past nationalists or ideologues made use of terrorism to prove authorities bankrupt or to force them to have to negotiate.[32] Now, in contrast, in a cosmic struggle between good and evil in which some on both sides believe those confronting them epitomize evil, destruction—not conquest or conversion—has become sufficient as a cause unto itself. In fact, purging the world of evil may represent the highest possible good as far as numerous true believers are concerned, and we are up against at least some true believers these days.

Combine this drive to destroy America, then, with our adversaries having an easier time learning about us than we do fathoming them and *then* factor in Major Challenge #4—globalization makes it infinitely easier to destroy than to control: even if we succeed in dismantling al Qaeda and rooting out all of its progeny, we will still have done nothing to prevent future adversaries from being able to up the ante of destructiveness. Thanks to the widespread availability and miniaturization of the means of destruction, as well as the easy transferability of tactics, techniques, and procedures—spread as much by the media and Hollywood as by bad guys communicating among themselves—Pandora's box has been flung wide open.

Why Should *They* Call the Shots?

Without question, the United States remains militarily dominant in space, under-water, on the seas, and in the air.[33] This dominance represents an unparalleled historical feat; it is astounding actually. It guarantees us huge military advantages. Yet, what is missing from the list of domains we can control are two we can't: people and information, arguably the two most important domains of the twenty-first century.

Ironically, we Americans not only pioneered two of the greatest forces for lib-eration the world has ever known—self-rule and free speech—but it was Americans who also invented the tools to speed up their reach. Just think about what television and the Internet have wrought and what the digital revolution increasingly enables: global dissemination of real-time images shot by people armed with nothing more than cell phones. President Eisenhower and his generation never had anything like this to contend with. Thus, who might target the United States, how, to what ends, and with what media effects becomes a forecaster's nightmare. Indeed, as Francis Fukuyama summarizes at the end of *Blindside*—an inside-the-Beltway effort to bring together a group of very smart people to think about strategic surprise—"We can predict with certainty that we will be surprised; we can and do anticipate an array of catastrophic future events. Unfortunately . . . we can also predict with certainty that when they come, we will be inadequately prepared."[34]

Without being sure what to prepare for, those who think about strategic sur-prise for a living gravitate toward examining current trends and extrapolating from those they consider most robust. They favor demography, for instance, because, they contend, a population that is aging or not replacing itself quickly enough is not something countries can readily reverse. Similarly, even if new sources or substitutes for critical substances like oil or water are discovered, it will take time to develop them—so, if we examine resource distribution, that should point us toward likely flashpoints.

Another approach futurists use when thinking about what should be put in place today, in order for the United States to have the right force structure and offensive and defensive capabilities tomorrow, is to construct scenarios that impel decision makers to think through alternative futures. The rationale behind doing this is that "once we identify critical risks, we can create 'hedges' or 'strategic options' that will facilitate rapid course adjustments, should the United States mili-tary find itself in a substantially different competitive environment" fifteen, twenty, or even thirty years hence.[35]

Yet, even when such scenarios are constructed with the most solid story lines money can buy, they still rest on projected trends that, in turn, depend on assumed facts. Plus, as Colin Gray cautions, "trends move together, and even if you think you can identify them you are likely to generate misestimates."[36] For instance, take HIV: No one predicted a disease spread primarily by adults engaging in unpro-tected sex would lead to an AIDS epidemic in Africa that has resulted in orphans raising orphans, and community after community of subsistence farmers stripped of their most able-bodied members. Most viruses devastate the very young and the very old, not the strongest members of society. So, not only can AIDS itself be considered to have been an "unknown unknown" (it was only isolated and identi-fied after it had begun its deadly spread), but even if epidemiologists had accurately forecast the appearance of such a devastating retrovirus, they likely still would have gotten its target population wrong. Nor is there any way to know, to this day, what Africa's "new" demography portends for the future, especially since certain sub-regions (like Southern Africa) have been harder hit than others: Will AIDS make resource competition more or less likely? Could this make China's interest in Africa more or less mercenary? One can spin out scenario after scenario.

One other problem with using scenarios as a window into the future is that certain things always have to be held constant in order to make them work. And, in most scenarios the same things tend to be held constant. This means scenarios take for granted features like our military dominance, never mind our military dominance thanks to our superiority in conventional weaponry. Ironically, we tend to gravitate so quickly to the new and different capabilities we think we should develop that we deflect ourselves from considering what more might be made of advantages we already possess—like our conventional warfare edge.[37]

Here, for example, is one version of a current dominant vision of our future: "By 2025, the international system will be a *global multipolar one* with gaps in national power continuing to narrow between developed and developing countries. . . . Although the United States is likely to remain the single most powerful actor, the United States' relative strength—even in the military realm—will decline and US leverage will become more constrained."[38]

Pushing this assessment even further: "Transnational networks and forces of disorder are seriously redrawing the maps of the world—and the lines that demarcate nation-states are becoming increasingly notional, if not wholly fictional. At the same time power and authority are moving away from states to other actors."[39]

Consequently, "future military operations will likely differ from those in the past in a number of ways. They will be more fluid and more complex, the pace of operations will be higher, the importance of non-kinetic tools will increase, the operating space will be closer to centers of population, and the need for information will expand exponentially."[40]

To contend with such "realities," we therefore "need to achieve better balance between the military and nonmilitary elements of US national power, and to balance expensive but rarely needed capabilities for conventional war-fighting with cheap but frequently needed capabilities for stabilization, reconstruction, and unconventional warfare operations."[41]

The message in all of these prognostications? The U.S. security apparatus had better be overhauled—*now.*

In the last of the four passages cited above, David Kilcullen's advice is meant for the Long War against al Qaeda and Islamic extremism, or the global counter-insurgency as he calls it. But elsewhere in his book *The Accidental Guerrilla*, he is broader and blunter: "events since 9/11 have exposed the limits of the utility of force as an international security tool."[42] Kilcullen is hardly alone in this assessment. Others, too, see a future full of more irregular warfare, hybrid warfare, and "non-military means of warfare, such as cyber, economic, resource, psychological, and information-based forms of conflict."[43] Or, as Paul Bracken summarizes, drawing on lessons learned from the 2006 war between Hezbollah and Israel, "Hezbollah used technology to match its tactics, knowing that if it took on Israel in a direct, head-to-head war with conventional forces, it would not stand a chance. This is all very suggestive of what other countries are going to do when they look at the United States. Fighting the United States with advanced conventional forces is suicide. Fighting in other ways is not."[44]

Consequently, many believe that to beat asymmetric adversaries we had better become more like them ourselves: stealthier, more networked, with flatter hierarchies, and a smaller footprint (otherwise, we will create too many accidental guerrillas or we won't be able to dry up the seas in which extremists swim); while, to be more effective than our adversaries we had also better do our best to secure locals' trust and confidence, which in turn means working for (and with) locals to secure their neighborhoods.

But, wait. Is this *really* what American servicemen and women should be doing abroad: providing local services *to* local populations? That is one question this book will return to.

A second question has to do with *whose* twenty-first-century lessons we should be learning. Israel's encounters with Hezbollah and Hamas remain works in progress, as do our own incursions into Afghanistan and Iraq.[45] For instance, even if Iraq continues to go well, it will still have cost us the better part of a decade and over four thousand American war dead, while if things do improve sufficiently and most troops come home by 2012 *and* Iraq stays intact, that will only make it all the less likely anyone will question why the United States, with the most powerful military on the planet, found itself having to learn *any* lessons the hard way at all.

Many Americans no doubt hope that, once the United States has extricated itself from Iraq and then Afghanistan, we won't commit to this kind of warfare or to such "stabilization" exercises again. But in other quarters, closer to the heart of policymaking, there is the opposite view—we just must intervene in failed or fragile states sooner, in order to *prevent* them from becoming the next terrorist heartlands: "the United States needs to enhance its capacity to prevent state failure and deal with its consequences. This will require building and maintaining a larger military, one with greater capacity to deal with the sort of threats faced in Afghanistan and Iraq. In addition, it will mean establishing a civilian counterpart to the military reserves that would provide a pool of human talent to assist with basic nation-building tasks. Continuing economic and military assistance will be vital in helping weak states meet their responsibilities to their citizens and their neighbors."[46]

Inherent in such thinking is that future interventions will just have to be executed more smartly using smarter power. Yet, as one advocate of smart power himself acknowledges, "intervention, ranging from military advising and training to counterinsurgency and stability operations, is often inconclusive"—it "does not play to America's strengths . . . and yet," he continues in the same sentence, "it is likely to remain a fixture of the future international security environment."[47]

Why?

Why would any strategist want to base policy on something he or she already senses won't work? Why would anyone in Washington want us to adjust ourselves to asymmetries that advantage adversaries and disadvantage us? Or, to be really pointed about the questions that should stop all Americans dead in their tracks: why should *we* accede to anything adversaries might want us to do? Why should we allow *them* to determine anything? Shouldn't *we* be the ones to shape the environment to *our* advantage? Indeed, what kind of American would ever accept the verdict that others *give us no choice*?

Playing to Strength

There are certain things the United States is militarily capable of, but does not do— and then there are things it is not very good at, but tries to accomplish anyway. For instance, have we been effective at rooting out all of al Qaeda's leaders? Clearly not. But flatten Kandahar? That we could have done.

To return to the example of Israel in the summer of 2006: Israel had six years to prepare for a war with Hezbollah in southern Lebanon. Why did it fail so miserably? Clearly, Hezbollah made use of those six years to turn certain villages into killing grounds for Israeli forces. So, why did Israel allow itself to get suck(er)ed in? Why was its reaction to Hezbollah's rain of rockets so timid and its responses so incrementalist? Why didn't Israel strike back harder at the outset? Why didn't the Israelis issue an ultimatum and then level a Hezbollah village or two?[48]

Unfortunately, once you start to question why well-armed states don't leverage their strengths this way, you have ventured deep into politically unthinkable territory.

Who dares talk about this stuff? In no strategy under consideration in Washington does anyone seriously suggest flattening a village. That is not a twenty-first-century option. It is a technique barbarians like Genghis Khan or Tamerlane used. Never mind that all successful imperial powers employed overwhelming force to deter rebellion. Not even the most ardent neo-imperialists today dare publicly advocate such methods.[49] None comes close to arguing that the United States should engage in such behavior. The overriding concern, instead, is that America always secure the global moral high ground, go out of its way to prevent casualties, and do its best to court if not actively cultivate world opinion.

However, read through enough white papers on foreign policy and national strategy and something else they convey, regardless of the authors' political bent, is the general sentiment that the United States must remain a dominant player, even if not the world's predominant hegemon. Yet, no one really explains how the United States might dominate without being domineering. There are prescriptions aplenty about how the United States *should,* for instance, work with partners and help rebuild failed states. But dig beneath the platitudes and there is no agreement about how exactly we might accomplish even these goals, let alone what the terms of our partnering should be, who we should count on to do what in the global division of labor, or what precisely that labor should entail.

▲   ▲   ▲

In contrast, this book argues that we should eschew most of these *should*s. After all, if policymakers can't know for sure what the future holds, how much sense does it make to try to calculate what we *should* do, especially when we already know we will be surprised by whatever it is we haven't considered?[50] This is the blindside issue. Our argument: why not instead consider a series of "if . . . thens": *If* the United States more effectively monitored trends, movements, and rumblings abroad, *then* that would mitigate the likelihood of surprise. *If* America were to get hit despite this but citizens were prepared to absorb the blow, *then* the surprise wouldn't paralyze us. *If* the United States had a series of counterresponses prepared in advance, *then* no enemy could gain from our misfortune. *If,* meanwhile, the U.S. government advertised its preparations ahead of time, *then* who would want to bother attacking us at all?[51]

This, we will argue, is one way to address the compound problem of not knowing who might target us, when, how, where, why, or with what.[52] Corollary to this, of course, is that we Americans also pay closer attention to what makes us vulnerable. Without question, American policymakers need to rethink how the United States wields the sword. But hardening the shield is no less important.

Chapter 2

Divisible America

You're a clever non-state actor. You don't have interballistic missiles or even your own air force. You can't beat the United States in any sort of military slugfest. And economically, you can't torpedo us without hurting yourself and disabling your ability to move funds. So, what might you do? You're patient. And being non-Western, you don't just focus on immediate gratification. If change doesn't come in your lifetime, what does it matter? You're willing to expend your life and your children's lives in order to transcend us.

Alternatively, you're a state. Your economy is too entangled with ours to make a run on the dollar worthwhile. We out-produce you in high-tech weaponry. We can outfly you, outshoot you, and obliterate you were it ever to come to that. So, fighting us militarily or financially—conventionally or directly—makes no sense.

You take a close look at what's occurring in Iraq and Afghanistan, who's in bed with whom, and whom you would like to see benefit in the short term. You think: Iran.

Is there any country more ideally suited to make trouble for the United States than Iran? Iran borders both Afghanistan and Iraq. Encourage Iran and you encourage Shi'a Islam, while the more triumphant Iran's version of Islam proves to be, the more this should stir fears westward in Saudi Arabia, throughout the Gulf, and beyond. Likewise, the more things get confused in Afghanistan, the more this should heighten tensions in the United States' erstwhile ally, Pakistan. Of course, it doesn't hurt that the United States and Iran already have such a troubled relationship, given the United States' historic support for the Shah, followed by the hostage crisis when fifty-two embassy employees were held for 444 days in the late 1970s.

So—you think to yourself—by helping Iran just a little bit who knows how fast the benefits might accrue? Maybe you can bait the United States into invading. Alternatively, by continuing to bleed the United States in Iraq or Afghanistan, or, ideally both, you could help force America into another humiliating retreat . . .

Because the United States cannot be destroyed directly, any intelligent adversary would want to undermine us indirectly. And miring us in untenable foreign entanglements would be one way to do so. Indeed, challenge and stymie the United States over an extended period of time, and you should be able to fuel all sorts of domestic rancor.

Who might think along these lines? *Adversarial* grand strategists might.

From an adversary's point of view, what could be easier, or more frugal, than to divide Americans over foreign policy. Rewind American history and isn't this exactly the kind of Grand Strategy a clever adversary *should* engage in?[1]

⋏ ⋏ ⋏

Some experts argue that America's chief vulnerabilities are its unprotected infrastructure, lax port and border security, and over-dependence on foreign oil. Others see greater dangers in just how big and unwieldy government has become and how inefficiently information flows, so that one law enforcement agency over here has no idea what has been filed away in someone else's office over there. No question, all such gaps endanger us. But one reason they do so is because, *if* they are successfully exploited, we can be attacked again.

It is the "we" in the previous sentence that is critically important. "We the people" represent the ultimate target. Toppling buildings and blowing up airplanes is just a means to that end. It is *us* who adversaries want to demolish. Therefore, one of the United States' most pressing national security concerns should be how we can harden ourselves. How do we make "we the people" so resilient and indivisible that, should an adversary be foolish enough to attack us, that adversary will do this country no lasting harm?[2]

The fact that answering these questions is not already considered a pressing national security concern suggests that too few people recognize the very real vulnerability domestic divisibility represents.[3]

One premise of this book is that we Americans are already more divided than most of us might care to imagine, although not necessarily in the ways that some might believe. Yes, we belong to different classes and hail from different regions. We come at problems with differing levels of education. Race and ethnicity make for historically tense differences, and biases and disparities still limit who has access to opportunity. A clever adversary or set of adversaries might well try to exploit any of these latent tensions, and this is hardly an exhaustive list. But—how would they do so?

In many regards, deep-seated differences over foreign policy will always be the smartest wedge for outsiders to hit. Foreign policy is not only the realm non-Americans have easiest access to, but the realm Americans have the least hands-on experience with. Also, foreign policy increasingly maps on to moral, political, and religious divides, which are far more congruent with each other than are race, class, and ethnicity. The latter three may be divides journalists, politicians, and social science academics continue to fixate on. But our internal dynamics have shifted.

Proof of this comes in one hugely important but under-remarked fact: in much of the world, and in very young countries especially, the same historic divides still divide people. Yet, even if push came to shove in the United States, we would never re-fight our one and only Civil War. We couldn't. Even if slavery were revived, which is what it would essentially take for us to redraw the battle lines, too much else has changed since the 1860s. Cotton is farmed totally differently; descendants of Yankees, Rebels, and slaves live all over the country; regionally we have become astonishingly intermixed.

Not only does race no longer legally pigeonhole Americans, but class is not permanent. The majority of those below the poverty line in any given year do not stay there, while not even the majority of those who are unemployed remain permanently unemployed.[4] One can still find inequities, but the fact that both major political parties draw from all strata demonstrates that something beyond race, class, or ethnicity must be motivating Americans politically—something like ideology.

Significantly, both political parties are said to be less ideologically diverse than they were twenty years ago, while ideological differences that do exist between them have grown increasingly more pronounced.[5] "The great majority of voters now fuse their party identification, ideology and decisions in the voting booth. . . . More strikingly," William Galston and Pietro Nivola go on to note, "political polarization has become akin to political segregation. You are less likely to live near someone whose politics differ from your own."[6] For all its potential downsides, one thing our ability to self-sort reveals is choice. Individual choice—that we have the ability to choose whom we consort with and how we want to be identified—speaks volumes about what identity means in the United States. And this, too, makes us distinctive from most people elsewhere.

For instance, ask a roomful of former Yugoslavs what they think their most salient domestic divide might be and they would all likely answer "religion."[7] It was religious divisibility into Catholic Croat, Orthodox Serb, and Muslim Bosnia that greased Yugoslavia's slide to dissolution in the 1990s. Numerous Arabs and Africans would answer the "what divides you?" question with "lineage," "clan," or "tribe." Hundreds of millions of Indians would likely cite religion and, if they are Hindu, many, many millions would point to caste. And so it goes around the world. In contrast, we Americans would likely loudly disagree with one another about which of our identities matters or could be made to matter most. For some of us, race or ethnicity remains paramount; or class and occupation matter. For others, something so personally salient, but demographically negligible, as sexual preference overrides everything else. Flip this around and our very lack of uniformity speaks volumes. It says something very healthy about us. Ask what defines us as a people and our lack of consensus indicates we really do privilege choice.

Nor is it a coincidence that the United States is one of the few countries where it is possible to become a citizen in good standing without being born here or being born to American parents. That, too, means *being* American is not a function of some immutable trait. Instead, as Samuel Huntington pointed out in his history of who we are, we started as a settler society and our foundation is grounded in a unique set of values.[8] The fact that we then evolved into an immigrant society over time, drawing people in from all over, just further demonstrates how relevant the Founding Fathers' values remain. Follow this thread and it suggests that what unites and defines us as Americans must still be our collective commitment to the founders' ideals. Otherwise, without that commitment, and without our willingness to abide by overarching laws that protect us *as* individuals, we would be much more like any other country and eminently divisible along classically sectarian lines.

The downside to this uniqueness, of course, is that when we Americans do disagree with one another over how far and to whom to extend our values—or, worse, when we question whether our ideals should even remain our ideals—we have little left to hold us together at all. This is why it is worth spending at least a few pages examining divisibility *as* a national security issue.

Right and Left

Although political analysts might have a hard time determining whether today's "culture wars" are real or a figment of media sensationalism, one thing most would likely agree on is that the United States underwent a series of profound changes in the 1960s thanks in part to, or in concert with, a youth rebellion: "When you added civil rights, the Vietnam War, feminism, the plight of farm workers, a new environmentalism, a deepening animus toward materialism and corporate power, and a 'credibility gap' between young and old, you could easily make a damning case against adult authority. No previous generation had been served up a richer menu of social and moral 'contradictions' and 'hypocrisies' with which to hammer away at the moral authority of adult American society."[9] One legacy of shredding that old morality: to this day, no one has proved able to replace it with anything else. Thus, as far as many on the political Right are concerned, the country continues to flounder, while nowhere do they see this more acutely than when looking at our schools.

That education *has* a purpose and that a country uses the education of its citizens to accomplish that purpose would not have been contentious one hundred years ago when the very aim of public schooling was to create a more literate, responsible, better-informed citizenry. This aim was not just part of, but integral to, the West's "civilizing mission"—a mission that was thought to be foundational until it was called into question by those who believed that "America was founded on a genocide.... This is a passionately racist country.... The truth is that Mozart, Pascal . . . Algebra, Shakespeare, parliamentary government, baroque churches, Newton, the emancipation of women, Kant, Marx, and Balanchine ballets won't redeem what this particular civilization has wrought upon the world."[10] So much for Western advancement. Though, of course, one problem with jettisoning the idea of Western progress is that once you decide that no one system of thinking or living should be considered more advanced, better, or preferable to another, there is nothing coherent to strive for. And though the attitude "anything goes" might be exactly the philosophy those on the Left prefer, such relativism flies in the face of everything those on the Right believe in. For most on the Right, there *are* immutable truths. There are also definite rights and wrongs. Their religious convictions back them up on this.

These are the kinds of divides out of which enmity and incivility are built in America today.

Today, at all levels of government, those on the Right see religion routinely and legally discriminated against. Put aside for a moment whether or not you think these views are justified. Tens of millions of Americans believe they are. From their perspective, faith is zero-sum: You are either for faith-based practices or you are against them; you are either pro- or anti-religion.

It should not take looking into a crystal ball to see that the more religion can be used to incite and inflame people politically, the more useful it becomes to politicians, and the more partisan a topic that makes it. What torques this further is that our current Islamist adversaries are bent on invoking their religion at every turn, which renders faith both a foreign policy issue *and* a domestic concern. To conservatives, liberals' attempts to increasingly marginalize faith and secularize the country endanger us in profound ways, whereas for liberals, faith-based initiatives raise the specter of fascism and a theocratic, nonpluralist state. Throw in the role of the media as "fight organizer," and mutual suspicions only build.

Like many other institutions, the media, too, experienced a sea change beginning in the 1960s. Thanks in part to reporters' role in the Vietnam War, followed by the celebrification of journalists after Watergate, lines have increasingly blurred between objective reporting and news analysis, and analysis and editorializing.

> As one journalist has remarked about the change in his profession, "We don't deal in facts [any longer], but in attributed opinions." Or, these days, in unattributed opinions. And those opinions are more intensely rivalrous than was once the case. The result is that, through commercial as well as ideological self-interest, the media contribute heavily to polarization.[11]

To quote Bill Keller, the executive editor of the *New York Times*: "It is probably fair to say that the cacophony of today's media—in which rumor and invective often outpace truth-testing, in which shouting heads drown out sober reflection, in which it is possible for people to feel fully informed without ever encountering an opinion that contradicts their prejudices—plays some role in the polarizing of our politics, the dysfunction of our political system and the increased cynicism of the American electorate."[12]

Some role?

One consequence of there being so many media outlets today is that we all can now find coverage that reinforces whatever biases we possess. While a potential upside to this democratization of information is a much more healthily skeptical public, the downside is that we also have a population that is far more receptive to concepts that not so long ago would have been dismissed as belonging to the lunatic fringe. For instance, after years' worth of documentaries devoted to the idea that the federal government orchestrated Roswell, the JFK assassination, Waco, and the bombing of the Oklahoma City federal building, it should come as little surprise that some Americans now believe the government was also behind 9/11.[13]

It should be extremely disturbing that the United States has reached the point at which numerous Americans believe their own government could intentionally slaughter three-thousand fellow citizens.[14] But even more troubling should be the ease with which one can find ample corroborating "evidence" of such a heinous act across so many different media (television, Internet, and public libraries)—troubling because the more any kind of misinformation or disinformation proliferates, the harder it becomes to dispel. At the same time, the more anyone in authority tries to combat such misinformation, the deeper such reactions drive distrust: Indeed, anything Washington says in refutation only further convinces the already conspiracy-minded that the government is simply continuing its monstrous cover-up.

The dots should not be hard to connect. Why should any people who distrust government, mistrust one another, and get their information from irreconcilably different sources hold together in a crisis?

The aftermath of Hurricane Katrina offers glimpses of where such mistrust could yet lead. Think back to the days immediately following the levee failure in New Orleans. What does it say when so many Americans found media reports of widespread rape, murder, and looting in New Orleans to be credible? What does it say about the media's *assumptions* about what the public would believe that the media felt free to promulgate such misinformation in the first place? We know from previous episodes of blackouts and riots that unexpected or extended disruptions in service raise serious questions about government's ability to cope. But, as the images from New Orleans in the wake of Katrina made clear, if breakdowns of *local* law and order are broadcast widely and repeated often enough they can permanently undermine confidence not just in government at the local level, but in government at every level.

What, we should wonder, *would* happen if Americans' confidence in government's ability to perform were shaken long and hard enough?

The resurgence of the militia movement in the 1990s should remind us what can happen when Americans actively distrust government *and* disdain one another.[15] It is not inconceivable that in a prolonged future crisis we could see vigilante lawlessness erupt in ways that seem unimaginable today. As bad as Hurricane Katrina was, we have to remember that it was not *nationally* catastrophic and it really was not prolonged. High water devastated areas of three states—over a matter of days—and then receded. Within weeks the aftereffects no longer dominated cable news. In contrast, the World Trade Center Towers were toppled in mere hours, 9/11 did not knock out services in New York City, and everyone who survived the attacks was able to flee the Trade Center area and the Pentagon.

It is important to retain a degree of perspective, difficult and painful as that may be, because 9/11 has become such a political touchstone that it could well warp our sensibilities.

Without question, the country pulled together in profound ways in the immediate aftermath of that September 2001 morning. No politician who invokes those initial weeks after 9/11 is wrong when he or she describes how resolved and united Americans felt. However, al Qaeda's attacks against the United States did not continue. They did not leave Chicago burning. We do not know what the consequences might have been had the fourth plane reached its destination and had the U.S. government been decapitated. Nor do we know what kind of panic might have been instilled had more anthrax-laden envelopes been delivered to offices beyond the handful of sites that received them. What we do know is that our solidarity did not last much beyond the initial invasion of Afghanistan. But then, American solidarity rarely does last long during wartime.[16]

Here is yet another source of divisibility—and *the* source of divisibility adversaries can most easily affect: wartime unity has proved to be a vexing problem from our birth.

Disunity during Wartime

Even George Washington had a difficult time maintaining popular support. We tend to forget that the percentage of colonists who supported the American Revolution was never more than a bare majority, if that.[17] During the Civil War, divisions over war policy were even more acute and dangerous. At the time, "the South was fighting for its very existence, and knew it; there was never any lack of motivation there."[18] The North, by comparison, was deeply divided, with large numbers reluctant to go to war to save the Union, while in the aftermath of the Emancipation Proclamation, the antiwar rhetoric of the Peace Democrats (also known as Copperheads) went from spirited opposition to outright sedition.[19] Just imagine what might have happened had the Confederacy been able to marshal nonstop media coverage. Imagine if it—or worse yet, England—had had the ability to directly communicate with disaffected Yankees. The results could well have been disastrous.[20]

▲　▲　▲

Examine our history and it turns out we Americans have never experienced unanimity over any of our wars—not the Spanish-American War, not World War I, not even World War II. We forget that even at the outset of the Cold War there was a decided lack of unanimity when President Truman decided to send troops to Korea. In 1951, during hearings held by the Joint Senate Armed Forces and Foreign Affairs Committee, serious consideration was given to demanding that U.S. forces be withdrawn immediately: "The policy of the United States in Korea . . . is essentially immoral, not likely to produce either victory in Korea or an end to aggression. Only a nation without regard for the sanctity of human life could be committed to a policy of prolonged war with no intent at winning a victory."[21]

A little more than a decade later, President Johnson intentionally avoided mobilizing the will of the American people to prosecute the war in Vietnam. His concerns were of a different sort than whether the war was moral: he feared for his Great Society programs. As he saw it, "History provided too many cases where the sound of the bugle put an immediate end to the hopes and dreams of the best reformers: the Spanish-American War drowned the populist spirit; World War I ended Woodrow Wilson's New Freedom; World War II brought the New Deal to a close. Once the [Vietnam] war began, then all those conservatives in the Congress would use it as a weapon against the Great Society."[22] Not wanting to jeopardize the Great Society, LBJ obfuscated.

What does it say when a president does not believe that his domestic and foreign policies can be reconciled, or assumes that they cannot be explained in tandem to the American people and therefore should *not* be explained? Such a circumstance should raise a giant red flag. Certainly it sent all sorts of signals to the North Vietnamese, who recognized that if they just hung on long enough they could win. Indeed, the larger the American protest movement grew against the Vietnam War, the more emboldened and reassured the North Vietnamese were that the United States would eventually be defeated. As Colonel Bui Tin from the North Vietnamese general staff later admitted, Hanoi's aim was to break Americans' will to continue, and the antiwar movement turned out to be "essential" to North Vietnam's strategy: "Support for the war from our rear was completely secure, while the American will was vulnerable. Every day our leadership would listen to world news over the radio at 9 AM to follow the growth of the American anti-war movement. Visits to Hanoi by people like Jane Fonda, former Attorney General Ramsey Clark, and various clergy gave us confidence that we should hold on in the face of battlefield reverses."[23]

In short, not only did the North Vietnamese understand how to take advantage of America's domestic political differences, but they appreciated how to contribute to them by manipulating soft American hearts and sympathetic American minds.[24] Or, to put this even more simply, once it became clear the United States was too riven to single-mindedly pursue victory, the war became North Vietnam's to lose. All of which holds strong echoes for today, when everyone in the world is privy to our bitter political debates over whether and how to continue to prosecute our undeclared wars in Iraq and Afghanistan.[25]

Mixed-Up Messages

Every year sees new books that continue to debate the mistakes the United States made in Vietnam: The draft was not fair, the government was not honest about the war it was fighting, the military was not competent to fight the war the political leadership wanted it to fight, policymakers did not sufficiently understand the Vietnamese, and so forth. The litany is long and the claims and counterclaims continue to fly. But interestingly, what very few writers point out is that we Americans were never in Vietnam for the sake of the Vietnamese. Washington sent advisors and troops to Southeast Asia to stymie communism and contain Soviet and Chinese expansion, but the Vietnamese themselves, as a group of people, were largely incidental.[26] This is something that became apparent to even our most ardent South Vietnamese supporters over time.

In *Understanding Vietnam*, former USAID representative Neil Jamieson recounts how, after delivering a lecture in Vietnamese to South Vietnamese political education officers in 1970, he was peppered with startlingly hostile questions. The questions came from

> men selected, indoctrinated, and trained to provide political education to their units in the army of the Republic of Vietnam. The United States had lavished billions of dollars worth of equipment and supplies on that army. American aid had purchased the uniforms these men were wearing, the chairs on which they sat, the weapons they bore. These young men were far above average in education and intelligence. They wanted to resist the Communists, and they wanted the United States to help them in that effort. Why should they of all people feel such resentment?

To try to get his audience to open up, Jamieson recited a few lines from a well-known Vietnamese epic poem, which evoked this response from one South Vietnamese political education officer:

> I believe, sir, that you are right in thinking there is something behind all these questions, something which troubles us but which no one has put into words. Let me try to put our real concerns into two questions. The first question, the one really big question, is this: "Does the United States want to make Vietnam into a little America?" If the answer to that question is "yes," then the second question is "Why should they want to do such a thing?" If the answer to the first question is "no," then our second question is "Why do they consistently act the way they do?" We honestly cannot understand American behavior in Vietnam.[27]

Now, fast-forward from Vietnam in the 1970s to Mogadishu in the 1990s, and to Operation Restore Hope, which was the United States–led effort to help feed the starving in Somalia. Somalis recognized from the outset that the United States did not undertake this "humanitarian" mission because American leaders really cared more about them than they cared about Bosnians or Liberians, who were also embroiled in strife at the time. From the Somalis' point of view, the United States had returned to Somalia for the same reasons it had sent aid to Somalia in the early 1980s (when the Soviets were just next door in Ethiopia): location, location, location. Somalis weren't entirely naïve; they knew their geostrategic location was the only reason outsiders (including Americans) had ever had anything to do with them before.[28]

Move on a few frames to Iraq in 2003: many Baghdadis viewed our liberation of them in much the same way. There were other tyrants elsewhere in the world. There were other Middle Eastern leaders who disliked the United States. Clearly, George W. Bush did not single out Saddam Hussein just for the reasons he publicized. There had to be more to it than that—a suspicion that was affirmed for many Iraqis after the invasion; how else were Iraqis supposed to make sense of Washington doing nothing to prevent looting that they (poor Iraqi civilians) knew would occur? Clearly the country that had put a man on the moon could have stopped the looting if it wanted to, just as the United States *could* have gotten the electricity up and running again. To many Iraqis, Washington doing neither proved that it had some other motive for being in Iraq that had nothing to do with them: "No country with America's power could fail so miserably unless it meant to."[29]

⋏   ⋏   ⋏

The trend to be noted here is not people abroad being prone to see conspiracies, but people abroad increasingly reading into our actions what they assume we are not telling them.

Not only are U.S. pronouncements treated with far more skepticism than they would have been forty or fifty years ago, but policymakers seem oblivious to why this is so. For all the talk in Washington about the importance of strategic communication and public diplomacy, few officials seem to appreciate how what they say to one audience not only might, but *will*, be heard by others. Imagine, though, that you are a young Iraqi: What are you left to assume when you hear American leaders repeatedly tell American audiences that the United States is better off fighting the terrorists over there, in Iraq, rather than "here at home," meaning the United States? If Iraq *is* your home isn't this the message you hear: Americans consider you expendable and your country worth sacrificing so that their neighborhoods remain safe and pristine.

Is *that* the message U.S. policymakers really mean to convey?

Washington currently helps subsidize an entire sub-industry devoted to branding and marketing sophisticated messages about U.S. intentions.[30] According to many of those peddling these services, the U.S. government needs to be far more aggressive if it hopes to successfully combat our adversaries' very effective information operations. In the parlance of the day, not only does Washington need to improve *how* it tells its story, but it has to craft a far more compelling "counternarrative" than it has thus far. But—this concept rests on an odd assumption; namely, that by crafting the right story we will somehow change Muslims' opinion of us— as if we can reverse engineer cognitive dissonance for people whose experiences have already told them plenty.

Dig deeper and there is an even more serious problem: we Americans claim to have had the same guiding principles since our inception, more than 230 years ago. If the rest of the world does not know where we stand on an issue or what we stand for, and Washington needs to hire consultants to carefully construct narratives in order to brand and then "sell" policy, that signals one of two things: either our policy and our principles must not be as congruent as we think, or we must not be standing as firmly as we suppose.

Or, to recast all of this in somewhat broader terms and plainer language: when what we are doing in someone else's country does not live up to local expectations, we clearly have a problem. When adversaries can then use the mismatch between what we say we are there to do and what people see us doing (or not doing), this points to an even bigger problem. When American audiences also begin to disbelieve the U.S. government or cannot figure out *what* to believe or question who is telling the truth and, thus, what the truth is—for example, did we go into Iraq for WMD and democracy, or for oil, or for some other neoconservative purpose?—we have a divisible public.

▲   ▲   ▲

To return to the Vietnam War example: as successful as the North Vietnamese were at exploiting our internal divides, their methods have to be considered rudimentary compared with what is possible today, given the speed with which words and images travel. At the same time, however, not everything has changed. Consider certain features of our national character and temperament—these have remained remarkably stable over time. Few national security proposals ever take these or any aspects of our strategic personality into account. But consider what savvy opponents should be able to bank on: we Americans tend to have short attention spans, we are action-oriented, and we prefer direct over indirect approaches.

Given such a national character, lengthy foreign interventions with no clear end state are bound to be contentious. Disagreements over how much, for how long, and at what cost we should keep investing in war will always aggravate our political differences. These disagreements will also offer politicians exactly the issues they need to keep *their* partisan differences alive—which, if you are a thinking adversary, should be exactly what you want, since this tension is something that you, your diplomats, and the lobbyists they hire and befriend can then help exacerbate.

Just think about it: if a United States polarized is a United States paralyzed, then nothing should be more useful to clever adversaries than to get us to intervene in messy situations they can prolong and make even messier—not that this explains why we invaded either Afghanistan or Iraq. But surely those watching what al Qaeda and insurgents in both countries managed to do recognize the opportunities that inhere in ensnaring us and keeping us ensnared, especially when the sheer size and complexity of our bureaucracy works against us, too: "From Richard Nixon through George W. Bush, our foreign and defense policies, like sausages, have been produced by processes of chopping, grinding, churning and smashing. Secretaries of state and defense contest for influence with national security advisers of varying talents brokering between the two or pushing their own agendas. Meanwhile, the president and his cabinet are perpetually at war with the military and diplomatic bureaucracies over the formulation and conduct of security affairs."[31]

With human terrain like this, clever adversaries should be able to have a field day.

▲   ▲   ▲

We Americans would probably admit we like to see immediate results and we want to be able to quantify effectiveness: what we most prize in one another tends to be consistency, dependability, follow through, responsibility, and accountability— none of the things that can be said to describe our foreign policy. But say, for the sake of argument, Washington *did* apply abroad those things that work among us at the retail level. And say this led to a totally different approach for how we conduct foreign policy. So, rather than spokespeople worrying about how exactly to spin or explain what the president, vice president, Secretary of State, or Secretary of Defense *really* meant to say, they would all be able to invoke the same thing. And, say what they invoked was predicated on principle, namely on the idea that actions speak louder than words.

With deeds in lieu of words, not only could no one misconstrue or mischaracterize Washington's intent, but it would be that much harder for anyone to turn our foreign policy to political effect. Even more significantly, with deeds in lieu of words there would be no messages for Washington to have to *try* to manage. What exactly might constitute such a foreign policy—one that could not be spun or politicized? *Don't tread on me* meet *to each his own.*

Chapter 3

Why Sovereignty?

The Left/Right divide in the United States has never been limited to domestic issues. When it comes to how to safeguard America even the mainstream can be split. In a 2003 survey, seven in ten Republicans considered military strength to be the best guarantor of peace, while only four in ten Democrats agreed. More than half of Democrats but only 17 percent of Republicans polled believed that U.S. wrongdoing precipitated the attacks of September 11, 2001.[1] Splits like these are never good. "Democratic and Republican lawmakers now hold very different views on foreign policy. On the most basic questions of U.S. grand strategy—the sources and purposes of U.S. power, the use of force, the role of international institutions—representatives of the two parties are on different planets."[2]

When foreign policy begins to look red or blue—and thus partisan—that signals that national security has been politicized.[3] Not only will the political party in power then be tempted to adopt whatever course of action seems most politically expedient, but both sides will become so busy reading political gain into each other's position that neither will be likely to accept a course of action simply on its merits. Yet, for anyone with their eye on the national security ball, there should only ever be two overriding concerns: (1) What makes the United States vulnerable? We need to protect those vulnerabilities. (2) What and who might threaten the United States? We need to thwart those threats.

Devising policy need be no more complex than addressing these two requirements, though thwarting threats is clearly easier said than done—and arguably can't be done—if we are not systematically monitoring social movements and undercurrents abroad.

The Need for a New Capability: Deep Understanding

Despite all the billions of dollars that have been devoted to intelligence collection and analysis over the past several decades, the United States can still be taken by surprise. Did we expect the Shah to fall, Hezbollah to become a major player in the Middle East, or Hamas to win an election?

The United States desperately needs to develop a deep understanding capability unlike any it currently possesses. Here is why: Among everyone in government today assigned to pay careful attention to what may or may not be happening inside nuclear programs in Iran and North Korea, no one pays systematic, sustained attention to what is transpiring in the seams of societies throughout the developing world. According to Russ Feingold and Chuck Hagel, "On the map of the world, it's those hidden corners, about which we know so little, where some of the most dangerous threats against the United States may be brewing."[4] When these two senators wrote this they were referring to literal places and spaces—geographical hinterlands like remote valleys along the Afghan-Pakistan border. But in the twenty-first century, any kind of community can serve as a hideout, especially when no U.S. agency bothers to routinely monitor what is going on on university campuses or among restless pockets of foreign populations, even though these are exactly the kinds of populations shrewd governments pay close attention to if they hope to stay in power. One question this reality should raise is, can we rely on such regimes to pass information of interest along to us? Which begs the far tougher question, how can we possibly know what might be of interest to us if we are not keeping a close ear to the ground ourselves?

Quite often there are all sorts of things foreign governments do not want outsiders to know about. Sometimes this is for perfectly understandable reasons. Who wants to be badgered by hectoring Americans? But even when information is passed along, Washington remains at others' mercy whenever no one in our government can vet it.[5] This situation makes the United States vulnerable on multiple counts: first, locals always know better than we do what we don't know, which then becomes something for adversaries—and cunning governments—to exploit.[6] Second, because we don't pay sufficient attention to all the ways in which people *normally* associate with one another at the local—never mind transnational—level, our intelligence agencies have no way to judge whether and when such associations are being put to potentially nefarious ends.

For instance, there are scores of ethnic diasporas. They can stretch from Mogadishu to Minneapolis. The less familiar we are with what is normal and routine in any one network, the less capable we are of detecting shifts in patterns. Truth be told, U.S. intelligence services have never been particularly good at monitoring life at the grassroots in other countries—but neither have they ever had to be.

Such monitoring tends to be an imperial task. The British, for instance, excelled at it. British administrators—district officers, especially—concentrated on studying tribes, clans, secret societies, religious brotherhoods, healing cults, and any groups that had a formal or informal leader. This is what they needed to do if they hoped to effectively control and keep tabs on large foreign populations. Arguably, too, Englishmen knew to pay close attention to pecking orders just by virtue of having grown up in such a highly stratified society themselves. Not so we Americans. Our strong suit is not invisible social structure, but egalitarianism.

We Americans pride ourselves on trying to treat everyone equally and, at least in theory, we strive to live by the Golden Rule. These aims are incontrovertibly good but have a number of unintended consequences. For one, we assume everyone's motivations are much the same as ours and that all foreigners believe in American values even if they just don't realize it yet. Or, as Loren Baritz has written, "A whisper runs through our history that the people of the world really want to be like us, regardless of what they or their political leaders say."[7] Such optimism about others wanting to become like us helps explain how generous we are. But this idea that there is an American lurking inside all non-Americans just waiting to be liberated by us also makes us surprisingly parochial. Because we do not feel the need to steep ourselves in other cultures or languages—why should we when people elsewhere are basically just like us?—we tend to fail to appreciate how profoundly different we truly are.[8] From our perspective, whatever differences foreigners manifest are just surface ephemera—a matter of appearance, diet, quaint customs—while anything deeper, like poverty, can be fixed via education, an overhaul of the local economy, and/or better governance.

However, as we have been (re)learning the hard way in Iraq and Afghanistan recently, nothing is quite this simple and others' differences from us *do* matter.[9] With hindsight, most people in national security circles today at least seem ready to acknowledge that if only policymakers had been more cross-culturally aware prior to our invasion of Iraq, Washington would not have made as many mistakes as it did.[10] Consequently, there has been a massive push within the military to emphasize greater cross-cultural awareness. Considerable sums are being spent on cross-cultural awareness training service-wide. Yet, no one has stopped to ask how wise this is in light of who enlists, and whether there aren't serious contradictions in asking young Americans who value our way of life enough to defend it to also learn to respect the values of people who engage in behaviors many Americans abhor.

Nothing tends to be more eye-opening for young Americans than a first-time deployment to the Third World, into communities where women and minorities are openly discriminated against. This rubs large numbers of American youth the wrong way—as all liberal-minded humanists should hope. But, for this very reason it also isn't clear that impelling these young servicemen and women to try to be cultural relativists jibes well, or can be made to fit, with the proud, patriotic spirit most bring into military service with them. Nor is it clear that as many troops can be taught foreign languages as promoters of more language training would hope.

As anyone who ever sat through high school or college language classes probably remembers, some Americans have a facility for languages but large numbers of us do not. The idea that we can turn most members of our armed forces into culturally sensitive, Pashtu-, Dari-, or Arabic-speaking warrior-diplomats seems Pollyannaish at best—which is not to say that the military should stop trying to help troops become more cross-culturally savvy. Cross-cultural awareness is unquestionably useful for helping to prevent otherwise avoidable cross-cultural faux pas. However, such training hardly gets us what we most need, which is a small cadre of men and women dedicated to spotting trends *before* they mount into problems that demand a military response. In other words, while being able to ask for tea in a local language is good—it is nice, it is friendly, it indicates that the individual asking might care—it takes a lifetime of drinking tea with locals to learn what is really going on beneath the surface.[11]

▲ ▲ ▲

At the moment, the U.S. government registers too little of what goes on outside foreign capitals or among any but the elites.[12] Embassies fool themselves when they think they are getting diverse points of view by talking to members of the political opposition. In most countries those in opposition simply represent elite families who happen to be out of favor. And, while it is certainly critical to keep track of machinations close to the heart of power, such tracking does not help shed light on what might be burbling beneath the surface in shantytowns and hinterlands, among student populations or in the seams.[13]

It is essential to recognize that in many places around the world, people measure trust in ways radically different from the way we Americans do. Typically, they do so via lifelong associations. Often, too, people enmeshed in networks of this sort don't think twice about helping family members who ask for innocent-sounding favors; God (or the ancestors) will punish them should they not do right by kin.[14] Indeed, most people throughout the non-West are bound together by unbreakable moral obligations we simply don't have. Bonds like these, combined with global diasporas, can yield any number of ways for our adversaries to put traditional networks and allegiances to diabolical use. Just think Windtalkers in reverse.

At the same time we are underinvesting in keeping a finger on the local pulse abroad, the U.S. government is pouring ever more money into developing sophisticated software programs that can collate, cross-tabulate, and manipulate mounds of social network analysis data with an aim to help us identify and target our adversaries and their accomplices. Thanks to all of the neat things everyone says these computer labs and social network analysis programs should be able to do, few people object to the tax dollars being spent. But, without deep local knowledge to begin with, what kind of decent social analysis will be done?[15]

In *Plan of Attack*, Bob Woodward describes a group of high-ranking and well-placed Iraqis to whom U.S. operatives gave radios prior to the official start of the 2003 Iraq War.[16] Labeled "Rockstars," this Iraqi network's task was to report on the inner workings of the regime and pinpoint Saddam Hussein's whereabouts. Who exactly were these Iraqis? They apparently belonged to an underground religious network that we didn't know existed. Purely by chance, a CIA operative ended up working with a local contact who, fed up with dealing with intermediaries, told the agent he could place his entire underground network at America's disposal. To the CIA agent this must have seemed like an incredible windfall. However, what, if any, benefits actually accrued remains classified; some question whether there were any benefits, and whether these men weren't working for Saddam instead—all of which points to the difficulties when the United States doesn't know whether hidden networks do or don't exist and has to rely on "parachute" operatives to play catch-up by chance.[17]

This is yet another reason why it only makes sense to develop a human sensor net so that Washington has a reliable set of people who already know how to determine who's who and what's what.[18] Which *would* be great—but to what specific ends?

Inconsistency and Ambiguity—the Banes of Current Strategy

Let's say the United States did develop a much more sophisticated ability to identify potential sources of trouble, or to detect trends before they mounted into shocks. What would we do about them? And which ones would we do something about? Would we only respond to problems that pose us an immediate threat? In which case, how does this yield anything different from how Washington already tries to operate?

Walk this back a step: even if decision makers in Washington were to learn that trouble is brewing someplace, what would they do with this information? The crux of our problem is that Washington has no coherent strategy into which such information would fit.

For instance, let's consider some of the places the United States tries to exert its influence right now:

> *Sudan.* Official U.S. policy has been to pressure the government of Sudan to stop the genocide in Darfur. We are working through the international community to do this. We do not deploy force. We do not employ unilateral

sanctions. Rather, we work through a Security Council chaired by member states that openly back the government in Khartoum.

Saudi Arabia. U.S. policy has been to recognize and work with the ruling family. We waver between encouraging a more open society and ignoring the repressiveness of the regime.

Pakistan. U.S. policy has been to recognize the legitimacy and sovereignty of whatever government comes to power. We acknowledge Pakistan's status as a nuclear power, but don't like thinking about its complicity in nuclear proliferation.

Egypt, Yemen, China . . . compile any list of nations we have tried to influence and it quickly becomes apparent that American influence is hardly a sure thing; though we say we favor liberal democracy over illiberal stability, if you compare how differently we have treated different countries it is clear that no matter how important Washington says free and fair elections or more openness is, it is our own national interests that remain the real driver behind our actions and reactions.

Who and what we favor, when, depends. It depends on whether we are talking about a country that has the capacity to acquire and use WMD. It depends on where else the United States is engaged. It depends on who we think might come to power in an election. Washington's policy decisions depend on so many external factors that we project nothing like strategic clarity. Washington never comes right out and says that it will pursue U.S. national interests above those of any other people, which is, in fact, what all countries do, and what most countries expect us to do.[19] One reason Washington cannot admit this is because that would imply we do periodically behave just like any other country, and that is not how we either see ourselves or how we want to be viewed. And, yet, by not being more rigorous about matching our deeds to our words, or our words to our deeds, we give critics all the ammunition they need to shoot holes in even our most selfless acts.

For instance, we like to say we stopped ethnic cleansing in Kosovo. Yet, why have we done nothing in Zimbabwe? We overthrew the regime in Iraq. Yet, why not in Iran? Not only can our inconsistency be construed to make our actions look suspect, our unreliability makes us appear unprincipled. Foreign populations are not the only ones affected by our undependability and lack of follow-through—as we saw in the previous chapter, there are domestic political implications whenever Washington's credibility is suspect.

Some might try to argue that strategic inconsistency is actually extremely useful, since it not only helps keep everyone guessing, but our inconstancy is bound to throw even potential adversaries off balance. Yet, choose any subset of the following foreign policy crises and ask yourself how much better we might have been served had everyone known what to expect from Washington:

- Hezbollah claims responsibility for destroying the U.S. embassy and killing hundreds of Marines in Beirut. We withdraw.

- Al Qaeda takes credit for destroying two U.S. embassies and killing U.S. government representatives. We shoot missiles, but kill none of the culprits.

- Chinese fighter jets force down a U.S. patrol craft from international airspace and force it to land in China. Beijing impounds the sensitive aircraft and holds the crew hostage for weeks.

- North Korea fuels long-range intercontinental ballistic missiles (ICBMs) on the launch pad. We don't know what the warheads carry, but North Korea has a proven capacity for nuclear weapons.

- Iran rejects the international directive that it stop making weapons-grade radioactive material in violation of the Nuclear Non-Proliferation Treaty. At the same time, Tehran continues to fund insurgent activity in both Iraq and Lebanon.

Or consider this hypothetical example:

- Jemaah Islamiyah bombs the U.S. embassies in Indonesia, Malaysia, and the Republic of the Philippines.

Such scenarios are worth reflecting on because how does strategic ambiguity help detect, deter, or respond to such events?

It can't.

Let us consider the Jemaah Islamiyah example further. Presumably the governments of Indonesia, the Philippines, and Malaysia are already monitoring mosques and Islamist study centers. If the U.S. government had long-term ethnographic sensors in place they, too, would be plugged in to student circles, or perhaps they would regularly visit Muslim elders in remote communities. By being on the ground often enough they would develop the same kind of situational awareness locals have or, at the very least, they would pick up on the fact that locals are picking up on something worth being aware of.[20]

Because our sensors would be linked, ripples in the social fabric in one location would alert their counterparts elsewhere to pay closer attention in their locations. Clandestine intelligence collectors could then be tasked. And the United States could deploy its formidable technical assets to sweep and probe. Then, with whatever information has been gleaned, diplomats could knock on ministerial doors.

Under the current dispensation, diplomats rarely show their full hand as they pass along what Washington knows. In certain countries today, American diplomats can't show their full hand because they can't be sure who in a foreign government might be colluding with our enemies. In addition, under the current dispensation, it is unlikely an American ambassador would be authorized to say to a foreign minister or president, "Here is what we know. If we're wrong, prove it to us."

Language like that is too direct for diplomacy. The U.S. government is not even that direct when it is not being diplomatic.[21] Consider some of the ways we've signaled our displeasure in the past; for instance: "In response to Libyan involvement in the December 1985 terrorist attacks at the Rome and Vienna Airports, a March 1986 attack against U.S. naval ships in the Gulf of Sidra, and an April 1986 bombing of a discotheque in West Berlin, President Reagan announced that U.S. Air Force planes had bombed Libyan military headquarters, installations, and terrorist camps in April 1986."[22] Bombs dropped in this attack allegedly killed one of Qaddafi's adopted daughters. A debate still rages about whether the intended target was Qaddafi himself. A debate likewise rages about whether or not this punishment then led Qaddafi to modify his behavior. To many, Libya's bombing of Pan Am Flight 103 over Lockerbie, Scotland, in 1988 suggests anything but behavior modification.

Or, what about the seventy-nine-day-long air campaign in Serbia in 1999? Some claim that it was U.S. bombs that forced Serbian president Slobodan Milosevic to pull his troops out of Kosovo. But others point to a lack of Russian support, not America's use of force, as the reason he withdrew.

Understandably, diplomacy is rife with ambiguity. Traditionally even realpolitik is supposed to be practiced in the shadows. And certainly, when states were each others' greatest security concern, negotiating with ministers and rulers behind closed doors undoubtedly did make sense. Maybe diplomats still try to curb wayward behavior and successfully derail deadly intent this way. But the fact that it is impossible for the rest of us citizens to know with any degree of certitude or confidence what has been said behind closed doors should strike most Americans as increasingly problematic on multiple fronts.[23] For starters, just the intimation of secret deals leads to conspiracy theories and exploitable spin.[24] But also, non-state actors, by definition, are not part of the state-to-state equation. How do they fit into this minuet? How should they be dealt with? How should the states that shelter them—yet claim they can do little about them—be treated?

The Non-State Actor Problem

One of the greatest paradoxes of the post–Cold War world, and yet another reason to develop better grassroots, in-the-seams awareness, is non-state actors pose a graver danger to most governments today than do other countries' armies or navies.

In an era when communications are instantaneous and people can fly halfway around the globe in less than a day, when government records can be digitized and remotely accessed, and information sharing is, literally, a mouse click away, one might think states would also have the means to exert far greater control over their citizenries than at any time in history. Yet, in numerous countries non-state actors do not just compete with governments for communities' loyalty, they already own it.

Governments have succumbed to such a degree over the past several decades that, in some cases, they have actually granted safe haven to their own armed opposition. Probably the most glaring example of this occurred in 1998 when Colombia gave away a Switzerland-sized chunk of its territory to the FARC. But Sri Lanka, too, ceded its northern parts to insurgents it proved unable (until recently) to effectively, permanently smash. The Philippines alternates between negotiating and fighting with separatists in its southern islands. Pakistan has never had effective state-like control over large swaths of the Federally Administered Tribal Areas (FATA), a fact it has periodically openly conceded. And then there is Somalia, which has no central government and has fragmented into various pieces and parts.

Indeed, it is the self-proclaimed Republic of Somaliland in the northern part of what was once a single country that is more akin to an actual state than any that has tried to assert itself in Mogadishu, the former and still recognized national capital. What is even more telling about the Somali case is not that the international community has been willing to provide desultory peacekeeping support to a central government that cannot protect itself, let alone the Somali people, but that a whole host of countries do so in the persistent belief that someone can put Humpty-Dumpty back together again and make "Somalia" work. This speaks to the power that inheres in the concept of states: other states want the space marked "Somalia" to be a coherent state.[25]

▲ ▲ ▲

Not only is the world today carved up among 192 countries, but one of the most under-appreciated realities of modern existence is that there is not a space on the planet that does not nominally belong to a government somewhere.[26] Nor is there a government that does not want to be taken seriously and treated as though it is just as sovereign as every other. "We are living at a time when existing territorial jurisdictions are vested with exceptional international validity. The principle involved is that of *uti possidetis juris* ('as you have, so may you hold') according to which existing boundaries are the pre-emptive basis for determining territorial jurisdictions in the absence of mutual agreement of all affected state parties to do otherwise."[27]

All countries lay claim to borders, flags, currencies, capitals, and other appurtenances that signify their autonomy. The United Nations itself is predicated on the notion of separate but equal sovereign states. Regardless of size, system of governance, or behavior, all countries get a seat and a vote in the General Assembly, while membership in other international and regional organizations further cements countries' privileged position and points to states as *the* international unit of account. In fact, it is hard to imagine how the world might work these days without them.[28]

Yet, at the same time that every state is made to count, no state is really *held* to account. This renders sovereignty a global emperor with no clothes. "When leaders are afraid to take real action they go to the U.N., where they know nothing tangible will be achieved. Resolutions are routinely ignored without consequences and, in fact, are openly flouted."[29] International bodies can pass any number of international laws, and the International Criminal Court can issue all the rulings it sees fit. But without institutions to enforce these, they are easy to willfully ignore.

For instance, months before the 2004 presidential election, Secretary of State Colin Powell was said to have been told to use the term "genocide" when discussing the violence affecting Darfurians in western Sudan. Then, according to Gerard Prunier, as soon as President Bush was reelected, "the interest level of U.S. diplomacy on the Sudan question dropped sharply." But it wasn't just Americans who punted. The European Union did too:

> [The EU] presented a spectacle of complete lack of resolve and coordination when it came to Darfur. The French only cared about protecting Idris Deby's regime in Chad from possible destabilization. The British blindly followed Washington's lead, finding this somewhat difficult since Washington was not very clear about which direction it wished to take. The Scandinavian countries and the Netherlands gave large sums of money and remained silent. Germany made anti-Sudanese government noises that it never backed up with any sort of action and gave only limited cash. And the Italians remained bewildered. . . .
>
> Even on the question of deciding on the nature of what was happening in Darfur, the union could not manage to speak with any clearly recognizable voice, its parliament only declaring that what was going on was "tantamount to genocide." During several Darfur "cease-fire" or "peace" talks in Abeche and Abuja, the Europeans pushed for a "no fly zone" above Darfur. But even when it was accepted, they did strictly nothing to enforce it.[30]

This would seem to prove Robert Jackson's broader point, "There is no cosmopolitan 'law of humanity' that stands above the positive international law of sovereign states."[31] Further proof can be found in the indictment of Sudanese president Omar Hassan al-Bashir by the International Criminal Court in March 2009. As of January 2011, Bashir was still Sudan's sitting head of state, even though all 108 countries that ratified the treaty to establish the ICC "are obliged to help bring him to justice."[32]

With no enforcement capability, the international community is just that: an entity that communes. It wields neither clubs nor trumps to effect.[33] This means the bottom line remains much as it has always been: ultimately, only might makes right.[34] More often, it seems, might makes wrong. Then, when that happens, yet more force is required to overcome those bent on misusing it.[35]

Unpleasant as such truths are, no universal consensus has been or will likely ever be reached regarding what everyone agrees is right, wrong, fair, unfair, or intolerable. After all, if universal values did exist countries would already be abiding by them.[36] If a consensus existed there would be no need for an international cavalry to ride to anyone's rescue, not that any such thing as an "international" cavalry exists. Instead, cavalries launch from states, just as it is states that pony up the forces and the citizens to arrest and prosecute those who commit crimes against "humanity."[37]

When it comes to international governance; when U.S. sovereignty is violated we are our own first responders. That means prevention is also up to us unless we can shift the burden to other governments. But, given the current system, even if we could agree somehow on how to share governance with other states and with non-state entities, there would be no guarantee—and nothing *to* guarantee—that our preferences, never mind our principles, would prevail (especially not if we all abide by the sole principle all states do hold sacrosanct—sovereignty).

▲   ▲   ▲

Ironically, it is the very existence of states as each other's sovereign equal that renders international governance unworkable. What country would—or should—voluntarily trade away its prerogatives for another country's laws? Would the United States accept Islamic law or sharia as national or even state law? What kind of sense does it then make to assume that people who live by sharia would voluntarily abandon their system for ours? Meanwhile, the question of whose laws and morality should prevail is just one obstacle to a unitary world.

Reinvigorating Sovereignty

Sovereignty promises two things: a country's territory remains inviolate, and populations within a country's borders pledge their allegiance to it.[38] Essentially, it is the territorial contract *among* states that guarantees the sanctity of the social contracts *within* them.[39] In principle, what this means for us in the United States is that no citizen hailing from another country should be able to cause us harm, unless we are at war. At the same time, because Washington is not only responsible *to* but *for* us, our government's duty is to ensure that Americans don't defy this principle either (again, unless we are at war).

By rights, Washington should not even have to remind foreign leaders that they are responsible for anything that violates our sovereignty (including anyone who bears their country's passport). If any violation of our sovereignty takes place, those who helped or harbored the perpetrators should already be on notice that we will hold them accountable. Indeed, if Washington made clear that this was the First Principle of our foreign policy, it could then quite reasonably add: *And here is what holding you accountable means . . .*

Not only would spelling this out and then following through on holding others accountable clarify Washington's position for other countries but, just as importantly, such a demonstration of sovereignty would enjoin others to do exactly the same. This is the flip side of the sovereignty coin. In theory, every country is just as free as we are to set its own course without worrying about outside interference, which in turn means populations should be able to live under whatever system of governance they choose, to use their natural resources in whatever manner they see fit, and to run their economies according to the principles that most suit them so long as nothing they do violates others' sovereignty in terms of pollution, refugee flows, or inability to police their own borders.[40]

In theory, this is what sovereignty already promises; in practice, no one has systematically ever tried to make it work. Worse, by not holding irresponsible governments to account, the international "community" has helped encourage a whole array of non-state actors whose very existence defies the "to each his own—don't tread on me" quid pro quo of sovereign responsibility. Today, if a government cannot or does not deliver services to its citizens, non-state actors eagerly fill the void. Some do so for the age-old reason of saving souls. Others seek support as they struggle against the regime. And yet others are recruiting foot soldiers for battles elsewhere.[41] But all such non-state actors defy the separation of powers sovereignty demands. Another problem they pose is to undermine the social contract essential to any form of governance.

It is government that is supposed to provide or, at the very least, regulate services for its citizens—thereby securing their security. When non-state actors usurp this role they hollow out the state. They also confound people's loyalties. This makes a travesty of sovereignty. Worse, non-state actors create all sorts of ways for governments to avoid accountability—this, as we have seen with al Qaeda's ability to take root in country after country, is extremely problematic. Yet, it is also self-inflicted; after all, it is governments that have permitted (if not enabled) non-state actors to evolve to such a point that everyone now treats them as though they are beyond governmental control altogether.[42]

As Jakub Grygiel notes, small stateless actors have become "the long tail of international relations."[43] Ergo, the widespread sense that "the Westphalian state system is in a long recession. States, having reached the zenith of their power in the totalitarian systems of the twentieth century, are in a period of absolute decline."[44] Or, as Richard Haass has written, "one of the cardinal features of the contemporary international system is that nation-states have lost their monopoly on power and in some domains their preeminence as well. States are being challenged from above, by regional and global organizations; from below, by militias; and from the side, by a variety of nongovernmental organizations (NGOs) and corporations."[45]

Yet, in a world in which sovereignty demands the fulfillment of certain duties and doesn't just promise deference—*non-state* actors, literally, would not exist.[46]

How to achieve such a world, and get states to live up to their sovereign obligations, is the subject of the rest of this book.

ᐱ   ᐱ   ᐱ

First, a caveat: states may not be the ultimate solution to all of the twenty-first century's challenges. Just a brief glance through any atlas should make plain that few borders make good geographic let alone demographic sense. It would be foolish to argue that every country in existence *should* be a country. Some should be two or three; others should not exist at all. There are any number of African countries that will probably never be solvent within their current borders, given how few natural resources they have, including dependable rainfall. Nonetheless, until humans stumble or agree on a new way to arrange political space around the globe, states are the sociogeographic containers we have.[47] Nothing else at the moment has states' potential to box in "bad guys." Nothing else grants diverse peoples a freer rein to govern themselves as they see fit.[48]

From a purely U.S.-centric point of view, the U.S. government (like all national governments) is configured to deal with other states. From the outset, the executive branch has been organized to interact with foreign entities through state-to-state relations.[49] Thus, holding other states accountable and responsible for the behavior of their citizens would not require a massive rewiring of government in Washington. Instead, such a stance could actually lead to a much more sensible consolidation of a number of federal bureaucracies, though the more significant point is that strengthening state responsibility—which lies at the core of making sovereignty matter—fits with who we Americans are as a people and fits with our national personality. At the same time, the beauty of reinvigorating sovereignty does not impose this personality or our culture *on* anyone else.

In allowing us to remain ourselves and permitting everyone else to stay as different as they choose, sovereignty also fulfills Sun Tzu's dictum. As this most famous of grand strategists is so often quoted as saying, It is never enough to know the enemy; you also have to know yourself. This alone suggests we would do well to try to tailor our national security policy *to* our character and, at the very least, recognize our weaknesses as well as our strengths. It is worth considering that "coun-terinsurgency and imperial policing operations demand forbearance, personnel continuity, foreign language skills, crosscultural understanding, historical knowl-edge, minimal employment of force, and robust interagency involvement and cooperation. None of those are virtues of American statecraft and warmaking."[50]

What, meanwhile, would we say does make up our character? Or better yet, what could we agree as Americans characterizes us *as* Americans? How about: we tend to be direct. We like clarity. Or as John Wayne said in *The Shootist*: "I won't be wronged. I won't be insulted. I won't be laid a hand on. I don't do these things to other people, and I require the same from them."

Chapter 4

The Radical Shift:
The Relationship Framework

Two questions loom: How can our government—how can Washington—make sovereignty work for, rather than against, us? And how can the United States reset the conditions for global security in general, with or without others' assistance?

This chapter will turn a number of accepted conventions on their head. Almost every point made here is bound to raise questions. The chapters that follow will address them and will make clear that a sovereignty-based approach is not nearly so brutal as it may sound at first blush, though it does rely heavily on being willing to wield force.

Here, too, we add another plank to the "if . . . then" logic that lies at the heart of our argument: *If* the only way to put responsibility back into the sovereignty equation is to hold other governments accountable for anything and everything that crosses their borders, *then* that means that any government that has harbored, given a passport to, or otherwise assisted those who may have violated our sovereignty must rid itself of this problem—or the United States will be compelled to consider that government to be a problem, too. Washington has to make this very clear. American demands? Simple. The metrics? Obvious: "Eliminate al Qaeda." "Disarm and disable Hezbollah." "Turn over terrorist X." "Stop sending fighters to country Y." Essentially, "here is what we expect you to do. And here's by when."

For instance, say the worst happened:

> Chicago has been struck, and within minutes there are two postings to the Internet. A group calling itself "Caliphate Now" claims credit for the dirty bomb that just went off. Caliphate Now doesn't sound like a typical al Qaeda affiliate. Members of the U.S. intelligence

community initially suspect that Pakistanis were involved in the attack. Then their thinking swings toward Hezbollah masking itself as a Pakistani organization. In the interim, a reporter on Al Jazeera says his sources tell him Caliphate Now is "run" by a Bangladeshi cleric based in London. Within four hours of the attack, several intelligence agencies from other countries confirm this. Within six hours of the attack, so does Scotland Yard.

London immediately reassures Washington it is treating this incident as though one of its own cities had been struck. In a series of classified discussions, London outlines for the president exactly what it is doing and planning to do. Dhaka (Bangladesh) likewise makes it clear to Washington it intends to fully cooperate with the United States The United States finds itself needing to issue no demands to either country, but the U.S. ambassador to Bangladesh is instructed to press Bangladesh for more specific information about what it intends to do, and by when. The ambassador then reiterates Washington's expectations right before these are publicly announced.

In keeping with the sovereignty quid pro quo, it will always be up to other governments to choose how they want to comply with Washington's demands. If networks involved in supporting our attackers exist in other countries, those countries have to dismantle those networks. Equally simple and straightforward, all countries are given the same choice. All have the opportunity to respond to the United States in one of four ways: as a partner state, struggling state, failed state, or adversary. One benefit to such an approach is it accommodates any form of government. Other advantages are that it is totally scalable, eminently flexible, but unimpeachably nonnegotiable.

The terms used—partner state, struggling state, failed state, and adversary—are not new. People bandy them about in print every day. On their own they do not represent a departure; rather, what constitutes a radical rupture from the way Washington currently does business is taking seriously the nature of the relationships these terms *should* describe. Also, use of the word "demands"—as in "the U.S. demands"—is deliberate. The United States will *demand*, not request. Requests invite bargaining and are the sine qua non of compromise. They placate and are perfect for peacetime negotiations, but make no sense when dealing with entities that are determined to do us harm.

In a Sovereignty Rules world, one thing and only one thing matters. Regardless of how historic America's friendship with another country might be, that government's ability and willingness to meet Washington's demands in the wake of an attack perpetrated or assisted by its citizens determine whether we still regard that country as a friend, or as something else. Consider this scenario with

England and Germany: Terrorists actually manage to blow an American airliner out of the sky, they plan and plot the attack in Frankfurt and board the plane in Heathrow. Washington would issue the same kinds of demands to London as to Berlin—and these would not differ from those it would make to any government that unwittingly or consciously served as our attackers' host.

What would a list of U.S. demands to a *partner state* look like? They need be no more complicated than this:

- First, destroy the organization responsible for conducting the attack. This does not mean simply arresting individuals, or closing businesses and monitoring places of worship. Instead, thoroughly root out the organization. Render it inert.

- Second, redress whatever intelligence lapses allowed the attack to occur. Prove able to control the movement of citizens and noncitizens within your borders. This may mean changing how you issue visas and passports. It may mean stricter screening of who receives dual citizenship. It might require tighter airport and sealift security.

Again, how another country complies with these demands would be up to it. *That* it complies is our only immediate concern.

Under such a rubric bilateral relations would still matter—the United States would not suddenly throw current treaty obligations out the window. But Washington would no longer use trade or some other instrument of national power as leverage behind closed doors. Instead, sovereignty would be kept congruent with security, and security only—with *our* security being paramount to us. Thus, only one set of questions need be posed: we've been attacked, and you own the problem. What kind of relationship have you had with the United States? What kind of relationship do you want *now*?

Because it is not the past but the present and future that matter in the wake of an attack, partner states may well come to include countries we don't readily think of in conventional partner terms. Thus, as hard as it may be to imagine right now, Russia or Iran could well become partner states in the future, while, conversely, a historic ally that balks at meeting our demands could see its relationship with us redefined. Let a government hesitate, bide its time, or drag its feet about responding, and it will not be deemed a partner.

The real radical twist this introduces is twofold. First, in the wake of an attack it is up to *other* governments to demonstrate the nature of the relationship *they* want with us. Second, *their* willingness to act determines what we do—or do not—have to step in to do ourselves.[1] These two factors not only put the burden of responsibility back where it belongs—on other governments—but likewise toss the ball squarely (and publicly) into their court.

Without question, the United States would offer to provide whatever foren-sic or technical assistance a partner state might require. However, in all likelihood, and as the term "partner" implies, such help would probably be minimal; partners should already possess the will and capacity to do what needs to be done.

What might this mean for states that might want to meet U.S. demands, but can't? Maybe they lack the military wherewithal—insufficient airlift and limited firepower, or insufficient financial means. These are "*struggling states*"—willing but unable to fully assist. They will need to allow us to help. As in all cases, our dip-lomats would deliver a set of parameters along with U.S. demands: "here are our expectations. Here are the benchmarks we will use to determine when and whether they have been met." Once in possession of these, it will be up to that other gov-ernment to then request help from us, which might well include a lethal or armed response to be delivered by U.S. forces.

For example, the United States might need to send air or naval assets to cut off terrorists' escape routes, thereby enabling local government forces to pin them down. Or we might deploy B-52s and cruise missiles to destroy well-defended training camps. Alternatively, Washington might send in Special Forces advisors to travel with the host national military and provide logistical support. Or perhaps we would only need to provide aerial reconnaissance and signals intelligence.

What the United States offers will depend on the other government's capac-ity and what it specifically asks for as it addresses its "problem." Our only aim will be to ensure that the organization that attacked us is thoroughly destroyed. For operational security reasons Washington probably wouldn't reveal exactly how it plans to assist a struggling state in achieving this.[2] Thus, the state we're assisting can retain an element of surprise. But Washington will always make clear once we have been asked to help that we are, indeed, helping. In this way, foreign audiences and Americans alike will be fully informed. Additionally, everyone will know that if and when the United States deploys troops, their sole mission will be to stamp out those who helped orchestrate the attack against us. Once that mission has been accomplished, our forces will return home.

Adversary states, meanwhile, are those whose governments are either com-plicit in an attack against us or refuse U.S. demands to destroy a "problem." What distinguishes adversary states is that they have the capacity to meet Washington's demands but willfully choose not to. When a government itself explicitly supports or launches an attack, it engages in state-on-state warfare. Adversary states that openly attack the United States hardly require a list of demands. Their aggression short-circuits the entire sequence. The only thing such aggressors require is an unequivocal response.

The U.S. response following Pearl Harbor was to take the war to Japan. It is hard today to imagine any country directly attacking the United States, given

America's overwhelming firepower. None has since Japan. Instead, a hostile government would be more likely to seek to do us harm via shadowy third parties; presumably, the more that such a government *thinks* it could successfully bury its links to non-state actors, the more tempted it would be to do so. In such a scenario, ethnographic sensors, along with all our other means of gathering intelligence, would become critically important. Forensically we have to be able to quickly trace and untangle connections, and ensure that some "innocent" state or government is not being framed for someone else's deeds. At the same time, Washington needs to be ready to act on the intelligence it does possess, incomplete as this may be: if terrorist A has traveled to country X on a passport issued by country Y, then country Y and country X have a lot to answer for. Adversary states are those that either refuse to answer such questions, or openly defy us by refusing to hold anyone accountable for gaps in their security.

Again, it is important to remember that under the Sovereignty Rules rubric other governments will be on notice: the nature of our mutual relationship is in *their* hands. Should a government defy us by explicitly supporting attacks, that government invites the largest and loudest U.S. response: we target it. We don't bomb a little or fire warning shots and then wait to see if a regime that has consciously put itself in an adversarial relationship with us suddenly wants to negotiate. Instead, we make an example of it. We pummel it—this would include any proxy forces that it employs.

Suffice it to say here (with more to come) that the United States would act forcefully and decisively, and the U.S. government's overriding aim should always be to knock out an opponent with our first punch. In a Sovereignty Rules world the United States would never launch cruise missiles just to send a message. Nor would we bomb buildings at midnight to express our ire. Incrementalism is no way to achieve a decisive result.[3]

▲   ▲   ▲

When thinking about how the United States would apply this framework—Is country X a partner state, a struggling state, an adversary, or a failed state?—it is vital to bear two things in mind. Once the United States adopts this approach, all governments (and their populations) would be on notice that it is their choices that will determine our subsequent treatment of them. Second, two events will have had to occur before the United States uses force, and both are triggered by others, not by us. First, U.S. sovereignty was violated. A sovereign government elsewhere intentionally or unintentionally lent attackers support. Second, that sovereign government will only incur our armed wrath after it *refuses* to meet our demands. In other words, this is not a policy of mindless punishment or destruction. Its intent is not to wipe out or even threaten every unlucky, inept, or corrupt regime. Nor is the demand-response-reaction sequence the least bit vindictive. It does not aim to exact an eye for an eye. Instead, it is completely iterative. Washington demands; the government we hold responsible responds; how it responds determines how we react.

States with Too Much Power (Nuclear Weapons) and Too Little (Failed States)

Clearly, a special category exists among adversary states: those equipped with a nuclear arsenal. It would be irresponsible to promote a national security strategy that does not address the threat of nuclear attack or the specter of nuclear weapons falling into hostile hands. But here, too, the demand-response-reaction sequence is transparently consistent—and all governments face the same choice. They can sign the Nuclear Non-Proliferation Treaty and open themselves up to inspection, thereby engaging in transparent activities, or they can choose to hide—or act as though they are hiding—enrichment and weapons development programs, in which case they invite suspicion and distrust.

When the latter occurs, Washington's course of action needs to include putting any and all such countries on a public and well-publicized nuclear suspect list. Then, in the event the United States is attacked with a weapon of mass destruction and our analysts cannot quickly determine who precisely is the source—perhaps the uranium was stolen, maybe the engineers came from two different countries and those delivering the device from a third—*all* states on the suspect list would receive the same simple ultimatum: immediate transparency.[4] The onus would fall on them to open themselves up to immediate inspection and prove they had nothing to do with the attack.[5] Otherwise, they should consider themselves targetable, as adversary states.

Again, under the relationship framework described above, all countries are afforded ample opportunity to choose the nature of the relationship they want with us. A state on the suspect list could, for instance, get itself removed from the list simply by opening its programs to inspection. This, too, is squarely in keeping with the transparency and accountability that go hand in hand with sovereign responsibility. But states that choose to behave like adolescents, those who display the look, but not the maturity or self-control, of adults need to be treated as such, just as those who play the troublemaker invite suspicion *as* troublemakers—*that* is what the nuclear suspect list represents.

At the same time, sovereignty does permit states to develop whatever arsenals they choose. Just because a state seeks nuclear weapons and engages in vile rhetoric does not grant us the right to attack it.[6] For instance, what has actually been gained by the six-party talks with North Korea, which are "only the latest iteration of a two-decade effort to stunt North Korea's nuclear program"? According to South Korean president Lee Myyng-bak, they haven't worked: "The North Koreans have gained, or bought, a lot of time through the six-party-talks framework to pursue their own agenda." What is especially remarkable about this assessment made in 2009 is that this was the first public acknowledgment of failure by a national leader since the talks began in 2003. That in and of itself testifies to how illusory talk masquerading as "collective action" can be.[7]

▲   ▲   ▲

We three coauthors need to be clear. We are not advocating that there be no penalty for proliferating nuclear weapons. Rather, we believe there are better methods by which to curtail proliferators' actions and curb their ambitions.[8] For instance, if North Korea or Iran, or some other country that acquires nuclear weapons supports or harbors individuals who use lesser weapons and kills Americans, that alone should set the demand-response-reaction sequence in motion. All one need do is reflect back on recent history: Americans have been killed in the DMZ. They have also been killed by Iranians in Iraq.

It is rare to find governments that preach death and destruction on a large scale but don't also support murders on a smaller scale.[9] If anyone has been ambiguous about its reactions to violations of sovereignty, it has been Washington whenever it has overlooked small transgressions because it fears bigger, more catastrophic events.[10] Under the sovereignty rubric, a violation is a violation. Violating the *principle* of sovereignty is all that should matter. Scale doesn't enter into the demand-response-reaction sequence at all—it can't; if it does, then once the United States calibrates its reactions according to the type of action taken against us, we are the ones who wind up at the bottom of an ethical slippery slope. Yes, on the face of it, 3,000 dead in the 9/11 attacks *is* worse than 3 or 30 or even 300 dead in other incidents. But one day there may be 30,000 killed. Should that mean we do nothing in the face of mere thousands of casualties?

It is important to remember what distinguishes us as Americans. The ethical imperative we live by is to treat everyone the same. We should be grateful we live in a country that strives to treat everyone equally; that is a noble thing. Yet, we have seldom responded as though an attack on just one American who is abroad representing the United States is an attack on all. Rhetorically Washington may posture as though we do, but our actions rarely match our bluster. Sometimes, too, for political reasons Washington takes greater pains for private citizens than for government employees, or for some private citizens over others. One need only think back to efforts made on behalf of Heather Mercer and Dayna Curry, who were arrested by the Taliban in August 2001 on charges of illegally preaching Christianity; or the attempts made to rescue missionaries Martin and Gracia

Burnham kidnapped by the radical Islamist group Abu Sayyaf in the Philippines in 2001–2; or the 2009 case of U.S. journalists Euna Lee and Laura Ling accused by North Korea of illegal entry. In each instance, timing and other agendas help explain why Washington initiated a full-court press on these citizens' behalf, for during the same period any number of other Americans were likewise being held for whom the U.S. government did much less.

Unfortunately, all such inconsistencies cost us. They help explain why the sovereignty quid pro quo—"Don't violate our sovereignty and we won't violate yours"—lacks teeth. Yet, nothing is more likely to impel others to police their own than our being resolute on this as well as other points.[11]

▲   ▲   ▲

As counterintuitive as it may seem, even failed states should be able to self-police. If struggling states are those that are willing but unable to meet our demands in the wake of an attack, *failed states* are unable and unwilling and so fractured that there may be no central authority to which we could deliver demands at all. This does not mean, however, that there is no one to hold to account in what are referred to as "ungoverned" or undergoverned spaces.[12]

To return to the world's most vivid exemplar of a failed state, not even Somalia lacks centers of power. At the moment, Mogadishu, the capital, may be under the nominal control of a governing body that claims to represent the rest of the country, but as the existence of the Republic of Somaliland suggests, the northern part of what used to be Somalia is under someone else's control. The same holds for Puntland, another independent-acting, self-governing region in the northeast. Consequently, though neither Somaliland nor Puntland have (yet) received international recognition, that does not mean that there is no authority in the country formerly known as Somalia. There is just no singular source of authority—which points to something else that is true the world over. Wherever there are people, there is always someone or some group of "someones" running things. Every population center on earth has some sort of governing body even if it bears no resemblance to what we think of as a sitting government and is instead "just" a council of elders who meet under a shade tree.

All societies have rules and means of dealing with rule breakers. Where the rule of law typically breaks down is *between* societies, tribes, clans, and ethnic groups, especially when competing groups can't agree on whose rule set should prevail. This, as much as anything, describes the situation in Somalia—and Iraq, Afghanistan, the former Yugoslavia, and elsewhere: competing clans, tribes, religious communities, and so forth do not agree on who should run the central government or whether they all even belong together in the same country. But hone in on any one set of people; take a look at their social structure: not only should it be possible to identify the troublemakers, but there will always be an individual or two who *can* police the rest.

This means there is always someone to hold to account. There is always someone who not only knows who violated U.S. sovereignty, but who could have either stopped an attack or passed on information that would have thwarted it. *That* is the individual or set of individuals Washington needs to hold responsible in a failed state. That is whom we should deliver our demands to. That is whom, if they defy us, we make an example of. In this sense, Washington would not react to violations that emanate from failed states any differently than it would respond to violations that originate in states with strong central governments. The only difference comes in whom to single out.

It is at this juncture that ethnographic sensors would play a major role. They would help point to and identify local sources of authority—something we should be monitoring anyway so that we do not get taken by surprise as trouble develops in a place we consider insignificant, bearing in mind that often places remain insignificant only because no incident has made them matter yet.

▲   ▲   ▲

To reiterate: this strategy does not advocate targeting anyone until parties who shirked their sovereign responsibility (maybe by accident, maybe through neglect) have been offered the opportunity to rid themselves—and thereby us—of our attackers and have refused to do so.

Nothing cuts through ambiguity like force. But also, reinvigorating sovereignty sets rules that are very difficult to game, to include rules for behavior in unconventional realms like cyberspace. Should U.S. government computer systems be hacked or attacked, that is a clear violation of sovereignty and demands a U.S. government response—just as does any violation of federal, state, or municipal property. In a Sovereignty Rules world, any network the government relies on to conduct its official business has to be protected at all costs—and the government needs to make this clear.[13] As for what should happen to violators when they attack U.S. commercial interests, the rhetorical counterquestion is, what happens to criminals who attack U.S. commercial interests right now via espionage or theft? Perpetrators are taken to court; the United States does not declare war.

Just as corporations, businesses, and citizens are responsible for securing their physical property, it seems reasonable to assume they should remain responsible for protecting their property in cyberspace. Arguably, the government might patrol the portals, much as police patrol our streets, but otherwise the market can determine how much risk businesses and consumers want to assume when we conduct so much of our life online.[14] Alternatively, should the American public decide to make cybersecurity a *protected* public good, then the American people would have to be clear about what this means: The United States would then need to react to *any* cyber violation from abroad as if the country itself had been physically attacked; and once the demand-response-reaction sequence was set in motion, reaction (if it came) could well be military.[15]

One advantage the United States has is we can already react to cyber violations with conventional counterforce if we so choose, whereas other countries with lesser capabilities would have to face up to the fact that they may not be able to defend themselves in cyberspace, or if they did decide that being online was as critical to them as it seems to be to us, they would then have to develop the capabilities to protect what they claim belongs to them. But this, too, is in keeping with the congruence built into sovereignty's twin pillars of choice and responsibility.[16] Or, to put this in a pithier but also classically sovereign frame: as you defend so may you hold. Indeed, as has always been the case, countries' ability to react to transgressions using real force in the real world may be the only way to set the boundaries they don't want others to cross.[17]

▲   ▲   ▲

Fast-forward a few frames and consider all the permutations the demand-response-reaction sequence should be able to handle. Not only would sovereignty force non-state actors back into roles that make them subordinate to states, but also it would force war back into a much more explicit and containable form.[18] If, for instance, agitators and rebels stage from country X or country X lends support to opposition movements trying to undermine country Y's government, these represent clear breaches of sovereignty, while any covert support represents just as much of a violation as overt support. Or, as Robert Jackson reminds us, "Sovereignty is not a matter of degree . . . it is categorical: either/or."[19]

Meanwhile, how realistic is it to think that any such framework might prevent rival countries from interfering in each other's affairs? Or, to couch this somewhat differently, if the United States did decide to operate according to this framework, what on earth would compel others to?

The short answer is: nothing. No *framework* can prevent one country from meddling in another country's affairs. When it comes to ineffectual governments with capable neighbors, interference will still loom as a very real possibility; examples include Somalia with a strong Ethiopia next door, the Democratic Republic of Congo (DRC) with a resurgent Rwanda, Nepal under the shadow of China. If we bear in mind that the only foolproof guarantee of security and longevity any government has is that its citizens prefer its rule over rule by someone else, the threat of a ruthless neighbor would pose the same danger in a Sovereignty Rules world that it does today—with one slight twist. The threat of trouble from without *could* prove exactly the goad many governments need to become more responsive to their own citizens since, if a government is fair, equitable, and inclusive, outsiders who seek to subvert it from within should find no one with whom they can work.

In thinking about how reinvigorating sovereignty could serve to help sort out those who can—and thereby deserve to—govern from those who don't, consider the world's most totalitarian state, North Korea. North Korea is hardly self-sufficient. The regime in Pyongyang blackmails other countries into feeding its population. It leaks defectors. It also forcibly abducts South Koreans and others, murders South Korean soldiers, and the list goes on. In a Sovereignty Rules world, South Korea or China should have responded to North Korean incursions years ago. And, had there not been such a strong U.S. presence in the region to complicate matters, regional political pressures might have ensured that they did respond.[20]

▲ ▲ ▲

Without question, few governments work as hard as they should to be inclusive and equitable. Locations far from the seat of power usually only matter when they boast lucrative resources or shelter transnational terrorists; in fact, both reasons help explain why the United States worries so much about failed states today.

Alternatively, consider what one imaginary dictator might say while holding an imaginary conversation with a neighbor,

> I'm corrupt and don't sufficiently take care of all of my citizens. But I do a pretty good job of crushing my political opponents. That's why they seek sanctuary and support across the border with you. And you—you have exactly the same problem. That's why your rebels come to me for assistance. So—I support them. They try to unseat you; and the rebels you back try to get rid of me. All of them chew up our borders and, in the process, lay waste local villages. The "world" hasn't figured out how to stop this. All it can do is send in humanitarian aid, which (the speaker now chuckles) is lucky for us. Not only does aid help prolong the fighting, but even better, if we siphon off enough of it for our soldiers and our cronies, and charge protection money so that the do-gooders can deliver the rest, well, it keeps us going, too. And we both stay in power—don't we?

Leaders do not even have to have this kind of conversation for such quid pro quos to work, although South African and Ukrainian pilots flying old Soviet gunships in Africa might. With so many of them working for anyone who pays them well, those serving on opposite sides of a conflict allegedly do say things to each other over the radio such as, "hey, I'll be working in Sector XY today, make sure you're flying somewhere else." That way they deconflict the likelihood of causing one another harm as they go about the *business* of shooting up the locals.

Although the world has been wringing its collective hands over Darfur for almost eight years, fighting devastated southern Sudan for the two previous decades. Yet somehow, in stunningly sophisticated humanitarian assistance operations, international aid organizations managed to get supplies through to feeding camps and to hundreds of thousands of internally displaced people. The aid industry moved veritable mountains of aid. But tellingly, none of this stopped the fighting; if anything, it may have helped prolong it. For instance, in 1997 Alex de Waal wrote of Operation Lifeline Sudan (which began in 1989):

> By 1994, the diversion of relief supplies by all the SPLA factions and the Sudan Government had become so systematic that some experienced relief workers canvassed the proposal that a certain proportion of all supplies be formally consigned to the military. ... Publicly, OLS continues to maintain the fiction that it does not supply soldiers. The final result is that relief is inextricably bound up in the political economy of war in Southern Sudan. Relief is provisioning both civilians and soldiers, is influencing political mobilization and military strategy, and is one of the prime foci of international diplomacy.[21]

Nor was the resourcing of war necessarily the worst of it. In 2007 Jok Madut Jok pointed out that donor countries that had been funding OLS for over sixteen years would invariably refer to the amount of money they had already spent—whenever they were confronted about their unwillingness to do more to help end the fighting—"as if throwing money at Sudan's conflicts was going to put out the flames of war."[22] In other words, they used aid to buy themselves an "out."[23]

It is equally revealing that over the course of all those years, the Sudanese government never once declared war on Ethiopia even when Ethiopia supported Sudanese rebels. Nor did Ethiopia declare war on Sudan despite Sudan's support of its insurgents. We could point to the same kinds of "arrangements" across Africa, or between pairs of countries in Asia and Latin America, or anywhere where insurgents find a cross-border "enemy of an enemy."[24] A cynic might well conclude from this that one reason governments do not directly target each other is because that would render war too *obviously* unwinnable. Yet, not only do wars seem to *have* grown increasingly unwinnable, consider what happens when no one forces those orchestrating and benefiting from wars to push fighting to a winnable conclusion—hostilities then go on and on.[25]

Embedded in this post–World War II paradox of inconclusive warfare has been considerable profit for some, a true humanitarian travesty for others, and a set of what should be discomfiting realizations for those of us who have not been directly caught up in such fighting.[26] Among such discomfiting realizations is that intractability may be all but guaranteed whenever the parties to conflict *refuse* to go all out. But intractability is also compounded whenever one or both sides receive external assistance. By no means do we want to suggest here that governments should be encouraged *to* go all out; rather, if those in power were at least forced to have to fear for themselves and for their families and cronies in capital cities and other safe locations, it is hard to imagine they would sacrifice hinterland communities quite as readily and as willingly as they do.

A case in point is Sierra Leone, where rebels turned children into soldiers, raped countless women, lopped off limbs, and did incalculable damage in the countryside. Civil war ebbed and flowed throughout the 1990s. Only after rebels rampaged through the capital and raped and pillaged their way through the city center did residents of Freetown fully appreciate what their lack of attention had helped foster. To this day, firsthand memories of that violence probably does as much to keep war at bay in that West African country as anything else.

▲   ▲   ▲

To be absolutely blunt, very few rulers govern today thanks to their followers' belief in their divine power.[27] Instead, those *in* power clearly know how to wield power to both get and stay where they are. For the moment, we in the United States have more power—power that is both more mundane *and* overwhelming. No one else is in as strong a position to say to heads of other governments "Be more responsible for and responsive to your own people, or else." Address their concerns. If you don't, let just one of them target us out of a sense of justifiable frustration or anger with you. If you don't then rectify the situation, you and your regime are finished.

What if we operated according to this principle? Wouldn't there then be a chance—maybe even a good chance—others would follow suit?

Chapter 5

Renewing America's Vision of War

merica's Founding Fathers engineered a brilliant thing. The system of governance they devised for us not only still works, but the principles they committed to paper—and thereby fixed for all time—were crafted flexibly enough so that the Constitution remains just as relevant and central today as when they signed off on it 230 years ago. If a document like that still endures, given all the changes in the world, we should be able to come up with a twenty-first-century national security strategy that endures from one presidential administration to the next.

The relationship framework outlined in the previous chapter offers one means toward such an end. The Constitution offers another.

The United States has issued formal Declarations of War eleven times and has followed each declaration with a victory.[1] Not a single Declaration of War has been issued in the past sixty years, yet the United States has pursued political objectives through military force almost continuously. The correlation should be striking. Declarations of War appear to be the proven method for reaching political objectives through military means. When Congress has issued them, the United States has succeeded in war. When Congress has not, the United States has reached inconclusive end states at best.[2] This track record alone suggests the United States should return to constitutionally mandated Declarations of War and points to why we should pursue military objectives under only such authority.[3]

If we were to consider this from a slightly different angle, for fifty years presidents and Congress have declared "war" on poverty, hunger, crime, drugs, and—most recently—terrorism; but our government has waged "real" war only under the banner of "authorizations of force." We currently have close to 200,000 troops deployed in designated hostile fire zones. We spend billions of dollars each week in support of military objectives. And we bury casualties from Afghanistan, Iraq, and elsewhere weekly, sometimes daily. It defies common sense that any American should be able to legitimately question the nation's strategic footing, or question whether or not America is "at war." However, without a formal Declaration of War, what should otherwise be considered absurd has become routine. Tens of millions of Americans do not seem to realize the United States is at war; rather, they might acknowledge, our armed forces are.

The Federalist Papers make it abundantly clear that the Founding Fathers considered war to be inevitable and part of statecraft, that government must have checks built in to prevent the abuse of power, and that, because the people are sovereign, they must be kept informed. From the founders' perspective, war was serious business and no single branch of government could be entrusted to prosecute it without the support and agreement of the other two branches. Yet, surprisingly, all three branches of government have, at different times, argued against the use of Declarations of War. Sometimes this has occurred because one branch has sought to maintain its power at the expense of the other two. At other times, a branch has objected in order to avoid accountability.

A Declaration of War requires that Congress act. Article I, section 8 of the Constitution defines the role of the legislature. Among its duties is the power "To *declare War*, grant Letters of Marque and Reprisal, and make Rules concerning Captures on Land and Water" (emphasis ours). The president, as chief executive and enforcement tool of the federal government, serves as the commander in chief "of the Army and Navy of the United States, and of the Militia of the several States, when called into the actual Service of the United States." The division of labor is clear: Congress's responsibility is to enact and empower. The president is supposed to lead and execute.[4]

Unfortunately today (and for the past six decades), rather than Congress arming the president with over 250 statutes under U.S. Code, our elected representatives have apparently preferred that the president conduct statecraft through executive fiat. Under the War Powers Act of 1973, Congress "permits" the president to pursue military objectives so long as Congress is informed of progress within a mandated timeframe. Ostensibly, Congress created the War Powers Act in order to curb executive power. Conveniently, however, what the Act has done is enable individual members of Congress to hedge their collective bets by taking no unequivocal position on military efforts until such time as either victory can be declared or defeat looks assured. Witness the run-up to both the 2004 and 2008 presidential campaigns—how else were candidates able to explain "yes" votes as "no" votes when it came to their support for (or, was it opposition to) the Iraq *War*?[5]

Meanwhile, in the ambiguous environment of no clearly declared war, the judiciary branch inherits all sorts of power.[6] The courts determine the extent to which the executive branch may prosecute a war, with what means, and to what degree. Consider all the recent and still pending court battles over the status and treatment of "unlawful" enemy combatants, detentions, surveillance, targeting, and so forth—and then reflect on how ill-served we are by this patchwork approach to strategy. Strategy needs to be clear and purposeful if commanders and diplomats are to execute it effectively. Strategy should not be left up to the courts to fitfully whittle away.

The Sovereignty Solution calls for a return to Declarations of War.

Rigorous debate about the merits of taking coercive action should have to occur *before* the first soldier is deployed or before the first "launch" button is pushed.[7] *Is* there an obvious reason the United States should go to war? *Has* war been declared against the United States? Was our sovereignty incontrovertibly violated? Has another government publicly refused to meet our public demands?[8] If the reasons for deploying force pass Americans' commonsense test, the answers to these questions will be obvious, the debate will be short, and the decision quick. If not, then the standards for declaring war clearly will not have been met, and if they cannot be met the executive should not want, never mind press, to take action.[9]

Another set of reasons for formal Declarations of War is that, without them, military pursuits remain just one among a series of ongoing activities that compete for government attention and tax dollars. Where is the national urgency during a time of "executive decision"? Which government agency leads during an "authorization of force"? Who can compel all the various government bureaucracies to cooperate? Who holds whom accountable to ensure that priorities are met? With anything less than a formal Declaration of War these questions cannot be answered; without accountability and a clear chain of command, the government becomes nothing more than a bunch of fingers and cannot act as a fist.

We Americans are an inordinately busy people. And while tens of millions of us contribute time and money to all sorts of local community-service activities, we do not openly pull together as a nation, except in a crisis. By definition, crises never last very long and, as discussed in chapter 2, few affect the entire country in the same way for any length of time; for example, 9/11 posed one kind of crisis. So did levee failure in New Orleans. War is a significantly different prospect, one difference being wars involve other actors who operate outside our legal system, beyond our borders, and beyond our control (at least initially). Maybe the United States military can prevail with an air strike or two, but if not, what, other than a collective commitment to either win or to surrender, guarantees that "we the people" will persist—despite whatever setbacks our military forces might experience?[10]

History demonstrates that Americans will expend a tremendous amount of blood and treasure in the pursuit of political and military objectives. Scan any national cemetery. Multiply the number buried there by the family members they have left behind. The widely held belief that Americans will not stomach casualties is patently false. What Americans do demand, however, is a legitimate reason for their sacrifice and an understanding that the successful outcome of a conflict *can* be achieved.[11]

Nothing short of a formal Declaration of War can deliver this because only the process of publicly declaring war ensures sufficient scrutiny and the careful determination *beforehand* that ends, ways, and means *will be* aligned. Will politicians commit enough soldiers, armor, resources, or whatever it will take *for* the duration? With Declarations of War there is no room for nuance and little room for ex post facto equivocation. If the United States issues a declaration, what that declaration promises—its point, actually—is that this country will prosecute that war until our announced political objectives have been achieved, or until we openly accept defeat.[12]

Admittedly, the very nature of a formal Declaration of War—and its promise that the United States will relentlessly pursue a clearly defined objective—goes against the first rule of politics: never make a hard promise you can't break. But this is also exactly why, in an age of unrelenting media posturing, the United States absolutely must return to issuing Declarations of War.[13] Declarations of war preclude secret promises and cut down on shady political deals. They likewise prevent waffling in the face of unexpected, but inevitable difficulties. Or as the late William F. Buckley put it, in a somewhat different context, "To declare war is not necessarily to dispatch troops, let alone atom bombs. It is to recognize a juridically altered relationship and to license such action as is deemed appropriate. It is a wonderful demystifier . . . [leaving] your objective in very plain view."[14]

▲　　▲　　▲

If any national security strategy is to have a shred of deterrent effect there must exist a government action that immediately signals to the rest of the world, *Enough.* Declarations of War flip that switch.[15] Could a Declaration of War lead to endless war? It is unlikely because, by declaring war on a physical enemy as opposed to an idea, a concept, or a method (e.g., terrorism), Washington would automatically be defining success, how to achieve it, and what would be needed before the state of war could end: the enemy submits, or we do.

Here it is worth noting, too, that there is no constitutional limitation on whom or what formal war can be declared against. Just because Declarations of War have not been used against non-state actors in the past does not mean that, in a case where there is no viable government to hold to account, the United States couldn't declare war against whatever local authority we did hold responsible for a breach of our sovereignty. Nor do Declarations of War come with a statute of limitations. A government might go into hiding, a substate organization might scatter across a region of states, and perpetrators might disappear into the population. Until our enemy has been permanently disabled, the declaration would stand.

Standing Declarations of Preemption

The United States might, at some future point, need to move faster than the time required to secure a Declaration of War. How, then, should the United States address a clear and present danger? How do we respond to an impending attack as it is in the throes of being launched?

Using the same constitutional authority that establishes formal Declarations of War, Congress could issue "Standing Declarations of Preemption."[16] A Standing Declaration of Preemption would amount to congressional pre-approval for military force to be used against a pre-identified threat. The power of the standing declaration would be strictly circumscribed. The president would have to identify to Congress the organization or state that poses a specific threat, what specifically constitutes that threat, what would be required to neutralize it, and what the trigger would be that would require the United States to take immediate action. In a nutshell, congressional pre-approval would grant the president the authority necessary to preempt an impending attack, but only when and if specified and pre-identified "red lines" are crossed.

One example of the need for a standing declaration would likely be North Korea today. Given North Korea's demonstrated nuclear and ballistic missile capacity, the president could ask Congress for a standing declaration whose trigger would be North Korea readying its long-range ICBMs for launch without being willing to verifiably divulge their payloads. In such a case, with a Standing Declaration of Preemption, Congress would pre-authorize the president to use sufficient force to destroy the missiles prior to launch, while any further action against North Korea would require a formal Declaration of War.

As with votes for (or against) formal Declarations of War, votes for (or against) Standing Declarations of Preemption would be a matter of public record. There should be nothing hidden either about the congressional debate, or the pre-authorization process. Operational details would have to be kept classified. But, as should be standard with everything done in a Sovereignty Rules world, the American public would be fully briefed on what overall effect to expect should specific "red lines" be crossed. In turn, this transparency would put foreign states and "non-state" actors, to include would-be attackers, on notice—which is also the point: "Don't, or else."

⋏　⋏　⋏

Of course the two most important challenges associated with adopting and then sustaining any such policy would be, first, Washington would have to demonstrate its willingness to be decisive. And second, it would have to follow through. *Will* the U.S. government respond to all attacks on national sovereignty with the determination that a formal Declaration of War requires? Will the American public support the use of force necessary to rid some other country of a proven threat if authorities there can't be compelled to act responsibly—even if, perhaps, the initial attack only killed a handful of Americans? These are legitimate questions that are impossible to answer because the United States has never attempted to implement a policy like this. But reflect on what will continue to happen if Washington remains hesitant or acts as though there is some threshold that has to be crossed before America *will* respond forcefully: transnational networks, organizations that infiltrate weak or willing sovereign hosts, and insurgent armies that hover just below the horizon of seeming to matter will continue to flourish.

From Hezbollah to drug-running gangs like MS-13, non-state actors have willfully killed American citizens. Meanwhile, the only reason such organizations continue to survive is because we, along with other governments and communities, allow them to. That is the ugly, but inescapable truth.

The Ugly Nature of Twenty-First-Century Warfare

No set of violent non-state actors can operate without a sympathetic or intimidated population in which to hide, arm, plan, train, and whenever possible, fight. Our current adversaries, for instance, are *of* the people. As Edward Luttwak matter-of-factly notes, "if insurgents do not receive, or cannot forcibly exact, at least the passive collaboration of the population at large, they normally cannot survive at all."[17]

Non-state actors understand that they cannot be eliminated so long as they burrow into the population. They take full advantage of contemporary discourse that says targeting population centers in any way, shape, or form is barbaric and, therefore, immoral—and not to be done.

Barbarism has been given a very wide definition in recent years. For instance, according to one definition, barbarism is "the systematic violation of the laws of war in pursuit of military or political objectives . . . its most important element is depredations against noncombatants."[18] Accordingly, Washington can be accused of barbarism as soon as it goes after terrorists and causes harm to anyone who does not *look* like a soldier. "Just War" theorists have split an awful lot of ethical hairs over the years differentiating between factory workers making munitions—without which war cannot be fought—and rations—without which soldiers can't be fed. According to many, the former are targetable, the latter not. Populations stuck under authoritarian rule make ethicists' determinations seem even easier; civilians with no say can't be considered culpable. However, according to this kind of logic, where people rule through their elected leaders—in democracies, for example—all civilians would be fair game. Indeed, this is the argument some among our current adversaries make, which is not dissimilar from the PLO's attitude toward Israeli Jews, any of whom it used to consider to be legitimate targets because all Israeli Jews were expected to perform military service at some point in their lives.

▲   ▲   ▲

Key to any definition are its connotations. *Are* civilians always noncombatants?[19] In virtually all societies the willful targeting and killing of innocents is considered indefensible, but the rub comes in who is considered "innocent."[20] Women are often considered innocent just by virtue of their gender, ditto for children under a certain age. But, what happens when women and children lend active support to combatants? What about women and children who refuse to turn in known insurgents? Or, how about women who volunteer themselves and their children for use as human shields?

Terrorists, insurgents, and others have not only figured out how to take the very precepts of Western "Just War" theory and turn them against us, but they now excel at this.[21] "The reason terrorist groups such as Hezbollah use human shields is elementary. They try to exploit the respect for innocent human life that is the hallmark of any civilized society to place that society in a no-win situation. If, for instance, a government fails to respond to terror attacks, it endangers its own citizens. If it responds, it runs the risk of killing innocents, earning world opprobrium and inviting diplomatic pressure to stand down."[22]

One thing that should be clear to anyone who pays attention to the news (no matter what brand of news) is that legal discourse has not caught up to these sorts of challenges. Or, as the *Wall Street Journal* once put it, "accusations of U.S. atrocities against civilians occur after almost every military operation."[23] Certainly, ethical murk is one reason the status of detainees at Guantanamo has proven so difficult. International law does not address non-state actors or their supporters. Yet paradoxically, as a set of norms, international law still has a powerful impact. We see this with countries' unwillingness to declare war: "Even states in a de facto war do not declare war, so as to avoid breaches of international law." The paradox Hew Strachan points to in this sentence has everything to do with Just War concerns about non-combatants.[24]

Strachan does not broach the subject of how to re-regulate war. But if we look at the problem through the sovereignty lens, the only legitimacy non-state actors have is thanks to states that permit or can't stop them from operating. Significantly, when (and where) governments fulfill their sovereign duties, armed non-state actors should find no legitimacy at all.[25]

▲   ▲   ▲

To be clear, *The Sovereignty Solution* does not argue that non-state actors be made to disappear through some semantic sleight of hand. Rather, the point is that non-state actors deserve no special status.[26] Nor should any foreign government be able to support someone else's non-state actors unless it is willing to go to war on their behalf.[27]

Again, without forcing war back into the open—which is what reinvigorating sovereignty would do—it is too easy for war by proxy, or sneaky war, to remain the chosen instrument of both the powerless *and the powerful*.[28] Lest we forget, proxy war is what Washington and Moscow indulged in throughout the Cold War—to our ongoing detriment in Afghanistan, North Korea, and elsewhere today. Worth remembering, too, is that so long as proxy war remains available to us, it also remains available to potential adversaries, and others would be foolish not to use it against us. Our aim should be to make it unavailable—to everyone.

For just one example of how out of hand the status of non-state actors has grown, consider the following assessment of Hezbollah: "though probably capable of taking over the weak central government of Lebanon, Hezbollah has preferred to maintain its sub-state role, thereby limiting its responsibility and hence its vulnerability to attacks."[29] Perhaps this seems justified in the eyes of many around the world because Israel is so strong and the Palestinians so weak. But the status that is accorded Hezbollah doesn't just make life difficult for Israelis. So long as sneaky war is countenanced anywhere, civilians *everywhere* remain in jeopardy. In no small part this is because the whole point of sneaky war *is* to jeopardize civilians.

⋏   ⋏   ⋏

What has to be remembered is that, in a Sovereignty Rules world, what would apply abroad would apply to us as Americans as well. Washington, for instance, would no longer be able to surreptitiously support some group it favors in its bid to unseat a government we don't like.[30] The only time we would be justified in removing a government is if it fails to meet Washington's demands in the wake of an attack it couldn't or didn't stop. If our response then enabled others on the local scene to step into the power vacuum we create, so be it. The chapters to come will have more to say about this. What is important to reiterate here is that non-state actors pose a twenty-first-century security problem not just because no one knows what to do about them, but because the West has enabled them to paint us into a Just War corner.[31]

Readjusting Just War Philosophy

Because neither the Hague Convention Accords from the turn of the century nor the 1977 Protocol Additional to the Geneva Convention address the issue of non-state actors conducting transnational attacks, combatant status is still defined by what fighters wear (e.g., uniforms and military insignia) and whether they answer to a chain of command. Ironically, definitions from the 1700s and 1800s do a better job of accommodating today's realities. In past eras, writers as varied as the eighteenth-century Swiss philosopher Emmerich de Vattel and American Civil War general Henry Halleck agreed: what people did, not how they looked, branded them combatants. Thus, Vattel, Halleck, and others considered any individual who hid, sheltered, fed, scouted, or provided intelligence to an enemy organization to be a legitimate target.[32]

There is a rule of discrimination under the *jus in bello* concept of war: who or what is the intended target sets the parameters for the degree of counterforce to be applied. But even this has proved problematic in today's environment.[33] How *should* an army handle kids with rocks, or widows who shrug their shoulders about the location of their insurgent sons? Think, too, about what happens when the enemy subdivides into small groups and *purposely* embeds itself in villages. Or consider what has happened since the dawning of the precision strike era.

Thanks to technological advances in precision-guided munitions there is now the expectation that the world's most sophisticated militaries can easily avoid what has euphemistically been called "collateral damage." In an inadvertent twist, the military itself has done much to feed these expectations. Since the first Gulf War—when briefings included footage showcasing successful strikes while bombs dropped down airshafts or missiles struck third-floor offices after turning corners around city streets—audiences have been led to believe our military can target and kill anything it sees as soon as it sees it.[34] As a consequence, if just one individual who is not a weapon-carrying, military-aged male is killed, this immediately serves as broadcast-worthy proof that the United States is not just *purposely* targeting civilians, but waging war against them.

Unfortunately, it doesn't matter that accidents occur or that intelligence can be faulty. As soon as people who look like civilians die, the speed with which the international media reacts delivers our adversaries a propaganda coup of incalculable worth.[35] Worse, such "mistakes" help reassure our opponents that they can't lose—in fact, our adversaries should only hope there will be more "unfortunate" incidents. Or why hope when they can facilitate this by locating weapons caches in schools and hospitals, emplacing command centers in embassies, using apartment complexes for firing platforms, and positioning snipers in religious buildings. Any targeting and subsequent destruction of any of these facilities by us only guarantees swift apologies, something that, these days, we then let restrict us all the more.[36]

What is doubly ironic about the condemnation U.S. forces experience when they try to be discriminating is that, although the United States is signatory to a number of treaties and conventions regarding the conduct of warfare, non-state actors are not.[37] Technically, however, reciprocity can be binding on only those who agree to it. This means that, through the principle of double effect, civilian structures and sites that are used for the purposes of waging warfare *can* be intentionally targeted and destroyed. Already, American military forces apply "breach of contract" rules at the tactical level. Whenever soldiers or Marines on the ground are caught in a firefight they respond with counterforce. If an enemy sniper is shooting from a church bell tower, that bell tower will be attacked. What the United States has not yet done is apply the principle of double effect at the strategic level. Local communities aren't treated as hide sites or sources of shelter; but, for this reason, that is precisely what they have become.

The American people need to be made both more fully and graphically aware of the degrees to which Just War philosophy has been outstripped by twenty-first-century realities. Only two decades ago during the first Gulf War, Americans had no problem treating conscripts chained to the insides of their tanks and uniformed boys held in fighting positions against their will as combatants. Saddam Hussein deployed them as cannon fodder and we decimated them. Yet, were such youth any more culpable than are civilians today who knowingly hide or raise money for al Qaeda, Hezbollah, Jemaah Islamiyah, or any such organization you could name?

Rethinking Non-Combatant Status

Insurgents, terrorists, and other fighters could not exist or function without enabling communities. Here is where *veritas* about *bello* (truth *about* war) needs to modify the Just War stand-bys of *jus in bello* and *jus ad bellum*.[38] Whenever an organization, a movement, or a network willfully jeopardizes a community, the deaths of any *true* innocents belong on the heads of its members.[39] The United States needs to make this the third rail for states. Washington needs to convey to populations abroad and to Americans here at home that it is not up to us to effect distinctions that our adversaries prevent us from being able to make.

Without question, the United States should always strive to be as discriminating and precise as possible in whom and what we target. That is a constraint no one should want lifted. Given who has to live with the eyewitness imagery for the rest of their lives—namely, our servicemen and women—it is critical that we never become cavalier about violence. However, this is just one more reason why Washington needs to make it crystal clear to other governments and local authorities that *they* are the responsible parties should we have to take action, and that we hold them as culpable as anyone who pulls a trigger or plants a bomb. Otherwise, squeamishness about what to do when communities act as accessories to murder will continue to stymie us and will remain one of our opponents' most useful weapons. Or, to put this somewhat differently, the clearer we can be about whom we cannot *avoid* killing, the less likely it may be that we have to face these difficult circumstances.

The argument here is that, in an era when combatants do not hesitate to turn residential neighborhoods into armed camps, it should not be up to us to have to differentiate between non-uniformed militants and militant "civilians." If a terrorist organization (or regime) blurs the lines in order to confound us, a Declaration of War (which comes only after a state proves unwilling to meet our demands), puts everyone on notice that we will treat alike anyone who belongs to or supports those who attacked us. This is yet another advantage to specifying who we are at war with via a Declaration of War: in the wake of a declaration, everyone who is an associate, or who might fear we will mistake them for an associate of those we are targeting, will have been warned.

Otherwise, without the United States adopting such a policy, it is hard to see our way out of our current bind in which communities, civilians, innocent, and innocent-seeming, sympathetic, empathetic, or just plain apathetic citizens offer adversaries the ultimate twenty-first-century cover.[40] Because we have permitted war to (d)evolve to the point of opponents situating themselves in the heart of densely populated neighborhoods *in order* to get us to inflict as many civilian casualties as possible to prevent us from even trying to root them out, opponents present us with a devil's choice. We play into their hands when we attack. But we also play into their hands when we don't attack and they remain free. They win either way—but only because we have helped them attain an unassailable advantage.[41]

▲ ▲ ▲

To readers who, at this point, wonder, *would* the United States ever strike a community without giving it fair warning first, the answer should be obvious: no, not even if civilians were actively and openly supporting terrorists. That is because Washington would have already continuously broadcast the same simple message: *don't* support those who seek to harm Americans. Don't support those whom you suspect might seek to harm Americans. Don't support those whom you can't know for sure *won't* seek to harm Americans. Otherwise, you may suffer the consequences along with them.[42]

▲ ▲ ▲

Ideally it is the responsibility of other governments to prevent our needing to take any action against those who violate our sovereignty. But where other governments do not have sufficient clout or courage, in failed states for instance, it seems only fair to warn populations directly—loudly, clearly, and continuously. To underscore how serious we are, we also have to make clear that should expatriates, including American citizens, choose to live and work among people who plot against the United States or should they hide and harbor those who do, such expatriates, too, have been forewarned and knowingly choose their fate. The U.S. government cannot take extra measures to spare them. Nor will the United States be held hostage just because they can be. Choice and responsibility: for individuals, communities, and governments. These are the twin pillars on which reinvigorating sovereignty rests.

Worth remembering, too, is just how many steps would be taken *before* the United States engages in military action. Not only will Washington have clearly and continually issued warnings about what governments and communities should expect if they hide or support violators of U.S. sovereignty, but Washington will have made it equally clear that the United States will accept no blame for any unintended casualties in the wake of an attack against us—all casualties are the responsibility of those whom we declare war against.

1. Our sovereignty is violated.

2. In the wake of an attack, Washington makes demands of the witting or unwitting government(s)/authorities it suspects, or knows, harbored our attackers. The demands are simple and public.

3. Those in authority reject Washington's demands or drag their feet.

4. The president asks Congress—and the American people—for a Declaration of War.

5. Congress issues a Declaration of War.[43]

6. Only at this point does the U.S. military tailor its means to achieve U.S. ends, which are to decimate those we are at war with. Our military forces will spare innocents to the best of their abilities.

⋏　⋏　⋏

How might all of this work in practice? Here are two potential scenarios.

First, a replay of the 1979 seizure of the American embassy by the Iranian Revolutionary Guard had we been living in a Sovereignty Rules world at the time.[44] Following the seizure of the embassy and in the shadow of a rapidly changing relationship with Iran, the United States would have delivered a list of demands to the new Iranian government: immediate release of U.S. prisoners and property, with all damages to be immediately repaired and repaid. The Iranian response—Iran's decision to respond as a partner state, a struggling state, or an adversary—would have then triggered the corresponding U.S. reaction. If the Iranians agreed to our demands, the United States could have provided assistance in order to help them get their house in order and rid them of their "student problem." If the Iranians had waffled or refused, then the entire Iranian government network—personnel and infrastructure—would have been immediately targeted in coordination with a full air/ground package to retrieve American personnel. The Iranian Revolution would have either been short-lived or de-fanged. Hezbollah would either not exist or would not have attacked the Marines in Beirut. The militant Shi'a revival likely would have withered on the vine.

Next, consider a variant of a more recent example: Suppose Hezbollah strikes targets on U.S. soil. In the wake of such an attack, our diplomats would deliver a list of demands to several different players: the government in Beirut if Lebanon is the country from which our attackers launched, Syria for being an enabler/supporter, and Iran as the sponsor. All three governments would have the opportunity to "redefine" their relationship with the United States. In agreeing to Washington's demands, the Lebanese government would have to thoroughly dismantle Hezbollah's capacity to bear arms—if it could. Maybe it would ask for our assistance. Maybe, like Syria and Iran, it would reject U.S. demands instead. In that case, all three governments would be targeted.

What if the Israelis had pursued such a strategy in July 2006? The Hezbollah threat might have been destroyed, Beirut's (non-Hezbollah) government liberated, and the Assad government toppled. Israel certainly would have fared no worse than it did from the precision-strike, incrementalist strategy it chose, which left its government politically and militarily weakened, Iran considerably strengthened throughout the region, and Hezbollah an invigorated model for non-state actors elsewhere to follow.

ᴧ   ᴧ   ᴧ

In both these scenarios the United States would be reacting to acts perpetrated against it in complete accord with the 1929 Kellogg-Briand Pact and the UN Charter, each of which recognizes that defensive war is fully within a state's sovereign rights. In fact, the parameters for the right to declare war were agreed upon well before either the UN Charter or the Kellogg-Briand Pact were penned. At the Hague Conventions of 1907, the "contracting powers" stipulated "that hostilities between themselves must not commence without previous and explicit warning, in the form either of a reasoned Declaration of War or of an ultimatum with conditional Declaration of War."[45]

One hundred years later, it would seem we have regressed if one considers that, today, it is non-state actors who are more likely than states to issue Declarations of War and ultimatums. Also, unlike one hundred or even fifty years ago, there are no longer any counterbalanced sets of allies, ententes, or blocs to count on: the United States is as unprotected by others as anyone is, and arguably even more so because, in terms of global force projection, we really have only ourselves to count on when it comes to our defense. That is why, as our own first responders, the best possible scenario would be that no sirens ever go off—which, presumably, they wouldn't, if only we could get other countries to effectively self-police.

Self-policing is, like everything else, about choice and responsibility. In the United States we prefer to undertake choice and responsibility as individuals; many Europeans and Asians are willing to cede more of each to government. Traditionally in Africa, choice and responsibility are local and collective. In a Sovereignty Rules world there would be no expectation that one style of choice and responsibility must fit all. Indeed, precisely because sovereignty allows for differences, reinvigorating it would deliver a far more reasonable means of resetting global security—and getting populations to self-police—than anything else being bruited about in Washington, especially since it offers a security formula with nothing to hide.

Deterrence

Everything about the relationship framework—are we dealing with a partner, struggling state, failed state, or adversary?—is predicated on the demand-response-reaction sequence being made explicit. The point is to always be transparent and congruent: what the policy promises, it delivers. Deterrence is a side benefit, though a potent one: "He [the opponent] has to be convinced that even in the face of his own counter-measures the targets he values will be found and destroyed, and that even if he can bear their loss you will escalate by attacking targets of even greater value to him."[46] This is one way deterrence is described. Another approach would be ours: attack targets of the greatest value first. Hit them, and the demonstration effect should preempt, dissuade, and compel those who think they don't want to self-police to think again.

One reads very few white papers these days about deterrence, perhaps because it remains too closely associated in most people's minds with nuclear war. Yet, the United States' conventional arsenal is of sufficient scope and size that deterrence should not require the use of nuclear weapons. Unfortunately, it seems we have not only lost sight of this fact, but worse—thanks in part to the Cold War–era linkage between deterrence and nuclear weapons—we have also succumbed to the syllogism that has non-state actors holding all the asymmetric cards. But this is only true if we forget our conventional arsenal *and* refuse to rethink Just War theory.

Of course, to some Americans anything even hinting at willful destruction as a course of action will be too unsettling to contemplate—it is too direct, too unnuanced, too primitive. In contrast, others who believe we should have turned certain countries into parking lots by now will say not even regime decapitation or obliteration of our attackers is sufficient punishment. This gap alone exposes a serious split. It is a divide that the strategy presented in this book strives to bridge by setting the conditions for strategic clarity—and not because the United States should ever seek revenge in retaliation for American deaths. Rather, in a Sovereignty Rules world the United States would act based solely on the "don't, or else" principle.

Additionally, "don't, or else" is not preemptive, or even slightly pro-war. Instead, it is decisively anti-sneaky and anti-long war.

▲   ▲   ▲

Without question, citizens the world over would be better off if wars were never fought. In a more ideal world, war's absence would be achieved by all governments behaving in a mature, responsive, and responsible fashion, with heads of state being responsive to and responsible for their citizens, and citizens willingly pledging support to just and well-functioning governments. But until then—or rather, to help precipitate that—the United States needs to develop a much more mature vision of what deterrence effectively requires: the unequivocal, principled use of decisive force.[47]

A maturing of Americans' vision, so that more Americans appreciate why decisive force is so critical in the twenty-first century, requires that all Americans more firmly grasp what is at stake. At the moment, it is not clear that the public fully understands the long-term costs of sending young men and women abroad to police other countries, or why it would be incomparably better for all involved if other governments voluntarily policed themselves. For one thing, international policing is not our forte. Being occupiers rather than defenders of liberty flies in the face of what we say we stand for. At the practical level, asking young Americans to do a job with no clear end state and no lasting rewards takes an inordinate toll— a toll whose costs we won't know until this generation, which is only just beginning to wrestle with PTSD and the other effects of combat, passes on. Members of the military themselves are thus another reason to mature the American vision: what *are* citizens' duties to this country? And who should bear this burden? The clearer we could be on this score, the more likely it is we would agree about what really jeopardizes national security—and what doesn't.

Chapter 6

Indivisible America

From some of what we have previously described, it might seem we three coauthors inhabit a black-and-white world, do not recognize how complex politics actually are, and are thus being utterly unrealistic about how the United States should go about its foreign relations. However, such an assessment of us would be dead wrong. Not only are we cogs in two massive bureaucracies—the Army and the Navy—but we have spent more time than most people in areas where nothing is black or white. Perhaps that explains why we are so eager to think our way through the murky gray of inconsistent policies.

Our experience definitely explains our conviction that cutting to the quick *can* be done. If not, quick reaction forces could never be deployed; trapped SEALs couldn't be plucked off of mountaintops in Afghanistan; and the Navy wouldn't be able to sail shiploads of assistance to tsunami victims in Indonesia. When crises occur it is amazing what the military can simplify, while what the United States is currently caught in is a slow-roll national security crisis. Between flare-ups that could require immediate attention—Russia invades Georgia, North Korea launches missiles, the global economy takes a nose dive—and too many competing theories about how international relations *should* be conducted, it seems safe to say that if the United States has a Grand Strategy it isn't working very well, or, if it is working, then whatever it consists of hasn't been conveyed to the American people. Either way the country is in some degree of trouble.

Here is where the Sovereignty Solution can effect a rescue. The United States already has most of the military hardware and technical know-how to make the "or else" part of sovereignty's "Don't, or else" promise stick.[1] All we lack right now are the eyes and ears to detect trouble so that we can mitigate another jolt like 9/11 or know who to hold accountable in the event our sovereignty is violated on a smaller scale. By definition it would take time for ethnographic sensors to reach their full potential, but setting up the program to field them would be easy, with the right kind of political sponsorship. Much more challenging—and what the United States does not yet have—is sufficient national will or a sufficiently compelling sense of its own purpose to meet the rest of sovereignty's requirements.

The contention in this chapter is that there is the world "out there"; then, there is the state of the union here at home: the two cannot be treated as though they are either unrelated, or one and the same.

We'll Be Us, You Be You

Academics can quibble over how exceptional America may or may not be. But ask most Americans—or most people, period—and among the things that distinguish us is the unique nature of our government as well as our identity. As Samuel Huntington pointed out decades ago, while some of our values can be found in other places, nowhere else are liberty, equality of opportunity, constitutionalism, liberalism, limited government, and private enterprise all found together as they are here.[2] This American creed or, as some describe it, our civil religion, is rooted in a fairly simple social contract: We citizens owe loyalty to the state so long as the state protects our unalienable rights; the state protects us *as* individuals, not as members of groups; and though our government rests on a religious base, it is never to be dominated by a single denomination.

Where did such concepts come from? Americans' common moral understanding is grounded in Judeo-Christian thought, and in Christianity even more than Judaism. Or to be even more specific, the founders' moral understanding can be traced back to dissenting Protestantism with its emphasis on individual freedom and a strong work ethic, as well as certain moral prescripts and an abiding interest in reform.

This heritage not only makes Americans significantly different from people elsewhere, but the argument at the heart of this book is that we Americans need to retain, not mute, these differences. What the United States represents has to remain unequivocal: a country where personal freedom and responsibility are paramount, where the individual remains the unit of account, where government stays limited, where Judeo-Christian values inform our rule of law, and where equality of opportunity is guaranteed. Does this mean immigrants from countries that don't subscribe to these values do not belong here? Absolutely not. But to live here, all citizens must accept that these are the definitional traits of the country to which they have come.

By being much more forthright about which specific values we Americans adhere to, we would simultaneously bring about two very different kinds of liberation. First, we would free ourselves from having to try to be all things to all people. Second, the more distinctly and resolutely American the United States becomes, the more that frees people elsewhere to remain distinctively *them*selves. Indeed, this gets at the ultimate quid pro quo reinvigorating sovereignty offers: don't expect us to embrace your values in this country and we won't expect you to embrace our values in your country; or to be even more blunt about it: we'll be us. You be you.

"You be you" means there would be no more government-sponsored proselytization of the American Way abroad. There would be no more inveigling by the U.S. government to get others to change. This buttresses the respect that sovereignty is supposed to accord, whereas self-respect requires a much more concerted focus by us on our domestic problems. Imagine how much more inspiring a model we would offer if we could clean up our own broken cities, feed all of our own hungry children, and take care of other social issues. Getting America's house in order would be one way to reprise our role as an exemplar—which does not mean we would have to stop trying to pull people our way either literally (let immigrants come), or figuratively (let others copy us). But what the sovereignty quid pro quo does mean is that the U.S. government would have to stop trying to push others to become more like us on their own soil.

Without question, hundreds of millions of people around the world seek to benefit from what we Americans make and are keenly interested in the freedoms we stand for. We should continue to extol both. But we also have to acknowledge that this attitude does not mean people elsewhere want to become us or to adopt our system of governance. Nor does everyone want to practice our version of capitalism. Most Europeans don't; nor do billions of Asians. Or, as those who contend we are on the verge of—if we haven't yet entered—a post-American era like to point out: "The second world's first priority is not to become America but to succeed by any means necessary."[3]

Where declinists are wrong, however, is about the inevitability of America's decline. Indeed, they are only likely to be right if our aim is to remake other countries in our image.

For the past fifty-plus years Americans in and out of government have been striving to get societies elsewhere to change. Yet, from Baghdad to Port-au-Prince populations have only responded piecemeal at best. Common sense alone suggests that if other people wanted to Westernize they would—in which case the non-West would be withering away. It clearly is not. But what this reality also indicates is that we have it backward: we Americans stand to lose nothing by accepting non-Westernness outside the United States. On the contrary, home is where being Western and having common values and ideals matter. *Here* is where we need to proselytize and make sure everyone really does harbor an inner American. Otherwise, if we persist in trying to remake people abroad, we will be even less able to keep ends, ways, and means sufficiently aligned, while those misalignments are what will jeopardize our way of life—a way of life predicated on "freedom of choice for individuals, democratic procedures for government, and private enterprise for the economy." Without preserving these, we *will* decline.

Being American

"We'll be us" is one reason it should trouble all Americans that illegal immigration has become so divisive an issue. One reason it is so divisive is because it affects blocks of constituents in ways that politicians find difficult to reconcile. But also, not even economists can agree on the most relevant figures for how many undocumented aliens there are in the United States.[4] Without accurate figures it becomes impossible for any politicians to say what impact illegal aliens have on our economy, never mind our social fabric. This situation helps further paralyze debate. Yet, the real showstopper should be the fact that the authorities have no idea whether there are 10 or 12 million such individuals in the United States.[5] From a national security perspective, the discrepancy in these figures should absolutely stun us. How can so many people hide out and remain undocumented—so many that no one knows how to even calculate their numbers?

The obvious quick answer to the question of how we have reached such a point is that no one must be looking hard enough at or for undocumented aliens—except to hire them. Their ability to hide out thus points to a broader societal problem, which is that there are now so many neighborhoods and communities that replicate the language, habits, and culture of "home" that illegals clearly do not have to try to act any differently from legal residents, or—to be totally politically incorrect—so long as the system does not require *legal* residents to assimilate, illegals don't have to, and authorities then have no good way to tell legals and illegals apart.

This is not at all what the founders had in mind.

George Washington certainly would not have understood how we could have reached this point since, as he noted in a letter to John Adams, "the policy or advantage of [immigration] taking place in a body (I mean the settling of them in a body) may be much questioned; for, by doing so, they retain the language, habits, and principles (good or bad) which they bring with them. Whereas by an intermixture with our people, they, or their descendants, get assimilated to our customs, measures, laws: in a word, soon become one people."[6] Teddy Roosevelt would have been apoplectic: "The one absolutely certain way of bringing this nation to ruin, of preventing all possibility of its continuing to be a nation at all, would be to permit it to become a tangle of squabbling nationalities." Though it is Woodrow

Wilson who may have summed up the situation best: "You cannot become thorough Americans if you think of yourselves in groups. America does not consist of groups. A man who thinks of himself as belonging to a particular national group in America has not yet become an American."[7]

These days most immigrants hail from our hemisphere: "for the first time in at least a century, one country and one language have dominated the influx since the early 1990s. Mexico accounts for 31 percent of the foreign-born, while, over all, Spanish-speaking Latin Americans make up about half of the total."[8] If this represents Shift #1, Shift #2 is that the United States is not necessarily most immigrants' final destination. Rather, for many we are but an economic way station to a better life. Family, friends, and property await them "back home"—all of which has implications for where we can expect people's loyalties and allegiances to lie.

Most of the concerns raised about illegal immigration today fixate on our porous borders—a clear problem, especially when everything from drugs to weapons to bad actors flow too easily in both directions. But the concerns that all three presidents—Washington, Roosevelt, and Wilson—voiced point to something else that can be even more corrosive of national security: unassimilated individuals and communities *stay* different. This makes them easy to treat as *theys*. *Theys* invariably invite backlashes, particularly when stirring up a backlash proves too politically tempting for some politicians or rabble-rousers to resist. But also, on principle, *theys* defy the unit of account on which the American system rests (and depends): the individual.

Something else usually missing from the illegal immigration debate is what the debate itself reveals about our divisibility. Consider that some U.S. citizens voluntarily patrol sections of our southern border, determined to prevent illegals from crossing into U.S. territory. At the same time, other activists do everything they can—from setting out barrels of drinking water in the desert to offering sanctuary—to ensure that illegals reach the United States safely and then, once in the United States, can stay here safely.[9] These conflicting actions reflect more than just a political difference of opinion. They reveal a fundamental disjuncture between what different groups of Americans consider to be right or fair, without considering what might be best for the country. What goes unsaid (but should be obvious) is that, if only we all agreed on what it means to *be* American, we would then agree on how immigrants should *become* American; the fact that we don't (or can't) agree brings us to another problem.[10]

Conservatives would say we Americans don't agree on what it means to be American because our education system is broken; schools fail to produce citizens who believe their country is worthy, let alone worth defending. One cure conservatives then offer is large dollops of civic education.[11] Some conservatives have even proposed establishing subcommittees at federal and state levels in order to develop standards for civic education. Failure to meet those standards would result in a loss of federal or state funding, and students would have to pass tough civics exams every year in order to advance to the next grade. Other conservative proposals are less intrusive and include greatly expanding school choice. But even conservatives are split over education as a solution. While some fear that an increase in alternative forms of education, like home schooling, is counterproductive to creating national unity, others contend that giving parents more choice will force the "establishment" to have to adjust. Meanwhile, none of these stances even broach what, specifically, *should* be taught. But what, for instance, would be wrong with a singular approach to *a* multicultural history?[12]

If these are the issues conservatives wrestle with, what of liberals? They typically don't like any such proposals. The question to pose to them, then, is, How would you instill a common understanding of what it means to be American? Or, if the very idea of a common foundation rubs them the wrong way, What would you propose investing in instead to prevent us from falling prey to irreparable divides?

If, for instance, liberals don't like conservatives' suggestions for providing every American with a more robust civic education, what method would they offer to ensure that all Americans share a common appreciation for the rule of law? Perhaps some among them can come up with an alternative not yet proposed. But consider the irony that whenever the United States is hit by an unexpected natural disaster it is the National Guard that is called out. Presumably National Guard units are summoned because they are trained; members of the Guard not only know what to do to maintain and restore order in the wake of natural or man-made catastrophes, but thanks to standard operating procedures and years of training they know how to work together. In other words, they operate from a common base of knowledge. The same holds for all first responders—which begs the question: why wouldn't we want all America's citizens to understand their duties in a democracy to this same degree?

Restoring Credibility

Instilling a common foundation for what it means to be American does not mean teaching people *what* to think or subjecting citizens to nothing but government propaganda. In fact, nothing is more critical than to *not* whitewash instances when the federal government has failed to live up to its principles. Indeed, only by studying past misdeeds and misjudgments is it possible to impart a sufficient appreciation for why responsibility and accountability matter, and what they should consist of.[13] For instance, consider Tet, a watershed event in the Vietnam War. "The Tet offensive was Hanoi's desperate throw of the dice to seize South Vietnam's northern provinces using conventional armies, while simultaneously triggering a popular uprising in support of the Viet Cong. Both failed. Americans and South Vietnamese soon put down the attacks, which began under cover of a cease-fire to celebrate the Tet lunar New Year. By March 2, when U.S. Marines crushed the last North Vietnamese pockets of resistance in the northern city of Hue, the VC had lost 80,000–100,000 killed or wounded without capturing a single province."[14]

To this day, North Vietnam's 1968—*1968(!)*—offensive haunts the ways in which the United States conducts, and the media reports, war.[15] That is, in part, because the whole series of surprise attacks that made up Tet totally belied the Johnson administration's depiction of reality. For years, the administration had been shaving the truth, never *voluntarily* squaring with the American people regarding the strength of our adversary (North Vietnam), the weakness of our ally (South Vietnam), or how well or ill prepared our own forces were for waging a "people's war." Even though, in the end, Tet constituted a clear military defeat for North Vietnam, that is not what the American press conveyed.[16] Instead, Tet's shock value overwhelmed any deeper analysis. Thus, it was North Vietnam's ability to take the media by storm—not beat our forces in battle—that helped undo us there (and, some would say, here).

Probe a bit deeper and one might question how deep the American people's commitment to the Vietnam War ever really was. From the outset, none of our political leaders consistently explained what winning in Vietnam might require. But nor did the "silent majority" fulfill *its* civic duty and hold political leaders to account for a credible explanation.

Ironically, it wasn't too many years before the first Americans went to Vietnam that Secretary of State Dean Acheson had used the phrase "clearer than the truth" to describe the stark (even exaggerated) language he thought the Truman administration needed to use when describing the threat communism posed the United States. Google the phrase "clearer than the truth" today and more references to the war in Iraq come up than to the Cold War. One might say officials in the Bush administration only meant to borrow a page from Acheson's book when they emphasized WMD in the public's mind as the reason for the invasion of Iraq in 2003. However, once the administration used this as the most pressing rationale for the war, and the expected WMD then weren't found, no other explanation gained traction.[17] Worse, once it was the media and not the administration reporting that there were no WMD in Iraq, many in the public—along with the president's political opponents—accused the administration of having willfully lied, a charge from which that administration never recovered.[18]

▲　▲　▲

Under the Sovereignty Solution no such thing could happen. The media would rarely—ideally never—be first to break a national security story. For one, there would be a Declaration of War or Standing Declaration of Preemption prior to U.S. action; full debate about ends, ways, and means would have already occurred in the public eye. The sovereignty rubric itself would already be familiar to audiences here and abroad. Thus, Washington's responsibilities would be clear, and there would then be nothing to prevent the government from squaring with the American people.

Only by presenting itself as an unimpeachable source of timely, accurate information can Washington retain the legitimacy to make demands of us—as well as of others. In fact, one of the chief missions for public affairs officers and spokespersons should be to ensure that the government has a jump on reporting any untoward event or operational error the media might discover—not with the aim to quash reporting, but because the only way for government to preserve its credibility is to break all hard, bad, embarrassing news first. Clearly, operational details about ongoing missions need to remain secret. But, so long as the government owns up to, and then proactively corrects, whatever mistakes it makes, it will earn sufficient trust from the public to keep operational specifics classified.[19]

Such directness is congruent with everything the Sovereignty Solution promises. So is the likelihood of many fewer errors. One reason there would be fewer errors is because responsibility for the deaths of any innocents under a Declaration of War (or Standing Declaration of Preemption) would belong to those who chose to invite an American attack in the first place. The attack itself could then be overwhelming, with the aim of being decisive. This is important because, as Richard Betts reminds us, "credibility is most impressive when power is husbanded and used undiluted."[20] Under the sovereignty rubric, if Washington's actions are sufficiently direct and decisive, the results not only should, but will speak for themselves. Or, to reframe this in "if . . . then" terms: *If*, after having to engage an adversary, Washington finds itself needing to explain why it did what it just did (note the past tense), *then* it will have failed.

Why Civic Responsibility Matters

Numerous proposals exist for how to renew a sense of national purpose. As already mentioned, promoting a more robust civic identity has long been a critical component of the conservative agenda. Conservatives seem especially keen to strengthen ties between the American people, on whom the military relies for support, and the military, on whom the American people rely for protection. Some conservatives—and even many liberals who worry about the state of our social fabric—like the idea of universal national service and would either make such service compulsory or make participation a prerequisite for receiving federal assistance.[21]

Here, for example, is Margaret Mead arguing for universal service in the mid-1960s: "Universal national service, if set up in such a way that units were a cross section of the entire society, could compensate for the increasing fragmentation, ignorance, and lack of knowledge of their fellow citizens and the rest of the world which is characteristic of those reared in our economically segregated residential pattern, in which both the poor and the rich, the highly technologically gifted and those with obsolescent skills, the white collar and the blue collar, are each reared in almost total ignorance of the other."[22]

Here, in not much contrast, is a 2009 pitch for universal national service (which would include community and not just military service): "The opportunity for all men and women between the ages of 18 and 24 to dedicate a year and a half to national service could have a transformative impact on the fabric of the nation. It could change the way individuals view their responsibilities as citizens, create stronger ties across divisions of class and culture, and instill a deeper understanding of the sacrifices required in the defense of the nation."[23]

Or, Margaret Mead again: "Universal national service, in addition to solving the problem of fairness for those who are asked to serve in the military, in contrast to those who are not, is above all a new institution for creating responsible citizens alert to the problems and responsibilities of nationhood in a rapidly changing world."[24]

One advantage to making participation in some kind of national service mandatory is that it would automatically become an *all-American* rite of passage. That alone would help broaden, deepen, and mature America's youth. Indeed, for all the recent attention accorded the "Greatest Generation," many Americans forget that one of the most useful things World War II–era conscription did was force individuals who never would have had to interact with one another, to interact as codependents. Hollywood has probably over-romanticized just how diverse the stereotypical combat platoon really was—with a Pole, an Italian, an Ivy League blueblood, and a southerner all serving side by side as brothers in arms. But the great public works projects undertaken during the Depression did much the same thing. They not only exposed young people to new places and new experiences, but required them to pitch in and invest sweat equity in *their* country.

Just floating the idea of universal national service, however, raises many Americans' hackles—even when those promoting the idea make it clear they don't mean mandatory military service.[25] Americans who object to any kind of compulsory service say it smacks of loyalty oaths, Hitler Youth, McCarthyism, and the like. In their view, nothing should be forced on everyone—that, they say, is utterly un-American, which is why they prefer voluntary service and suggest incentives like college tuition credits as a way to attract young people.

Examine all such suggestions, however, and what they have in common is the promotion of a much tighter connection between civic responsibilities and civic rights. Maybe this should not be national service in exchange for student loans and grants, Social Security, or Medicare. Maybe English language classes should not be a prerequisite for citizenship. Perhaps students should not have to pass civics classes to advance to the next grade. But then, imagine how it would help clarify government's role if, whenever someone invokes what they think are their "rights" ("health care is a right"), the immediate rejoinder would be, what is the civic responsibility that grants you that right?

▲   ▲   ▲

There is another reason we should want to reinvigorate Americans' sense of civic responsibility: it builds self-reliance. The more responsibly we Americans behave, the more likely it is that communities will *want* to look after their own, should some tragedy befall us. The more willingly communities look after their own, the more such action would help reduce the demands everyone makes of government. The less Americans need to ask of government, the less pandering politicians will have to do—or will be able to get away with.[26] The less pandering politicians do, the more able they should be to keep ends, ways, and means aligned, the better Washington will work. Ultimately, the better Washington works, the safer we all will stay.

Under our federal system of government, Washington is responsible for our collective security. For there to be a collective to secure, however, Americans have to want to feel tied together and not just tied to government. Without a collective sense and a national sensibility *to* defend, all we are left with in common is a federal cash register.

Other synergies to be gained from (re)instilling pride in self-reliance and personal responsibility relate to resilience. As Stephen Flynn always emphasizes, "a focus on building a more resilient society immunizes us against overreacting when disasters occur, thereby allowing us to remain true to our ideals no matter what the future may bring."[27] Done right, knitting communities together at the grassroots level would mean neighbors would have no reason to fear neighbors in the wake of an unforeseen disaster. If, meanwhile, the American people were demonstrably well prepared to withstand a bad event, no adversary would stand to gain anything by trying to cause one. Or, to return to the "if . . . then" refrain from chapter 1: *If* the United States more effectively monitored trends, movements, and rumblings abroad, *then* that would mitigate the likelihood of surprise. *If* America were to get hit despite this but citizens were prepared to absorb the blow, *then* the surprise wouldn't paralyze us. *If* the United States had a series of counterresponses prepared in advance, *then* no enemy could gain from our misfortune. *If*, meanwhile, the U.S. government advertised its preparations ahead of time *then* who would want to bother attacking us at all?

Put like this, it is hard to see the downsides to wanting to weave a stronger social fabric that would take seriously all four "ifs" and concentrate on the "thens." The aim? To safeguard our system of "liberty under law."[28] In the American context, "liberty under law" applies to individuals. The founders' conception was that individuals "would compete with their different abilities within a framework of equal civil rights, within the framework of the Constitution and the law."[29] But "liberty under law" can also be used to describe our American brand of federalism and our commitment to states' rights. Alternatively, it could be expanded to include states in the global arena—with the caveat that there is no constitution for the "United Countries of the World"—though with the reinvigoration of sovereignty, there also wouldn't need to be one. The premise of reinvigorating sovereignty, which protects people's right to choose their own fate, includes their choice about who they *let* choose their fate.[30]

▲   ▲   ▲

Contrary to what some might imagine, weaving a stronger social fabric in the United States does not demand the kinds of central controls some Americans might fear. Rather, Americans from all walks of life and from across the political spectrum simply need to agree there are certain kinds of ruptures we can't risk. We need to recognize that certain kinds of uncivil discourse and democratic fractiousness make us vulnerable. Knee-jerk partisanship is dangerous. Disbelieving the government is dangerous.[31] A government that does not fully disclose why it acts as it does is dangerous. Being divided into mutually distrustful, irreconcilably opposed camps is dangerous. If we Americans can agree that these four conditions represent exploitable vulnerabilities, we will already be that much closer to achieving the kind of cohesiveness the country needs—a cohesiveness that is easy to foster when government policies are consistent, dependable, clear, and simple to convey, the hallmark of "to each his own—don't tread on me."[32]

Of course, one additional advantage to building a more Indivisible America is that indivisibility itself sets a powerful example. If the United States' security depends on no one being able to use our differences against us, why shouldn't we want to see others strive to achieve the same thing?[33] Washington claims to want to see a united, functioning Iraq and a coherent, stable Afghanistan. But, an "Indivisible Russia," an "Indivisible Kenya," an "Indivisible Pakistan," and so on, would be no less critical, particularly since the very quest *for* indivisibility may be the most powerful tool there is for reinforcing the social contract between people and their rulers.[34]

We say this because the domestic bargain that lies at the heart of sovereignty for any people is that *a* government meet *its* citizens' demands. How it accomplishes this is up to it to work out with them. That a government does so, though, is the only guarantee that none of its citizens will want to drag it into dangerous predicaments by rebelling, thereby purposely or inadvertently attracting others' interest and support.

When countries have viable social contracts designed *by* and *for* them, indivisibility results.[35] Ultimately, we should want all other countries to achieve this for at least two reasons: first, the world is too diverse for anything less.[36] But second, the world needs to stay diverse. Without diversity there is no distinctiveness.[37] Should the U.S. lose its distinctiveness not only would that be bad for us, but, in any kind of world, our loss would not be good for anyone else either—as the next few chapters will reveal.

Chapter 7

To Each His Own:
The Ultimate Freedom Agenda

Two things help make Americans among the most generous people on earth: our egalitarianism and our bounty. As we look around the world, how can we not want to share our formula for success with others? When we see how others live, how can we not want to help improve their lives?

In a Sovereignty Rules world, the United States would continue to strive to demonstrate how great our combination of freedom and capitalism can be. However, our main aim would be to demonstrate that concept here, in the United States. Elsewhere, Washington would stop trying to admonish or cajole others to adopt what we have. If others choose to learn from our example, fine. But no matter how committed we Americans are to rights and freedoms we believe should be made universal, sovereignty—as the term has been used in this book—allows people elsewhere to live as they, not we, would prefer.

We need to remember that others' values matter to them just as much as ours do to us. So long as our sovereignty is not threatened or attacked, what difference *do* our differences make? In the twenty-first century, this is no longer a libertarian question; instead, it goes to the heart of why we have adversaries at all.

A foreign policy based on principled noninterference would remove the crosshairs from our back. Beyond this immediate benefit it would impel others to develop abilities too many currently shirk. These "others" include our allies. Indeed, as some contend, "America's allies still depend on the United States to solve problems they could tackle themselves. They lack the incentive to act responsibly."[1] Fifty years ago, no less an authority than Dwight D. Eisenhower advocated that the United States reduce its contributions to NATO. According to Stephen Ambrose, Eisenhower felt that "by pulling out Americans, the United States could force the

Europeans to do more in their own defense."[2] Sixty years later, it can't be a coincidence that we remain NATO's largest contributor.

Or, from the other side of politics, talking about the other side of the world, Democrat Chester Bowles once wrote, "a politically stable Asia can be assured only by the Asians themselves. Not only must they make an all-out effort to provide better living standards for their people; they must also learn to work with other Asian people for common objectives. A nation that cannot keep peace within its own borders is unlikely to maintain its sovereignty for very long. This, in the long run, is a sufficient reason alone why the United States should not become involved in the internal civil wars of Asia or anywhere else."[3] Bowles was writing in the shadow of Vietnam, thus the reference to civil wars in Asia, though several decades later, Owen Harries quoted John Stuart Mill to even more pointed effect: "'the only test possessing any real value, of people's having become fit for popular institutions, is that they, or a sufficient portion of them to prevail in the contest, are willing to brave labor and danger for their liberation.'"[4] In other words, people have to be willing to fight—and labor—for their own liberties. Our doing so for them does them no lasting good.[5]

▲   ▲   ▲

Humanitarian assistance and foreign aid can be touchy subjects, in part because the last thing anyone should want to do is criticize those who seem so willing to sacrifice their own health and comfort in order to assist others. Nonetheless, foreign aid pumps billions of dollars through corrupt foreign governments every year.[6] According to the World Bank, "about $40 billion of government money is stolen by officials each year, an amount equal to 40% of global foreign-aid budgets."[7] A good portion of this is World Bank money. According to one Indonesian journalist, in Indonesia alone "it is widely believed that around 30% of foreign loans disbursed in the past were stolen. The World Bank has given $25 billion in loans to my country since 1968, which means almost $8 billion of these loans ended up in the wrong places."[8]

Whether we want to acknowledge it or not, U.S. tax dollars help fuel this dysfunction. Aid projects seldom get off the ground without bribes being paid, and bribes can come in many forms. Government officials might agree to green-light a project only if it enables them to skim off the top, or they will do so in exchange for a one-time payoff, or the arrangement is that their relatives get jobs. Invariably, whoever is responsible for giving U.S. agencies permission to start a project gets *something* out of the deal, or the deal does not happen. How, meanwhile, do foreign governments benefit by outsiders coming in and taking care of basic social needs? By not having to do so themselves.

Aid, especially in large amounts, can damage governance and make an economy uncompetitive. Like revenues from natural resources, it is manna from heaven for governments. When governments receive large oil revenues or aid, they have less incentive to be accountable to their citizens and governance suffers. In theory, donors impose an alternate form of accountability. In practice, donors' motivations are sometimes a mixture of the murky (think of the United States and Pakistan post 9/11 or the West and Zaire's Mobutu several decades ago) and the mindless (in 2000–2002, the Tanzanian government reportedly had to write a few thousand reports to donors every quarter). Even where motivations are honorable, recipients have infinite ways of circumventing donor conditions.[9]

Look closely—the aid industry not only enables governments to avoid having to fulfill obligations to their citizens, but it also fails to impel them to have to live up to their sovereign duties. Or, to put none too fine a point on it: aid not only corrupts, it undermines sovereignty absolutely.[10]

Pakistan's minister of finance, Shaukat Tarin, offers one example. While being interviewed by James Traub, he stated: "We have avoided the tough decisions, and we just keep hoping that something will happen, and we will get this infusion of foreign aid." According to Traub, "Tax-collection rates [in Pakistan] are dismal, and the country spends paltry sums on education and health. Little serious planning has been done on either agriculture or manufacturing. Infrastructure remains primitive. And the bureaucratic culture sedates the entrepreneurial spirit. 'There's no performance management,' Tarin said, 'no merit, a lot of nepotism.'"[11]

Or, consider the discomfiting example of Somalia: In October 2008, *The Economist* reported that "a slender hope, backed by Britain and some other EU countries, is that ordinary Somalis will eventually force their leaders to put national interest above self-interest and sign the proposed [peace] agreement in Djibouti." Two paragraphs later, *The Economist* continues: "The UN reckons 3.2m Somalis now survive on food aid."[12] Only someone totally naïve might wonder why those Somalis who are in a position to divert even a fraction of such aid flows would ever want peace.[13]

As with warlords, so it goes with governments: "A constant stream of 'free' money is a perfect way to keep an inefficient or simply bad government in power. As aid flows in, there is nothing more for the government to do—it doesn't need to raise taxes, and as long as it pays the army, it doesn't have to take account of its disgruntled citizens."[14]

▲ ▲ ▲

Westerners have spent decades promoting development scheme after development scheme: import substitution, export promotion, structural adjustment, and capacity building.[15] There has been almost as much churn in the aid industry as in the fashion industry—which should be an indicator that either the experts do not know what they are doing and therefore *are* experimenting with foreign populations or that they lack the stick-to-itiveness to make any one thing work. That experts do this with other people's lives should, but unfortunately does not, raise major ethical concerns.[16] That they do so with tax dollars should, but unfortunately does not, receive serious scrutiny. But then, that so many in the policymaking elite assume we now need to do *more* of this in order to deprive terrorists of potential recruits should defy common sense altogether. If there is little to no evidence development aid does good, why assume more is better?

On Sunday, November 4, 2007, the John Templeton Foundation ran a two-page ad in the *New York Times* titled "Will Money Solve Africa's Development Problems?" The foundation printed responses from eight prominent individuals. Here are the sentences that introduced each response:

> —*Yes.* If it is invested in enhancing African capabilities to integrate the continent into global networks of knowledge and creating prosperity and stability.

> —*No.* In fact, after fifty years of trying and $600 billion worth of aid-giving with close to zero rise in living standards in Africa, I can make the case for "no" pretty decisively.

> —*I thought so . . . But now I don't.* There is that threadbare maxim: If you hold a hammer in your hand, every problem looks like a nail. What happens, then, when all we hold in our hand is a checkbook?

> —*No.* Not as long as there are issues such as prolonged violent conflict, bad governance, excessive external interference, and lack of an autonomous policy space.

> —*Yes.* But only if the money comes as investment. Africa doesn't need aid from governments and international agencies.

> —*No.* By now we should have learned. Donor nations have spent billions of dollars for development schemes in post-colonial Africa, yet there is little to show for this beyond dependency and corruption.

> —*Only if . . . It empowers citizens.* African entrepreneurs are the key to solving Africa's development problems.

> —*No Way.* The problem in Africa has never been lack of money, but rather the inability to exploit the African mind.

At first glance, the split between *yes*es and *no*s might make it seem as though there is no consensus. Dig deeper into the solicited answers, however, and they point toward the latest trend in development aid: bottom-up entrepreneurship, microfinance, and direct investment. Or, as Iqbal Quadir, founder of Bangladesh's largest cell-phone company and one of the John Templeton Foundation respondents, wrote in the *Wall Street Journal:* "Aid empowers bureaucracies, promotes statism, and weakens government incentives to boost tax revenues through growth. Economic assets are often kept in the hands of the state, leading to monopolies, stagnation and extortion. All of this hurts entrepreneurs, who have the potential to create wealth and promote governmental accountability."[17] His implied message? Unleash entrepreneurs; once enough of them succeed, they will use their public-mindedness and clout to hold their governments' feet to the fire.

In the interim, though, "business" continues much as usual. Less than a month after Quadir's 2009 op-ed appeared—a year before Haiti's devastating 2010 earthquake—*The Economist* was reporting that donors were due to convene their first conference on Haiti since late 2006. In the wake of a series of catastrophic storms, donors had already doubled aid to Haiti to $800 million a year, on top of the UN mission's $600 million annual budget and Venezuela's fuel subsidy. More money would doubtless be promised, yet as *The Economist* reported, "Some things have been achieved in Haiti . . . but more should have been. 'We spend a lot of money doing capacity building, but it is not clear that this has an impact,' says Mr. Boutroue of UNDP. 'Maybe we are just buying social peace—instability has just as much to do with the well-being of members of parliament as with a deepening of poverty.'" As if Mr. Boutroue's comment about the well-being of politicians isn't troubling enough, consider *The Economist*'s conclusion: "It is surely time for outsiders to hold Mr. Preval [Haiti's then president] and the politicians to account."[18]

But if outsiders were not already holding Port-au-Prince to account two decades *after* the end of the Cold War, what was going to impel them to suddenly crack down in 2009? The obvious answer: nothing—as evidenced by hundreds of thousands of people still living in tent cities a full year after Haiti's devastating 2010 earthquake and ten thousand NGOs had descended or sprung up.[19]

Education and Training *Yes*, Development Aid *No*

Americans need to understand what happens whenever we send tax dollars abroad to fund schools, clinics, wells, and other seemingly worthy projects. We not only subvert what citizens of other countries need to be able to expect their own governments to do, but we contribute to immiseration. Another case in point: "Since its creation by the so-called Oslo Accords of 1993, the PA [Palestinian Authority] has garnered more international aid than any entity in modern history—more, per capita, than the European states under the Marshall Plan. The lion's share of this fortune has been siphoned into the private accounts of Fatah leaders or used to pay off the commanders of some 16 semi-autonomous militias. . . . The Palestinian people, meanwhile, languish in ever-deepening poverty and unemployment, while lawlessness plagues Palestinian streets."[20] In many respects, foreign aid is nothing short of welfare—but even worse, "outside assistance allows autocrats to circumvent the need to gain financial support and leverage from their own populations, and in turn makes the United States dependent on unstable individuals and regimes rather than on popular support."[21]

In a Sovereignty Rules world, dependencies like this would disappear. U.S. taxpayer dollars would no longer fund foreign aid—which is not to say foreign governments would have to forego all sources of foreign charity. Governments could still welcome Private Voluntary Organizations (PVOs) and non-taxpayer-supported NGOs if they so chose. Thus, church groups, human rights workers, and organizations like Save the Children and Oxfam would be free to do everything they currently do—including promoting Western values—but with the understanding that foreign governments would have the right to reject visa applications from private citizens and the United States would not lobby on these citizens' behalf. Consequently, if foreign governments don't want missionaries, don't like Habitat for Humanity, or kick out CARE, that is their prerogative. At the same time, our government's responsibility would be to ensure that all Americans traveling abroad understand they are responsible for abiding by the laws of countries they visit. Essentially, every passport holder would be told the same thing: Traveler, beware—preach where you're not supposed to proselytize, and imprisonment is a risk you accept; venture into a place where Americans are not well liked, and that is a risk you knowingly assume; assist people who are plotting against their government, and you may well share their fate. Choice and responsibility—again, these are the twin pillars of sovereignty.

▲　▲　▲

Just because the federal government stops funding foreign aid *projects*, however, does not mean it would stop doing two of the things it has always done exceptionally well: educate and train. The United States should do as much of both as possible. Education and training offer intangible benefits that can't corrupt. Nobody gets anything that can be pocketed or stolen from time spent in a classroom. Admittedly, foreigners who receive education or training in the United States do receive a leg up, and many who are sent here do have family or political connections that already endow them with all sorts of privileges; this is hardly very fair. But it is also exactly why we should then go out of our way to offer education to as many people as possible through as many different venues as possible, rewarding merit at every possible turn (which has always been the strength of our education system and of our society).

Because the United States' overriding goal should be to be exemplary, it makes sense to reach out in those fields we lead in, like health care, environmental science, and engineering—all of which are critical to strengthening sovereignty. The same holds for education and training in a host of subjects that appear less traditional, like security-sector reform. In an ironic twist, nothing may hold more promise for strengthening a state's commitment to its citizens than forging greater mutual respect between citizens and their security services. The United States is one of the few countries that has never experienced military rule; we should make much more of this than we do.

But regardless of whether education's focus is security-sector reform, medicine, or hydrology, the aim should be to expose others to fields of study that would directly benefit them—not us. This is critical not just for passing along the tools through which to build capacity, but because we do not want to be telling people we no longer proselytize and then proselytize in sneaky or surreptitious ways.

Some readers might equate an emphasis on education and training with soft power. Don't. Training and educating are strictly take-it–or-leave-it propositions, whereas according to the classic definition of power, power involves the ability to coerce and force others to do what they otherwise would not want (or choose) to do themselves. Despite the catchiness of the term "soft power," what soft power advocates are really pushing is "Crusader State Lite."[22] They *want* the United States to actively shape other countries; they just want to do so in gentler ways. That is not this strategy.

What this strategy promotes is *dis*entanglement. Hindu-dominated governments in New Delhi have never insisted we Americans stop slaughtering cows. Nor do officials in Taipei or Bangkok tell us we ought to do more to honor our dead. We don't tolerate criticism from Europeans about our methods of corporal punishment. Nor, in a Sovereignty Rules world, would we have any place telling others how to behave. The only time Washington would wag its finger is about matters that relate to our security; and if we see a potential security problem, then that is a matter for diplomatic discussion: "please, Minister or Prime Minister X, reassure us that A, B, and C are *not* likely to occur."

The topic of entanglements will come up again in the next chapter. For the moment, it seems more pressing to address whether Americans really could tolerate regimes that engage in rampant human rights abuses. Would we really be able to stand by if governments banned girls from school? Or permitted child labor? Or turned a blind eye to slavery? Unfortunately, the easy rejoinder to such questions is, what is the United States doing to halt such things right now?[23] Note that the question isn't what are activists *saying* we should do, but what is the United States *actually* doing about—or to—such regimes? The answer is, "nothing." Some suggest we are actually doing worse than nothing.

In a provocative argument about moral hazard, Alan Kuperman points to the very real harm caused by our rhetoric, which raises unreal expectations abroad. His logic goes something like this: ambitious and impatient opposition leaders, as well as local activists who seek a more equitable slice of the pie for disenfranchised or marginalized people(s), will sometimes stir up local violence to, essentially, bait a trap. They expect, and actually want, the regimes that are ignoring or oppressing them to overreact. What they are banking on is that once a repressive regime cracks down and applies overwhelming force against poor helpless victims, the international community will feel duty-bound to respond.[24]

But, as the crisis in Darfur, Sudan, so vividly illustrates, this scenario doesn't always pan out; not even a full-court press by glitterati, the worldwide media, world leaders, or the international public moved the Sudanese government to alter its behavior. Nor did cries of "never again" move anyone to meaningfully intervene. In 2006 President Bush "insisted there must be consequences for rape and murder, and he called for international troops on the ground to protect innocent Darfuris. . . . He spoke of 'bringing justice' to the Janjaweed, the Arab militias that have participated in atrocities that the president has repeatedly described as nothing less than 'genocide.'" "Yet," the *Washington Post* reporter continued, "a year and a half later, the situation on the ground in Darfur is little changed"—and that was already four-plus years after warnings were initially sounded that a major humanitarian disaster was in the offing.[25]

As Kuperman's argument implies, by allowing—and even encouraging—local populations to think that they might be rescued, do-gooders can unwittingly trap people in inescapable cycles of violence. This is because even the most corrupt states control means of violence local populations can seldom match. Almost always states possess the upper hand. Thus, too often locals who act in the belief that outsiders will help them end up sacrificing themselves or being sacrificed in vain.[26]

The unfortunate cold, hard reality is that Washington seldom steps in to reverse political facts on the ground unless it regards a repressive regime as inimical to our interests or until we think that regime is about to fall. Then policymakers might begin to hedge their bets. Otherwise, Washington avoids openly siding with opposition leaders. No doubt there are structural reasons for this, among them that our government is wired to deal with other governments. The bottom line? Respect for sovereignty continues to trump all else, regardless of how much sentiment the "responsibility to protect" might evoke.

National Security *Yes*, National Interests *No*

The Sovereignty Solution is predicated on facing up to just such uncomfortable realities as described above. Among these realities is, again, the dirty truth that no set of outsiders these days can maneuver through the "developing" world without contributing to dysfunction. For example, set foot as an official American in an airport in most countries in Africa and you will be met by an expediter whose job it is to facilitate your entry and exit through passport control and customs. The expediter is there to handle the locals so that those who travel on behalf of the U.S. government never have to pay bribes. How exactly does the expediter manage this? No one with an official or diplomatic passport ever has to know—and this is but the first arrangement made on behalf of official visitors. In other words, from the moment we set foot in the developing world, those of us there on "official" business become complicit in a system that is stacked against our kind of rule of law.[27]

This unspoken complicity is why—unless the U.S. government wants to keep supporting what it claims to want to change—its position needs to be: Enough! In a Sovereignty Rules world, we would share our values, ideals, and principles, and let people make of them what they will. But we wouldn't build or finance projects or inject large sums of anything that can be pocketed or siphoned off.[28] We would educate. We would train.

Those who fear that limiting aid this way might place an undue burden on incapable states should rest assured that the will if not the capacity to be sovereign exists, even in the capitals that seem most under-developed.[29] In fact, one of the things that stokes the anger of young educated, upwardly mobile males (especially) is that their own governments would rather pocket money from foreign aid projects and foreign assistance than rely on them—their own citizens—for development.[30] This anger is one reason why there are so many well-educated immigrant taxi drivers in the United States. Ironically, it is Western immigration policies—and loose visa enforcement—that help facilitate the developing world's continuing brain drain. So do offshore and foreign bank accounts—"the double whammy of graft in the poorest countries is that state funds are first diverted into private hands and then sent overseas."[31]

If, as one elderly Sierra Leonean once told one of us, the West really wanted to help Africa, it would make banking abroad much more difficult. How the West might legally restrict money flows he couldn't say, but the argument he made was compelling:

> If the international banking system limited Africans to no more than $20,000 in foreign bank accounts, the ruling class would have to invest their money at home. That would close off their escape hatches. Without big foreign bank accounts they wouldn't be able

to cheat us, or misbehave and then flee abroad. Ministers and other government officials would have to act much more responsibly. They'd be trapped. The people would be able to hold them fiscally and physically accountable. But also, civil servants would be able to carry out their jobs. And maybe they could even do honest jobs

Who was the individual who floated this idea to us? A custodian at one of Freetown's best-known hotels.[32] There is nothing naïve about populations in the developing world today; instead there is only growing cynicism—yet another reason why we should change what we do and grant populations elsewhere the opportunity to make sovereignty work.

▲   ▲   ▲

Of course, there is also growing cynicism in this country about a different, but not wholly unrelated, kind of behavior. When numerous Americans believe we have troops in the Middle East to protect access to oil, that conviction reflects an appreciation for the ugly truth that we all drive cars; however, when oil company *profits*—not just prices, but profits—rise to record heights and politicians have long-standing Big Oil ties, that rightly or wrongly leads to uglier suspicions. Throw in evidence of Saudi ties, Saudi money, and U.S. troops protecting Saudi oil (even if just from Qatar), and it becomes easy to assume that Washington has not only engaged us in unseemly entanglements but has also participated in shady deals.

In a Sovereignty Rules world even intimations of entanglement would become a historic artifact. The reason? The "to each his own—don't tread on me" framework for international relations separates security from trade. With the Sovereignty Solution, American security interests are clearly and unequivocally determined by one thing and one thing only—where a country places itself in the relationship framework dictates how we treat it. Whether we depend on that nation for oil or buy its bananas does not figure into the security equation at all.

Consider the implications, were the Sovereignty Solution applied. No longer would it be up to U.S. taxpayers to protect corporate investments or markets overseas.[33] If corporations situated themselves in difficult circumstances or located themselves in bad neighborhoods in order to increase their market share, the onus would be on them to use some of their profits to minimize their risk. In so doing, corporations would themselves have to figure out new ways to exert pressure on local, regional, and national governments to live up to *their* sovereign obligations if those corporations want their workers and profits to stay safe.

Let us consider oil and politics, for example. They already make for an unholy mix in the Gulf of Guinea in West Africa. Because it is said that as much as 25 percent of America's oil will come from that region by 2015, lots of players are seeking a piece of the pie. These do not include just local governments, but also local residents who feel cheated whenever others reap more benefits than they do from resources extracted from their backyard. Piracy, kidnappings, extrajudicial killings, and general thuggery have increased throughout the Niger Delta since the mid-1990s. Locals routinely accuse American oil companies of colluding with the central government to cheat them out of their fair share. Yet, it is not only Lagos that has benefited from granting the oil companies access. Local warlords have proved equally adept at squeezing oil companies.[34] One consequence? U.S. taxpayer dollars are now flowing into the region at unprecedented rates as the United States tries to shore up West Africa's security infrastructure in order to keep the oil flowing. A second consequence? Not only do these investments by the U.S. government signal just how important the Gulf of Guinea has become to Washington, but to shrewd observers and opportunists, they are also highly suggestive of just how much *more* money Washington will keep pouring into the region. In the grandest irony of all, we—American taxpayers—become the ultimate extractable resource.[35]

One argument often made for why the U.S. government needs to help American corporations abroad is the worry that if Washington doesn't protect our access to resources and markets, some other resource-hungry country will move in and corner the market in our stead. The Sovereignty Solution says, let them, because even if this were to happen, how would it disadvantage us, the American people? Suppose an economic competitor did pour billions of dollars into shoring up a corrupt regime; eventually it would face the same objections from local residents and warlords we have and would get mired in the same kind of commitment trap.[36]

▲ ▲ ▲

At the moment, one thing our ongoing financial crisis should make clear is that entanglements hurt all taxpayers, whether we are individually responsible for bad (or venal) decisions or not. Unfortunately, the blurred lines among the banking, insurance, and mortgage industries are not dissimilar from those used to define our national interests. How many Americans can distinguish among national, vital, and strategic interests? Tellingly, not even those in policymaking circles agree on which interest is which, never mind where on such a list the health of our economy belongs. For all the criticism leveled at former President Bush for admonishing the American people to go out and spend money in the wake of September 11, he actually had a point. If our economy had melted down in the immediate aftermath of that attack, our adversaries would have been able to claim a clear victory.

We would be fooling ourselves to think future adversaries won't try to hit us even harder on multiple fronts at once. Thus, no matter how much it might seem to go against the American grain to sever what we can agree constitutes our "national *security*" (emphasis on the word "security") from our "national (read:

economic) interests," we would be making ourselves that much more invulnerable if, as with church and state, we separated these two concepts.[37]

Nor is this separation of security from interests as fanciful as it might sound. Consider, for instance, the term "national interests." National interests are rarely collective interests, but, rather, are usually invoked to protect one industry, and can have a negative impact on others. Consider the dollar: The stronger it is the worse American businesses built around exports tend to do, while retailers whose bottom line is built on imports thrive.[38] One benefit to having such a highly diversified economy is that whenever some lose, others gain. The downside is that those who make the most money can then buy themselves political protection. This has all sorts of untoward effects—on subsidies, tariffs, trade negotiations and, ultimately, international relations.

The Sovereignty Solution would help change this reality by eliminating opportunities for politicians to play economic favorites via trade relations or by tailoring foreign policy to benefit certain industries.[39] Instead, it would be as if politicians' better civic selves posed the following set of questions. To individual Americans invested or working abroad, where do your loyalties really lie: Are you shareholders first and taxpayers second? Or, are you Americans first and shareholders second?

ᛚ   ᛚ   ᛚ

Of course, if such questions were asked today it is not clear what the responses would be, which is yet another reason why Americans' sense of civic responsibility needs renewal. At the same time, in a Sovereignty Rules world the rule for Americans would also be if you break foreign laws when abroad or are complicit with a corrupt government, you automatically forfeit taxpayer protection.[40] Enforcing this rule would be one way to underscore the twin pillars of liberty under law: choice and responsibility; it would also pretty neatly disentangle our collective *national* security from corporate, private, NGO, and other "interests."[41]

Under such a policy, consular officials would still be responsible for visiting all Americans detained by foreign authorities to determine whether or not they are being held on bogus or trumped up charges. But, say you are the consular official on duty in country X and the call comes in:

> The Ministry of the Interior has just detained three young Americans, and is charging all three with promoting Christianity, which is a crime against the state. You don't personally know these three Americans, but you are familiar with the organization they belong to. You remember that members of this same organization have run into difficulties elsewhere, since the group's unofficial motto is: "heal the body, save the soul." When you meet with them (a doctor and two nurses), one of the nurses admits that yes, they

prayed with two local staff members. They ask you to call their congresswoman. You tell them you will, but you also know that in a Sovereignty Rules world this will do little good other than to potentially win them decent treatment as they await trial. All three signed waivers before they left the United States accepting full responsibility for their behavior abroad. You also know that with their visa applications they received a written warning that country X forbids religious proselytizing. You tell them you hope they will be able to hire a good lawyer, but that they need to understand their defense is up to them.

Rewrite this scenario for "leftist activists" or anyone else, and under the Sovereignty Solution the U.S. government's response would be the same.

Natural Disasters and Humanitarian Assistance

In chapter 2 we listed some traits that most Americans could probably agree define us. As Americans, we tend to be impatient, we pride ourselves on being problem solvers, we don't mind getting our hands dirty, we quickly become frustrated when people refuse to help themselves. Add these up and it should be apparent that while we are not particularly well suited to sustain operations that may achieve only incremental and hard-to-measure results among people whose values and priorities differ from ours, we have exactly the traits needed to help anyone cope with the immediate aftereffects of large-scale natural disasters.

No country can ever be adequately prepared for the aftermath of a major earthquake, tsunami, or similar catastrophe. When these hit they don't distinguish among rich or poor, fundamentalist or communist, young or old. That they can make victims of anyone, anytime, anywhere, means there is not a country that could not use assistance in their wake. At the same time, no country has greater logistical reach *to* assist than the United States. None has greater stores of food, medicine, clothing, building supplies, or the ability to purify water than we do.

Imagine if, the morning after a major earthquake in Peru or a Category 5 hurricane bore down on Mexico, both countries knew an American fleet would be heading their way. What messages would the arrival of immediate assistance send to local governments, to local populations, and to the world at large? What messages would such acts reinforce?[42]

There are many reasons the United States should want to rush aid to victims during the triage phase of recovery from natural disasters. Not only is this what all good global neighbors should strive to do and what American citizens always seek to do anyway, but there is no surer way to show people elsewhere how well democracy and a free market economy *can* work—since without them we wouldn't have either surpluses or skills to share. Yet at the same time, caution is also called for. Responding to unprecedented five-hundred-year floods is one thing. When governments knowingly allow or encourage people to occupy low-lying areas that are in the path of annual monsoons or hurricanes, that is something altogether different.

Likewise, despite how they are often depicted, famines and genocides are *not* acute natural disasters. Both of these are man-made events. Neither happens without ample early warning. Each is also fully within a government's ability to control. Famines are political—food does not reach the hungry. A famine can start with a drought, which results from lack of rainfall, or it may be the by-product of war, as fields get trampled and crops cannot be sown or harvested. Localized food shortages will occur under both sets of conditions. But everyone knows this in advance. Governments *know* what the outcome will be if food is not redistributed in time; when those who need food can't afford it, they starve. Meanwhile, as horrific as starvation is, one reason it is so horrific is because it is so protracted.

Nor is there anything sudden about genocides. Like ethnic cleansings, genocides are *planned* orchestrated events. There is ample testimony, for instance, from witnesses who were working for the UN, the U.S. Department of Defense, and other agencies about how much early warning there was prior to the killings in Rwanda in 1994. Much was also known about the scale once the killings started.[43]

Of course, in a Sovereignty Rules world nothing of the magnitude of a genocide could occur without our being aware, since with ethnographic sensors keeping a close ear to the ground, our diplomats would have the information they need to make it clear to any government planning a campaign of mass murder or state-orchestrated terror that it faces a choice: opprobrium abroad and likely destabilization at home, or a mitigated disaster. Under these circumstances, no government could act as though it had been taken unaware. No guilty government could make itself appear innocent. Because, too, disasters like these invariably spill over and affect neighboring states—as soon as the first refugee flees across a border or the first body washes up on foreign shores (as was the case with waters flowing out of Rwanda), neighboring states would have a duty to *their* citizens to respond, a duty that all citizens everywhere would be aware of.

In real terms what this means is that if Myanmar imploded that would be an issue for India, China, and Thailand—its neighbors—to contend with. Likewise, should Burundi succumb to the same paroxysms of violence that have shaken it in the past, its neighbors—Uganda, Tanzania, and Rwanda—would need to react so that they would not be swamped by hundreds of thousands of Hutu or Tutsi refugees. Indeed, one reason India assisted East Pakistan (now Bangladesh) in attaining independence in 1971 was because refugees from Pakistan's civil war put undue strains on local supplies of food, water, fuel, housing, employment, and so forth.[44] This is also why, while on the face of it, the existence of agencies like the

United Nations High Commission for Refugees might seem to mark progress in world affairs—since as soon as refugee flows begin the international community galvanizes—what does the international community actually galvanize to do? Some refugees are kept in chronic limbo for generations. This has had all sorts of insidious effects, as the Palestinians' plight should make more than abundantly clear.

Again, the argument being made here is not that we could do away with famines or genocides by reinvigorating sovereignty, much as it might be nice to think we could. Rather, it is to point out how the timetable for decision making would be pushed up, forcing those in neighboring countries to take a stand—or not. If neighbors refused to take a stand, at least victims would then know *not* to wait for help. Ideally, this would spur them to then organize their own defense which, these days, they seldom do—perhaps because too many think that, given their helplessness, the world is bound to respond. Until it doesn't.

▲   ▲   ▲

As for those who might argue that distinguishing between acute and chronic, or natural and man-made disasters is unrealistic, never mind unfair because it again places an undue burden on incapable states, consider the case of Malawi. According to Celia Dugger, writing on the front page of the *New York Times* in 2007,

> Malawi hovered for years at the brink of famine. After a disastrous corn harvest in 2005, almost five million of its 13 million people needed emergency food aid. But this year, a nation that has perennially extended a begging bowl to the world is instead feeding its hungry neighbors . . . Farmers explain Malawi's extraordinary turnaround—one with broad implications for hunger-fighting methods across Africa—with one word: fertilizer. Over the past 20 years, the World Bank and some rich nations Malawi depends on for aid have periodically pressed this small, landlocked country to adhere to free market policies and cut back or eliminate fertilizer subsidies, even as the United States and Europe extensively subsidized their own farmers. But after the 2005 harvest, the worst in a decade, Bingu wa Mutharika, Malawi's newly elected president, decided to follow what the West practiced, not what it preached.[45]

For much less uplifting, but even more telling proof that where there is the will governments can find a way, Angola, Namibia, Zimbabwe, Rwanda, Uganda, Chad, Libya, and Sudan had no difficulty sending forces into the Democratic Republic of Congo in the late 1990s to assist warring factions in tearing that country apart. One aim, if not the chief aim, in these interventions was to participate in wholesale looting. Worth underscoring is that none of these other governments was motivated by peacekeeping in the usual humanitarian sense.[46] If one were to be truly hard-headed, the Congo case suggests one of two things. Either others clearly don't share our humanitarian impulses or values, and thus the only reasonable approach to inhabiting the planet together *should be* "to each his own." Or, alternatively, given such callousness and greed, we absolutely do need to do everything possible to ensure our brand of humanism *does* take root worldwide. But in that case, we had better first stop infantilizing other countries and instead permit (or force) them to grow up.

Either way, foreign aid is not the answer. Or, as Mukoma Wa Ngugi explains in a piece written for BBC *Focus on Africa*:

> Part of our tragedy is that in the 1960's and 1970's the Idi Amins of the continent were busy assassinating the future Sankaras and Steve Bikos. By the time it was time to cast a democratic vote in the 1990's, the voices which might have offered an alternate vision of change as opposed to working within a consensus of western capitalism had been silenced.
>
> But nevertheless we cannot afford to give up on the African state. If we do, we will be giving international non-governmental organizations, philanthropists and international corporations and capital a permanent place at our dinner table—and they are always hungry. Rather than give up on our states we have to demand more of them. Through a revival of people-powered movements, trade unions, farmer and women organizations, we can challenge our states into having a little more spine.
>
> Otherwise the alternative is not only economic and political dependence on Western capitalism, but leaders who are also psychologically beholden to their Western counter-parts. Nigeria's Umaru Yar'Adua humbled himself in front of George Bush recently and gushed "I feel highly honored and privileged to be here. This is a moment that I'll never forget in my life." Tell me, what demands could a prostrate Yar'Adua make of Bush?[47]

Not only is government-sponsored foreign aid pernicious, but from almost any perspective it undermines sovereignty.

Chapter 8

Alliances and Other Arrangements

While at first glance it might seem that the United Nations and other international organizations would become defunct with what we described in chapter 7, they would actually become more relevant, but in a markedly different way because their concern would no longer be what goes on *inside* a country's borders. Rather, their role would be to help safeguard the international sanctity of spaces *beyond* countries' borders.

Some level of international cooperation and adjudication will always be required to ensure shipping lanes remain clear; air traffic corridors are safely administered; the mail gets from point A to point B; and sensible rules are in place for currency exchange, banking, standardized weights and measures, and so on. Because these things do not impede any one country's sovereignty, but benefit all, international agreements concerning them are not just useful but necessary. Suprasovereign domains—the oceans, airspace, and deep space—all demand multilateral attention, as does the free flow of communications, transportation, and commerce through, across, over, and under those domains. Virtually everything else, however, belongs to states.

One reality worth remembering is that for all the producing, consuming, and to-ing and fro-ing people do, we all still live somewhere. Despite all that globalization is blamed for or credited with, it still has not—and cannot—change the fact that people live a physical existence *on* terra firma, *in* a physical location.[1] Nor will it change the fact that people and their property require physical (not just virtual) protection. These are among the immutable realities of human existence.

Ironically, international treaties, conventions, and agreements make such realities abundantly clear. Examine a random selection of these agreements and you can't help but wonder what purpose they serve, other than to remind people who are already in agreement that they *are* in agreement. One example is the Convention on Cluster Munitions signed by ninety-four countries in Oslo in December 2008. Countries that did not give up their right to use cluster bombs include Russia, China, Poland, Finland, Israel, Egypt, Syria, the Koreas, and the United States. More curiously, the treaty has built into it "an exemption for signatories to conduct operations alongside non-signatories, such as America." Still, the treaty was apparently considered a success by those who signed it because, if nothing else, it sets "a new global norm."[2]

▲   ▲   ▲

As for the international commitments the United States has made, try to name the major alliances to which Washington is party. As a signatory to nearly one hundred such agreements, listing our commitments should be easy to do. A somewhat tougher task might be to list the actions these require. If, for instance, North Korea lobs a conventional warhead into mainland Japan, is the United States at war with North Korea? Does the United States go to war with China over a blockade of Taiwan's ports? If members of a Pakistani paramilitary participate in a series of coordinated raids inside India and India takes military action against Pakistan, does the United States stand with India against Pakistan or with Pakistan against India?

If you find yourself unable to answer these questions with any degree of certainty you are hardly alone—neither can most U.S. government officials.

In a global environment in which pop-up dangers loom as large as unnamed threats, indeterminate arrangements like coalitions of the willing can appear to make sense. We had Allies or, more accurately, the British, the Free French, and the Soviets had us during World War II—*that* was a coalition of the willing. A coalition of the willing helped us win the first Gulf War. And the United States continues to make use of ad hoc associations in Afghanistan and Iraq, as well as to pressure North Korea, Palestinians, and others. However, the problem with pick-up groups is that they suffer from the same disadvantages that plague all alliances—inefficiency, disunity, clashing egos, and disagreements over priorities, and at the same time offer none of the advantages of a steadfast relationship. For instance, what exactly does Washington gain from several Central American countries lined up with it as we attempt to conduct foreign policy in the Middle East? Aside from a public relations "feel-good" photo op or two, and the ability to talk as though there is strength in numbers, we gain no advantage.[3]

On closer examination, not even those most deeply committed to multilateralism should like such adhocracy; after all, "simply allowing interest-based ad hoc coalitions of the willing to coalesce on a case-by-case basis opens the door to unilateral action where the most powerful states decide what they want to do and persuade a handful of supporters to go along."[4] Of course, too, there is never such a thing as just using others. Others, for their part, allow themselves to be used because they invariably get something out of the relationship.[5] Just consider NATO's ever-expanding membership: "The addition of small countries with murky political characteristics, trivial military capabilities, and dicey relations with neigh-boring states is a development that is especially pertinent from the standpoint of America's security interests, given this country's obligations as the leader of the alliance. Adding such members does nothing to augment the vast military power of the United States or enhance the security of the American people. All enlargement does is create another set of potential headaches for Washington."[6]

Is this really how we should be executing our foreign policy?

▲   ▲   ▲

Thomas Paine reminded readers in 1777, "It has been the folly of Britain to sup-pose herself more powerful than she really is, and by that means has arrogated to herself a rank in the world she is not entitled to: for more than this century past she has not been able to carry on a war without foreign assistance."[7] Reflecting on Paine's assessment, one can't help but wonder what it means if we Americans can now no longer fight without having to enlist others. Are we setting ourselves up to share Britain's fate? If so, who will we have to come along to rescue *us*?

According to our first president, George Washington, whose words were reit-erated by our sixth (John Quincy Adams), the United States would best preserve its own union by avoiding the entangling alliances of Europe. "Americans, Adams argued, should accept no binding obligation to align their long-term interests with those of any other state, or to pledge mutual assistance when those interests were challenged. Nor should the United States *overtly* cooperate, even in the absence of a formal alliance, even with a state whose interests paralleled its own."[8] For well over a century the United States successfully managed to follow John Quincy Adams' advice. Prior to the dawning of the nuclear age, the balance of power was shared by several European states, and the United States was formally allied to none. But then, in the wake of a nuclear-armed Soviet Union, Washington helped orchestrate a flurry of alliances—from SEATO to CENTO to, most famously, NATO.

What's in an Alliance

According to the definition the Department of Defense uses, an alliance is a "for-mal agreement [i.e., treaties] between two or more nations for broad, long-term objectives that further the common interests of the members."[9] This is an unusually straightforward definition coming from the Pentagon. Tellingly, it says nothing about cobbling together alliances for their potential public relations value. Nor, according to the Defense Department definition, should alliances be thought of as strategic ends in and of themselves. Rather, they are supposed to be the means *by which* strategic ends are achieved. Thus, even NATO's value is less than clear.

Certainly on the face of it, NATO's continuing existence would seem to defy the grand strategic imperative of aligning ends, ways, and means, because without a compelling, common objective—some military purpose that NATO's member-states *need* to pursue in concert—what is its actual function? The war for which it was devised—the Cold War—is over. Some now point to critical "other" purposes NATO serves, like preventing the re-nationalization of defense in Europe and providing "for an ongoing US-European security dialogue. If NATO did not exist opportunities would have to be found for official transatlantic get-togethers and grand summits."[10] But, in that case, why not admit that NATO is more of a "political honor society" than an entity capable of delivering security?[11] Especially since NATO *promises* the ability to deliver security, but then can't.

Among the most damning evidence: As late as January 2009, the International Security Assistance Force (ISAF, or NATO in Afghanistan) consisted of forty-one members "all of whom operate under differing rules and a myriad of national strategies and caveats," and still six years after NATO formally assumed ISAF command, "fundamental questions remain for both the international and U.S. effort: who is in charge? What is the plan? What does success look like?"[12] Yet, surely with one-fifth of the world's countries involved and six years into such a mission, NATO should have been able to point to a job well done —not to disarray.

▲   ▲   ▲

There are alliances like NATO, and then there are allies, such as "our good friend, Leader X from Country Y."[13] Ask most people to describe the attributes of an ally and they would probably cite shared language, common culture, or similar sensibilities. Yet, while affinity surely matters, liking others or being like them does not explain what makes an effective alliance work. Lest we forget, it was our own progenitor—England—who was our chief nemesis and rival for the first hundred years of our existence. Despite our shared heritage, it wasn't until after World War I that the bonds of the great Anglo-American alliance formally solidified. Cultural affinities may have predisposed us to want to work together, but it was our willingness to mutually sacrifice in the face of a common menace that actually cemented our ties.[14] The takeaway from this? Meaningful alliances require commitments beyond mere sentimentality.

The founders clearly understood this. The Constitution could not be clearer on the process of entering formal agreements with foreign governments: "[The

President] shall have the power, by and with the Advice and Consent of the Senate, to make Treaties, provided two thirds of the Senators present concur." In other words, the president, through his executive agencies, is charged with negotiating the terms of our foreign agreements, while the Senate is responsible for formalizing them through a supermajority approval process. In this way, alliances are supposed to be taken extremely seriously and, presumably, fully debated, so that "we the people" are fully aware of their terms.

The public's involvement needs to be considered critical for two sets of reasons: First, because we live in a representative democracy; and second, because alliances represent deadly serious business. Alliances directly embroil us in others' affairs. If, for instance, the United States has a mutual defense treaty with Country X and Country X is attacked, that obligates us to wage war alongside Country X. Likewise, our allies are obligated to join us whenever we react to an attack made against us, regardless of the source.[15]

For these reasons the founders considered alliances so problematic they built into our system the requirement that the Senate debate the merits, costs, and benefits of any treaty—just as our elected representatives are supposed to deliberate about Declarations of War.[16] As with Declarations of War, those arguing for or against a specific alliance should have to make an overwhelmingly compelling case, which is critical because, beyond committing us to something we are then obligated to remain committed to, the whole world needs to know that should ally X be attacked, the United States will respond as if its own sovereignty had been violated. It is hard to imagine a more powerful, or more useful, deterrent than our coming to the assistance of our ally with our full conventional arsenal.

A Twenty-First-Century Ally

What might a twenty-first-century U.S. ally look like in a Sovereignty Rules world? Such an ally would, first, have to be able to fulfill all the demands required of a partner state, which means being responsible for and responsive to its own population. Before signing on the dotted line of any defense treaty, we must be sure that a prospective ally not only can, but will, live up to these commitments and then, in addition, not renege on its obligations to us—all of which should lead readers to wonder whether the United States would even need allies in a Sovereignty Rules world. The answer is yes, at least initially, because before the global order resets— or, indeed, to help reset it—the United States might need to use another country's military bases, or we might need real-time access to raw intelligence feeds. Alternatively, other countries might decide that entering into a formal alliance with us would be the fastest way for them to help us recalibrate the global order.

Imagine, for instance, a series of complementary, bilateral defense treaties. An attack directed at any one country with which we are allied would guarantee our participation in a no-holds-barred response. Over time, two possibilities emerge. First, lots of countries might seek such treaties. That would be one way to achieve our ultimate goal of spreading accountability and responsibility—since to be our ally means agreeing to *always* self-police. Second, countries that harbor problems that their leaders fear might develop into transnational threats would be under that much greater pressure to come up with a method for dealing with whatever grievances gave rise to those problems, in order to avoid spillover consequences. Either of these possibilities would help reset the conditions of global security by both invigorating responsiveness *and* responsibility.

For the vast majority of countries, however, having what amounts to a formalized, ratified relationship with the United States would hardly be necessary.[17] Economic trade does not require a codified security agreement, and under the Sovereignty Solution, security and trade would stay detangled. Thus, all of the impossible questions about what constitutes a vital or national interest would atrophy. Better yet, an assessment like the following would no longer apply: "Throughout the Cold War, Americans broke each other's bones and reputations over what constituted mortal threats to our vital interests; whether to fight or, if not, how otherwise to deal with such threats; when to fight and die over less than vital interests; when to help *others* fight and die instead; what not to fight for; and what means other than military force to employ to foil serious threats. Well into the first decade of the twenty-first century, Americans are still embroiled in the same arguments."[18] What the Sovereignty Solution does is cut through these Gordian knots.

▲　▲　▲

What, then, of multilateral alliances? For instance, what if Mexico, Guatemala, Honduras, and El Salvador were to seek a mutual alliance focused on narco-terrorism and international crime in Central America and solicited U.S. participation because we are a destination for some of the drugs and almost all of the money? Washington might agree. But if so, we should not confuse Central Americans' objectives in this hemisphere with ours in Central Asia; the terms of any multilateral alliance would need to be very specific. In agreeing to terms of an alliance, what the American public would have to first weigh is whether we can count on all signatories to fulfill *all* of their commitments; if we cannot, we shouldn't sign. In other words, there would be no more arm-twisting, logrolling, or *trying* to sign people up to coalitions because broad support sells well and looks good. The truth of the matter is that more is never merrier when it comes to coordinating defense. More *is* better, however, when it comes to *self*-policing—the more countries that will self-police the better, which is yet another reason to insist that entering into any alliance with us be difficult.

Worth reiterating is that, given the world in which we live, there is no other set of people as likely to actively defend our country as we would. But—if we can get other countries to self-police, no other defense should be necessary.

What's Wrong with Multilateralism

Because major pieces of the strategy presented in these pages fly in the face of most other foreign policy proposals—which tout such things as "collective defense"—it is worth examining such notions just a bit more closely. Tellingly, most who write about multilateralism today treat it as if the pursuit of it is sufficient as a strategic goal in and of itself; for instance, "Power cannot be wielded [by the United States] unilaterally, and in the pursuit of a narrowly drawn definition of that national interest, because such actions breed growing resentment, fear, and resistance. We need to reassure other nations about our global role and win their support to tackle common problems." [19]

What is especially interesting about such passages and the broader report from which these particular sentences come is that they deliver no real-world context. Reports like these seldom enumerate which *specific* "actions" breed "growing resentment, fear, and resistance." Nor do they tell us within whom, exactly, these sentiments are growing. The presumption is that savvy readers already know that unilateral U.S. actions breed these things, that the former Bush administration is the guilty party, and that multilateralism is our only salvation. But—what if we were to take the report's sweeping language more literally? Do the authors *really* mean to suggest that Washington should *never* want adversaries and potential adversaries to fear the United States? Is fear *never* a useful thing?

In fairness, the Princeton Project on National Security, from which the above passage comes, does take a serious look at America's strategic options. To the authors, America's refusal to work well with others was the main source of anti-American resentment, fear, and resistance during the George W. Bush years, but, as a consequence, they overlook the possibility that it might have been Washington's lack of clarity or dependability that disturbed non-Americans as well (or that our consumerism, materialism, and boosterism—in other words, who we are and what we export—might be just as offensive as who we do and do not talk to).

An entire book could be devoted to exploring variations on the "more multilateralism" theme. Suggestions about how best to do multilateralism have ranged from "concerts of democracies" to a "Global Freedom Coalition" to "multi-multilateralism" to "multilateralism à la carte." Some authors favor regional concerts: "the first step is for the United States to abandon its attempt to be dominant everywhere. Instead, it should seek to retain global leadership by remaining the only great power that is present everywhere, and therefore has an important say in what happens everywhere."[20]

Other authors alternatively say "the United States should lead the international community to develop and use international institutions to engage and reach inside of states without using force and influence their development in a positive direction. These institutions, including a community of democracies, can bring more resources and skills to bear upon the problem and they can conceal America's role, showing that good governance is not an American project but a widely accepted step towards modernity."[21]

But how principled are such approaches, really? Would the United States *really* be pulling the wool over anyone's eyes by making ourselves "first among equals," yet pretending otherwise? And, if we aren't likely to fool anyone about what we are after—namely, primacy—why should we bother trying to be so indirect?[22]

Equally unclear is how more multilateralism would move us significantly beyond where we currently are. For instance, there have been

- U.S.-led "six party talks" oriented against North Korea. North Korea's response? Unafraid and nuclear armed.

- U.S. and EU efforts to prevent Iran from achieving a nuclear arsenal. Iran's response? Unafraid and building centrifuges.

- U.S.-led talks designed to settle Israeli-Palestinian land disputes. Palestinians' response? Militias fighting a civil war to determine who can best lead the effort to destroy Israel.[23]

Proponents of more multilateralism may claim that the more parties involved in talks, the more "pressure" those parties can bring to bear.[24] But, in reality, the pressure that tends to be applied is almost always on us—to *not* act unilaterally. Indeed, one doesn't have to be a cynic to see that those who advocate more multilateralism do so because multilateralism weakens our ability to effectively pursue our national objectives: "Does multilateralism risk partially tying America's hands, limiting Washington's freedom of action, and ceding some decision making power to other states and international institutions? Yes, and that is precisely the point. If the world's greatest power is not to be viewed as the world's greatest threat, the United States must find ways to convince others that they have some say in how America's power is used."[25]

Under the sovereignty rubric, however, there would be a much easier way to restrain the United States: don't violate our sovereignty. Only in cases when *others'* self-restraint fails would the United States ever need to act like the world's greatest power. Or to rephrase this, unless we are violating some other country's sovereignty—in which case we should be at war—no country or subset of Americans should have cause to want to restrain us. In other words, in a Sovereignty Rules world the international restraints many want to slap on us today would be totally unnecessary.

▲   ▲   ▲

What multilateralism's most ardent supporters miss is that collectivism can only be effective when there is a real and common bond among governments that share the same priorities with equal zeal. Otherwise, here is what we are left with—and *The Economist's* description of the EU response to Russia's 2008 incursion into Georgia is but a microcosm: "[France's] Mr. Sarkozy may have popped up in Tbilisi (as did Germany's Angela Merkel, who earlier met Mr. Mevedev in Sochi), but other EU leaders such as Britain's Gordon Brown and Italy's Silvio Berlusconi have been near-invisible. Worse, the policy response from France, Germany and Italy has been diametrically opposite to that of Britain, Sweden and the east Europeans. The French and Germans, eager to preserve their links to Moscow, have tried to be neutral, while the Italians have blamed the entire war on Mr Saakashvili. The British, Swedes and most east Europeans have loudly condemned Russia's aggression."

The Economist's conclusion is that "so long as EU members hold such divergent views, no amount of institutional tinkering can ever create a forceful common foreign policy."[26]

At the same time that meaningful action proves so hard for diplomats to orchestrate, police, treasury, intelligence, and other professionals working across governments do tend to work together surprisingly effectively. Allowing them to collaborate is among the smartest things governments do. Nor can it be considered a coincidence that where we see the most egregious violations of sovereignty—rampant insurgency, smuggling, and/or transnational crime—is exactly where there is a dearth of professionalism. Thus in much the same way that spillover transnational problems become the triggers to trip the "redress such problems, or else" switch, in a Sovereignty Rules world the results of a lack of professionalism should serve as the triggers for professionalize, or else.

In practice, how might this work? Take spillover violence from Mexico, for instance: At the moment, we Americans are being inundated with news about a total lack of professionalism and about rampant police corruption south of the border. The inference is that this violence directly threatens our security. But is this spillover violence solely Mexico's fault? From a Sovereignty Solution point of view, we are responsible for our southern border. Thus, the onus would actually be on us to get our own house in order. It would be up to us to do this before we made demands on Mexico. And here is why: violence engaged in by Mexicans living or transiting through the United States is something we—not Mexico City—make possible. It is, after all, our fault—not Mexico's—that we have a gang problem. Therefore, it is up to us, not Mexico City, to do everything we can to address this issue within our borders. Or, if we don't want to see the laws we already have enforced, we should repeal them.[27] Essentially, it is only after we have made our own words and deeds congruent that we have any right to make demands of the government in Mexico, though presumably if we were to reinvigorate Americans' civic sensibilities there wouldn't be any demands *to* make because Americans would no longer tolerate armed gangs *with* transnational ties operating *on* U.S. soil.[28] As for Mexico City, with the ball squarely back in its court and no drug money or guns flowing south from the United States, it should then have an easier time (re)professionalizing its forces and being a peaceable neighbor.

Civic Action (aka Nation Building) Redefined

When it comes to America's security concerns further afield, numerous countries that have their own reasons to fear violent Islamism—just to pick another politically sensitive topic—are clearly wary of us and very selective about how closely they allow their professionals to work with ours.[29] Often this is not just a public relations issue for them, but has to do with our public relations, too.[30] Can Rabat or Addis Ababa trust us?[31]

Unfortunately, we Americans have never proven particularly trustworthy. Brave, generous, capable, yes—but rarely does our enthusiasm last. Just consider Washington's track record when it comes to encouraging peoples elsewhere to revolt against oppression. Ask the Hungarians what happened in 1956, or the Kurds and Shi'a in Iraq in 1991. Military forces we have trained and equipped and then abandoned in the past include North Korean partisans during the Korean War, Tibetans during the 1950s, Cubans prior to the Bay of Pigs, Hmong circa Vietnam, and the Sons of Iraq more recently. Then there are the governments we have fitfully assisted, but only for as long as we deemed necessary—South Vietnam, Pakistan, and Iraq.[32] Some might even add Iran to this list.

Just consider what often happens when a foreign government comes under attack from its own dissidents and then cracks down on them in ways we don't like. Some in Washington immediately seek to put distance between us and them, others argue for a public scolding, and still others want us to continue lending the "offending" government support, but sub rosa. In sending all these mixed signals, one thing we convey is that the United States likes to hedge its bets. Maybe we will cut and run or maybe we will turn. Alternatively, something else others can read into our posture is that we have no coherent policy. Not only do all such interpretations then detract from any leverage Washington might *want* to wield, but, the less other governments feel they can trust us, the less they allow us to learn (or do).[33]

For example, in November 2002, the president of Yemen agreed to a predator strike on Yemeni soil against Qa'id Sunyan Ali Al-Harithi, an al Qaeda operative accused of helping to orchestrate the USS *Cole* bombing. The Yemeni president's stipulation was that the predator strike had to be unattributable. And, according to BBC correspondent Frank Gardner, the truth about the successful strike might well have remained "buried with Al-Harithi":

> had it not been for some loose tongues wagging in Washington. Officials there could not resist crowing to journalists in private about this apparent success in the War on Terror. A top terrorist was dead and without the loss of a single American life. The US Defense Secretary Donald Rumsfeld was clearly delighted. "He's been an individual that has been sought after as an Al-Qaeda member as well as a suspected terrorist connected to the USS *Cole*," he commented to reporters, "so it would be a very good thing if he were out of business." Yemen's President Saleh was less delighted. Faced now with angry questions from his own country-men, he gave orders that this sort of extrajudicial killing by the USA must never happen again on Yemeni soil.[34]

Perhaps it is merely a coincidence that, as the *Washington Post* later reported in May 2008, "none of the defendants convicted in Yemen in the 2000 bombing of the USS *Cole* remains in prison. Al-Qaeda member Jamal al-Badawi has escaped twice and slipped away at least once with the blessing of Yemeni officials. Another conspirator was secretly freed in Yemen, and two were released after serving partial sentences. Only two suspects, captured outside Yemen, are in U.S. custody, at Guantanamo Bay, Cuba."[35]

So who, ultimately, has come out ahead in Yemen?

▲　▲　▲

Here is where the relationship framework described in chapter 4 would effect a dramatic recalibration, predicated as it is on public disclosure from the outset. Suppose Yemen, as a struggling state, had sought our assistance after we issued our demands that it dismantle al Qaeda and turn over those involved in the USS *Cole* attack. We would have publicly assisted—but only after setting benchmarks that would have been publicized by us as well. That way we would have ensured all interested stakeholders were on notice. Automatically, Yemen's citizens would have been deputized to serve as monitors of progress: Is al Qaeda being successfully destroyed, dismantled, and/or disarmed? Is the Yemeni government accomplishing this without violating its own laws?

Also, it is worth repeating that only if the United States suffered an attack and local security forces were not up to the task would American forces ever act in lieu of them on foreign soil, or alongside them if they required logistical support. Otherwise, U.S. assistance would remain limited to education and training. Thus, what has transpired since the USS *Cole* attack in Yemen would not have occurred.[36] The United States would have been out of the business of launching catch-as-catch-can drone and air strikes. Washington would have instead insisted that Sana'a make the targeted area unlivable for our attackers in short order. Or we would have done so.

By the same token, the United States would not do what it is currently doing in places like the Trans-Sahel or the Horn of Africa, where our military is delivering humanitarian assistance to regimes that have not specified what they need—and where there has been no publicized list of benchmarks and no demand-response reason for our presence. The last thing we should want to do anywhere is enable regimes to either play us or use us to keep themselves in power.

▲   ▲   ▲

In country after country today, members of the U.S. military are digging wells, building schools, and setting up health clinics because this fits the counterinsurgency presumption that by helping others we can prevent them from hurting us. Yet, none of our assistance guarantees our winning over local populations. In fact, one unintended consequence of our going out of our way to work with populations ignored by their own governments (about whom we otherwise wouldn't need to worry) is that the non-Muslim communities we thereby bypass are left to wonder why they deserve to be penalized for being good. From their perspective, who are we rewarding? We are rewarding those who—unlike them—are either disinterested in Westernizing or who sympathize with our adversaries.

Yet, even if we were shrewder about understanding that this is one way populations read and misread our intent, the historical reality is that no "hearts and minds" campaign has ever been won when *our* military performs civic action in someone else's country. In fact, Col. Edward Lansdale, who credits himself with introducing the concept of civic action to the U.S. military in the early 1950s, was adamant, stating that the whole point of civic action is for the local military to demonstrate *its* credibility to *its* citizens, who are also its clients.[37] Thus, *the* critical thing that Lansdale did with Minister of Defense Ramon Magsaysay to quell the Huk Rebellion in the Philippines was to get the military to prove it could protect and would no longer prey on Filipinos. The military did this by, among other things, helping to police free and fair elections, thereby demonstrating its apolitical professionalism.

According to Lansdale, this should be the aim of every military: to help its government achieve and maintain *uncoerced* security. At best, the U.S. military might assist others to do this by conveying what a civic action capability consists of, and our soldiers and Marines could help train others to standard. But it should not be up to U.S. military personnel to dig wells or build schools. In fact, their doing anything beyond training defies the whole point. Worse, *their* doing civic action undermines sovereignty.

Again, sovereignty requires that a government live up to *its* obligations to *its* citizens. Only when a government's security services behave responsibly, and responsively, and are incorruptible will citizens feel sufficiently protected to uphold their end of the social bargain. Only then will the people deny support to insurgents, terrorists, and anyone bent on undermining the integrity of the state.

Chapter 9

Deeds, Not Words

Most Americans believe that we live in the greatest country on earth. The Sovereignty Solution is designed to see to it that the United States remains the greatest country on earth—for us. "For us" is the critical qualifier.

We Americans cannot force liberty on other societies—that is a contradiction in terms. We can demand elections, but holding elections does not guarantee the rule of law. We can breathe down people's necks, urging them to write constitutions, but charters alone do not represent the structures necessary to sustain freedom.

No matter how much we might want to, we Americans cannot goad people elsewhere to change their values or reorder their priorities without first altering existence as they know it. Altering their existence almost always requires either conquering them outright, which no people will stand for in the twenty-first century, or engaging them in a long, grinding "total" war after which it *might* be possible to install a new form of government that *might* take root—as we did in post–World War II Japan or Germany or even in South Korea. But it is worth remembering that any such endeavor requires massive sacrifice on all sides. Also, neither World War II nor the Korean War were initiated or engineered by us just so we could make over other populations.[1]

Because the wars in Iraq and Afghanistan and the broader war on terrorism will continue to shape national security debates for years to come, it is worth considering what their prosecution reveals about twenty-first-century preferences and capabilities. Without question, the United States achieved a string of military successes in April 2003 when it swept the Iraqi army from the field of battle in mere weeks. Equally impressive is U.S. forces having done so without causing widespread physical destruction. Indeed, the United States strove to apply force with extraordinary care. But also, from the outset, the military goal was to rout the regime's forces, then root out the *regime*, not to devastate the country. To accomplish regime change, the United States needed the Iraqi people to be on its side or to stay neutral at the very least.

Here is where, unfortunately, Washington's logic was questionable from the outset. First, how any policymaker assumed that Iraqis, who were not already for us, would stay out of Americans' way when we were in *their* country remains a mystery. But then probe a bit deeper, and it is even less clear that the United States could have gone in any differently than we did, given our objectives. On this score, Iraq exemplifies the paradox of waging war in a post-conquest age when any foreign occupation, no matter how benign, generates resistance. This is also why it may not necessarily be correct to blame looting as *the* turning point in the war, as so many authors do; nor is it necessarily accurate to presume that if only there had been more troops present, looting would never have occurred. Perhaps because these topics are still too raw, one seldom hears the counterfactual posed: if three times as many American soldiers had been present, would there have been no looting?

Would criminals who Saddam Hussein released from jail, along with Iraqis freed from years of living under repressive state control, really not have stripped vacated houses and unguarded stores? If American soldiers had nicely asked those who did get carried away to put down their booty and return to their homes, would the looters have obeyed? And if not, would Americans really have shot Iraqis dead in what we broadcast to the world were *their* newly liberated streets? Perhaps U.S. forces could have reassembled the Iraqi army at gunpoint and ordered *them* to shoot the looters. But had we piled the streets with several hundred casualties in those first heady days of Iraqi freedom, what would the international response have been? What would have been our own domestic reaction?

No matter how tempting it is to criticize the Pentagon for its lack of foresight or planning, it seems irresponsible not to acknowledge the level of force—not troops, but *force*—that would likely have been required to prevent mayhem from breaking out in Baghdad. Critics tend to forget that the rule of *Iraqi* law, corrupt as it may have been, was suspended in the face of "U.S. raiders turned liberators turned occupiers but not quite conquerors." Arguably, it was this suspension, along with the ambiguity of our presence, that was the price we and Iraqis *had* to pay for the United States not subjugating Iraq.

In one sense this might be construed as a sure sign that the world has made tremendous postcolonial progress; in another sense, not really—not if you consider how few lessons we have retained from our first overseas venture to liberate others. After all, human rights abuses were among the casus belli during the Spanish-American War, too. But back then, foreseeing complications, the

United States wisely chose to avoid freeing and then occupying Cuba. Not so the Philippines, where Filipinos initially greeted us as liberators, until it became apparent we intended to stay and not just liberate. According to the rhetoric of the day, Americans did not consider Filipinos sufficiently capable of governing themselves. Washington also needed a friendly government in place in Manila to support U.S. interests in the region; plus, who at the time could have predicted that it would then take seventeen years of brutal warfare to beat down resistance in the Philippines? Though, interestingly, U.S. methods and the costs inflicted on Filipinos and U.S. soldiers alike did generate strident debate. In fact, it is said this turn-of-the-century debate helped inspire President Woodrow Wilson to promote the principled notion that all peoples deserve the right to rule themselves.

Meanwhile, once President Woodrow Wilson lent the idea of self-determination his official imprimatur and made it the linchpin of American foreign policy in the 1910s, he essentially guaranteed that any foreign occupation anywhere would lead to nationalist revolt from that point forward—which it has. Just consider the great wave of anticolonial liberation struggles that followed World War II. More than a few peoples are still fighting to acquire their own state—including the Kurds. Thus, if anything should have been surprising about Iraqis' response to our incursion, it should not have been that our uninvited presence inspired resistance, but that anyone might have assumed it would not.[2]

In a more charitable vein, one potential explanation for why otherwise smart people in Washington may have ignored the possibility of Iraqi resistance could have been that once upon a time we Americans likewise broke free from a repressive regime and emerged as small *d* democrats.[3] Unfortunately, however, the situations of the distant and recent past are hardly analogous. For one, not only was it Americans who orchestrated and organized the American Revolution (with foreign support to be sure), but in the course of declaring independence, James Madison, Alexander Hamilton, Thomas Jefferson, and the other founders created a system of governance completely organic to the thirteen colonies. They tailored our rule of law to *our* realities. This is not a situation the Bush administration could have recreated in Iraq no matter how much it tried. In fact, no group of council, committee, or convention members in any country has been able to write a constitution de novo since the founders first wrote ours. Instead, there have always been constitutional experts and other "interested" outside parties peering over local lawmakers' shoulders. This, as much as anything, helps explain why so many constitutions read so similarly and also helps explain why we might not sufficiently appreciate that peoples elsewhere *don't* necessarily share our values even when their constitutions suggest they do.

For instance, just consider an act that continues to stump most Americans ten plus years after 9/11. Ask any American parent whether all parents the world over want the same things for their children, and most Americans will likely reflexively answer "yes." But the answer clearly can't be "yes" when you remind them that there are mothers and fathers in other countries who *want* their children to venerate suicide bombers and who will themselves glorify their children should they blow themselves up and kill others in the process. To be sure, no one's constitution sanctions suicide terrorism. But, to be equally clear, constitutions also don't make the rule of law stick. Only people can do that.

No Anti-American Violence

As an act, a concept, and a threat, suicide terrorism doesn't just challenge most Americans' sensibilities but presents us with real challenges. Among these real challenges are how can we make suicide terrorism unconscionable? How can we get religious leaders to make it taboo? How can we de-radicalize extremists?

For ten years and counting, U.S. policy has rested on the unrealistic notion that it is possible to separate "moderates" from "radicals," or reconcilables from irreconcilables. The guiding philosophy in Washington has been that if those espousing and participating in violent jihad—the radicals—can be isolated, it should be possible to woo moderates; and once the radicals have been isolated they can then be eliminated. To accomplish this, we or, ideally, progressive Muslims, just need to persuade moderates to stop lending extremists support.[4]

One problem with such thinking, however, is that it presumes that radicals and moderates are like tribes and represent two neatly distinguishable groups of people; but, this clearly is not the case—not when parents and siblings can express genuine surprise when they learn it was their son, daughter, brother, sister, or husband who just martyred himself or herself in a suicide attack. If family members in close quarters and tightly knit households can't tell or don't know exactly where each one is on the scale of radicalization, how can we make such determinations? More to the point still, why would we ever want to base our security on the presumption that we can?

Sometimes individuals make it obvious they hold extremist views; some wear their politics on their sleeves. But not all do. Most famously, the 9/11 hijackers didn't; nor did the 3/11 bombers in Madrid, or the 7/7 bombers in London. Further, just because someone is a moderate today does not mean he or she can't be radicalized tomorrow; nor is it possible to predict which sorts of events will trigger which sorts of reactions or in whom–it could be the fourteenth rather than the thirteenth time a young man is made to stand for hours at a checkpoint or the second rather than the first casualty a young woman sees that flips the switch. This is why not even the best-intentioned interventions through education are likely to prove sufficient, because, while education may inoculate some, "some" is not all.

Inadvertence compounds the radicalization problem. Just consider the release of the prisoner abuse photos from Abu Ghraib. None of those incidents should have occurred. Meanwhile, incidents that shouldn't have occurred were also recorded. Consequently, those images will continue to be available to incite people for years to come. Once incidents are logged into social memory they can't be deleted. In addition, as the Abu Ghraib debacle illustrates, there is no foolproof way to ensure abuses won't occur.[5] Worse, if unforeseen events can push buttons in people who themselves were not aware they had them till they were pushed, keeping "moderates" separate from potential "radicals" becomes either an impossible or a never-ending task.

In a Sovereignty Rules world, the United States would not engage in the same sorts of behavior that anger so many people today. We would not imprison people in other countries.[6] We would not indefinitely "detain." Nor would we occupy. But also, to return to this book's overarching premise: if no one can ever be sure what *won't* happen, then we need to be prepared to respond to *any* violation of sovereignty. The set point for when to respond itself needs to be reset. Under the sovereignty rubric people should be able to rant, rave, vent, and even hate. Let them act against us, however, and that is the trigger. That is what guarantees a set of U.S. demands—followed by either their government's reaction or ours.

There is a reason the Sovereignty Solution seeks to distinguish between words and deeds. Warning people to stop doing things we don't like—with no ability to punish them—makes no more sense than urging people to rise up without being able to protect them when their government then cracks down. Essentially, talk is cheap. Having said that, we Americans, who laud free speech, should never want to license other governments to stifle speech, even if it is hate speech. Better that people be able to vent than explode. Or, to invoke something American parents used to instill in American children: "sticks and stones may break my bones, but names can never hurt me."[7]

The relationship framework purposely places a premium on deeds. Yes, words are important. They are one reason we need ethnographic sensors—to monitor local moods. As moods shift, diplomats can ask for reassurances and remind other governments we will hold them (and their citizens) to account for any violations of our sovereignty. But the chief aim in concentrating on deeds, not words, is congruence. Under the sovereignty rubric, when it comes to *our* deeds, we act in accordance with what we *can* do, and we don't promise, threaten, or bluster to achieve things we can't.[8]

Decisive Action

In a Sovereignty Rules world clarity and congruence self-reinforce. What we say we are going to do, we do. Thus, when it comes to the application of force, there are at least four reasons why, should the United States have to engage in military action, it must do so overwhelmingly and decisively from the outset. First, no one is deterred by hollow gestures. Second, this is the only strategically clear thing to do: the United States promises, it delivers. Third, decisive action is the only form of military action that aligns our ends, ways, and means in *our* favor. And fourth, a direct, no-holds-barred response fits with our strategic personality.

Finesse is not an American strong suit. We are smarter than we are clever; the British can be considered clever. It took cleverness and a sure sense of superiority, not egalitarianism, to run the kind of empire they did—with just a few white men posted to exert control over legions of natives. But also, at the height of imperial power, when Britannia ruled three-quarters of the globe, the Crown was more heavily invested in certain locations than others. Today, any country can turn itself into a flashpoint. Who, for instance, would have considered Kosovo a key "country" as recently as 1990? In fact, by *not* paying sufficient attention to places most people would characterize as obscure—Somalia, Bosnia, Kosovo, Afghanistan—the local *has* turned global.

Under the strategy developed in this book, the etiquette of sovereignty proscribes playing favorites. In addition, with actions speaking louder than words, there would be little room for mixed messages or cross-cultural confusion. The aim of the relationship framework is to make the nature of our relations crystal clear. Or, as Richard Betts has pointed out in a different context, "many messages can be transmitted and understood across cultures, especially if they are stark rather than subtle—for example, 'Surrender or die.'"[9] Or, to once again invoke the man who oversaw the most important alliance of the twentieth century, General Eisenhower, consider his attitude during World War II. According to Stephen Ambrose, Eisenhower, like General Grant before him, was a fan "of the direct approach and put his faith in the sheer smashing power of great armies. He was once accused of having a mass-production mentality, which was true but beside the point. He came from a mass-production society, and like any good general he wanted to use his nation's strengths on the battlefield."[10]

Worth noting is that the United States still possesses smashing power. We have an incomparable arsenal, but only if we are willing to use it. If not, then the military strength we do possess can hardly deter.

As mentioned in chapter 5, one aim of deterrence should be to dissuade people from even thinking they have anything to gain by attacking us—something that will work only if current and future (or potential) adversaries understand they stand to lose *everything* should they try to fight us. We tend to forget that one of the things that rendered deterrence so effective during the Cold War wasn't just the specter of nuclear annihilation, but tens of millions of people—including Soviets, Western Europeans, Asians, and millions of Americans—had just lived through a war marked by horrific devastation. In other words, World War II not only taught all sides what everyone else was capable of, but by doing so also instilled a visceral appreciation for what total destruction means.

We Westerners do not engage in total destruction these days. Instead, we occupy a nether world in which we try to make impossibly precise separations. Worse, we have turned war into an impossibly wicked problem.

> Wicked problems have the following characteristics: 1. There is no agreement about "the problem." In fact, the formulation of the problem is the problem. 2. There is no agreement on a solution. In actuality, stakeholders put forward many competing "solutions," none of which have stopping rules to determine when the problem is solved. 3. The problem-solving process is complex because constraints, such as resources and political ramifications, are constantly changing. 4. Constraints also change because they are generated by numerous interested parties who come and go, change their minds, fail to communicate, or otherwise change the rules by which the problem must be solved.[11]

Alternatively, Rupert Smith offers an apt description of the catch-22 we've created: "the trend of our recent military operations is that the more the operation is intended to win the will of the people, the more the opponent adopts the method of the guerrilla and the more complex the circumstances, the longer it will take to reach the condition in which a strategic decision can be made and a solution found. And while it is being found the condition has to be maintained, and since in part at least it has been arrived at by force it must be maintained by force for want of the strategic decision."[12] Yet, force is exactly what proponents of population-centric warfare say we should try to avoid.

The above example is just one impossible challenge our current policies pose for young men and women sent to serve in Afghanistan and Iraq, only two of the front lines in a war that many in Washington say has no front lines and where winning remains undefined.[13]

Who Fights for Us and Why This Matters

As everyone in the military knows, anything required to keep troops moving, fighting, and protected itself requires continual repair and refurbishment—from tanks to personnel carriers to trucks, helicopters, jets, and computer systems—you name it. On this score, we are fortunate. At least when the equipment is worn out, the United States can manufacture or purchase more. In contrast, when those in uniform are depleted, no amount of check writing will suffice; it is not possible to hit a button, turn on the assembly line, and generate new divisions of volunteer professionals—especially not when it requires years to turn privates and lieutenants into worthwhile midgrade and senior leaders.

Men and women in uniform are worth highlighting because if we accept the Grand Strategic imperative—align ends, ways, and means—then it becomes essential to take into account the capabilities of those in uniform today. They *are* our means. Let's think about, for instance, a typical young soldier or Marine—a truck driver, say. Not only does that young person have to know how to use four different types of communication devices, work a global positioning computer, read a map when the GPS breaks, handle several different types of weapons, and be able to repair the truck when it breaks (which it will). But add to this the list of tasks necessary for staying sane in an irregular warfare environment; a tremendous amount of investment by the services, not to mention by individuals themselves, goes into getting such a young person to even a minimal level of proficiency. Now consider this young soldier or Marine's platoon sergeant. He or she would be an individual with something like seventeen years in service and *multiple* tours in complex environments—an absolutely irreplaceable national asset, as is true of his or her peers in the Air Force and Navy.

None of the services are easily augmented today. This means that despite what some outside the military advocate, a draft would do nothing to boost our military effectiveness in the near term. For better or worse, the armed forces we have are simply too skilled.

Nor is this the only sobering new reality worth noting. In today's volunteer professional force, those who make up the career backbone of the military commit themselves to twenty or more years of service. This means that the men and women who choose military life do not just grow up, mature, and develop *in* the military, but they grow and raise their families there, too. Not even the most dedicated military families can be expected to adjust to mom or dad being deployed to a hazardous combat zone twelve months out of every thirty. The stresses and strains of continuous deployments will either increasingly break families apart or impel otherwise patriotic and committed Americans to leave the service. There is evidence that both trends are already well under way. In other words, a hard reality is that the makeup of our forces represents a very real strategic constraint.

Meanwhile, something else that will prove increasingly debilitating over the long term is sending servicemen and women to the same theater over and over again, particularly if they see themselves making only incremental differences, if that. You can hear this sentiment among even the most committed officers today. No one wants to be ineffective. What happened to the morale, esprit, and capabilities of the Israeli Defense Forces once they began to serve as a holding, rather than a fighting, force is highly suggestive of the potential corrosiveness to come.[14]

▲　▲　▲

Although there seems to be general recognition in policy-making circles that today's military is ill-suited to making the sorts of distinctions between moderates and radicals or "real" and "accidental" guerrillas that effective counterinsurgency is said to require, many in Washington continue to want to believe that, with just the right changes, it should be possible to develop forces who *can* do this.

Consequently the push is being made to "revitalize our military to operate in a more whole-of-government context, particularly giving people the training and the education they need to operate in a very interagency environment, in an international environment, and in an environment where members of our military will often be called to do a number of things that are not nearly military in nature, as we've seen in Iraq and Afghanistan, from mediating community disputes in a local village, to rebuilding damaged infrastructure, to managing detention centers, to securing free and fair elections."[15] Yet, not only does such an approach totally ignore Edward Lansdale's prescription for civic action—it is not *our* military that should be doing any of these things—but, even if Washington's policies were coherent, no one seems to want to pay attention to what our military is *already* well suited to do. Or, to be totally impolitic, why is everyone so afraid to devise a strategy that makes use of our known strengths?

▲　▲　▲

As military historians have long pointed out, there *is* a tried-and-true American way of war: namely, the application of overwhelming force. As for the benefits to direct, decisive action, here are some: Clarity for our adversaries, clarity for those who might otherwise aid and abet them, clarity for "we the people," and clarity for members of our military. The latter are, again, especially important because, if policy is either too complicated or too impractical, can't be understood by those tasked with applying it, or, worse, involves a concept that a young officer in the field can't grasp, then it is useless precisely where it is most needed—at the point of contact, on the ground.[16]

The unspoken truth is that the United States *can* project overwhelmingly decisive conventional force—when, where, and how we choose.[17] Our air, space, and naval supremacy lend us enormous advantages. In fact, the United States is not just supreme in these realms, but supremely dominant. Our military can control the pace, tempo, duration, and intensity of how it delivers force that, by definition, yields tangible proof of success or failure. Direct decisive force can be applied via waves of B-52s and tons of aerial bombs. But this force doesn't have to be delivered from on high. If the strategic objective is to destroy a terrorist organization operating from some mountain fastness somewhere, aerial bombardment alone will probably not suffice. The better option might be U.S. Special Forces teams working with local tribal chieftains and their armed men. Or it might be light ground forces backed by a swarm of American aircraft. Or it could instead involve enforcement of a total quarantine, utilizing American space assets to direct shoot-to-kill drones whenever movement of any kind is detected.

One defining feature of decisive action is that it is of short duration. Its timing and delivery might require surprise, but the effects would be readily apparent and the aims well understood. In a Sovereignty Rules world, under the relationship framework, the only kinetic (armed) mission for U.S. forces abroad would be to get in, break, and get out—not to fix. Anyone who seeks to survive will surrender, while our military would keep targeting those who refuse.[18]

If this sounds daunting, it isn't. Consider what the United States *could* do, should it find itself at war with an array of different actors. For instance, to return to the example of a Hezbollah-orchestrated strike against U.S. targets—with a Declaration of War against Hezbollah, and with Israel as a partner state—here is what might happen:

In Lebanon, U.S. Army Special Forces advisors would work with whatever effective forces non-Hezbollah factions of the Lebanese government could muster to shut down the Syrian border and prevent ground traffic moving north of the Beirut–Damascus highway. Israel, for its own protection, would doubtless ensure that Hezbollah would not flee south. Combined air and land operations would be launched against all known Hezbollah locations and villages and would be followed by a sweep through southern Lebanon and the Bakaa Valley. Anything or anyone carrying, waving, or moving weapons—or openly flaunting a Hezbollah affiliation—would be targeted and engaged. All structures would be seized and searched and, if found to be militarized, demolished. Because speed matters, U.S. forces would not slow down for urban resistance. If a town did not submit and gunfire was taken from a window, that building would be targeted. If opponents shot from a building, the street would be at risk. This would be one way to handle Hezbollah.

Another way to address Hezbollah would be to deliver the same ultimatum, village by village: surrender, agree to dismantle under supervision—or else. If a village chose "or else," it would be demolished. Tight time demands, overpowering strikes, and an unrepentant projection of force would make this option completely militarily feasible.

As for Hezbollah's sponsors—Syria and Iran—defiance by both governments would invite targeted responses. The strategic objective for U.S. operations would be to decimate both regimes and continue to destroy Hezbollah's resources. The airpower provided by two aircraft carrier groups and long-range bombers should prove sufficient. Under air cover, ground forces moving from Lebanon and Iraq, and through Syria, should be able to quickly obliterate military resistance—should any force actually choose to resist. Again, the aim would be to destroy, not to hold or pacify.

The United States would likewise interdict any contraband or fighters trying to enter the area. And here it is important to add that the United States would no doubt ask Russia, one of Iran's major arms suppliers, to stop selling arms to Tehran. If Russia refused, citing economic hardship or preexisting contracts, it, along with all other countries trading with Iran, would be reminded that while the United States is not at war or about to go to war with them, given our Declaration of War against Iran we reserve the right to interdict any road, rail, and sea shipments entering Iran. We would not specifically target Russia's or anyone else's trade and certainly would not touch Russia's trade anywhere else. But anything and everything entering Iranian airspace, crossing its borders, or approaching its shores would be considered fair game.

Once U.S. operational objectives had been met—with Hezbollah destroyed as an organization and Iran's and Syria's regimes removed—U.S. military forces would immediately withdraw. They would remain just-over-the-horizon for a time, in case any fighters reemerge (complete annihilation of a non-state entity and total destruction of foreign governments may never be fully possible). However, the damage U.S. forces would have done in the first round of fighting would have been so thorough that surviving elements should have permanently disbanded. The moment support for a rearmed Hezbollah were to resume, or the remnants of the governments against whom we declared war attempted to reassemble without *first* suing for peace, U.S. forces would return to finish the job.

Not only are existing U.S. military capabilities ideal for the application of this kind of decisive force, but such operations capitalize on our other military strengths: speed and agility. Applying overwhelming force, especially from standoff distances, would not only help keep U.S. casualty figures low, but the speed and ferocity of our operations would likewise ensure service members do not again have to be deployed for years away from home.

↟   ↟   ↟

Until the day the United States chooses to adopt universal conscription, it is not only critical to optimize the All-Volunteer Force, but politicians and the public need to understand *who* joins the military and why. This understanding is vitally important when it comes to what the United States can—and should—ask its armed forces to do. Consider those who volunteer for the combat arms, for instance—infantry, artillery, armor, and combat engineers, fighter pilots, bomber pilots, Special Operations Forces, and Marines: all join in order to fight. In a black hat world, they want to wear the white hats. They also want to shoot guns and blow things up. Only a small fraction feel comfortable "dealing in the gray," as Special Operators call it, and many of them prefer direct action to civic action when given the choice.

It behooves American politicians, policymakers, and the public to bear in mind that men and women in the military are the thinnest of thin lines standing between us and harm. They deserve all the support we can muster. Support that counts means freeing them to use the tools of their trade to the best of their abilities, which is what decisive action does—occupations and fighting long, unwinnable wars "among the people" never will. "Upon occupation the military force loses the strategic initiative. Once all the tangible objectives have been taken or destroyed, and the land held, what is there left for force to achieve strategically, or even operationally? The initiative moves to the occupied."[19]

Decisive action fits with America's strategic personality in another sense. One need only remember back to the days immediately following 9/11. If another attack on U.S. soil occurs, the public's demand for justice will be deafening. Americans will not care about good intentions or noble pursuits. Instead, most will want Washington to hit back at those who struck us. It is at such a critical moment, when American idealism is knocked flat, that the national demand for justice—even retribution—will make the public ready and willing to unleash our military arsenal to its fullest. It is at this precise point, when all others shudder at the thought of what might come, that we would do well to make them truly shudder— not because we hit back blindly,[20] but rather because we are absolutely clear-headed about what we need to accomplish and then go about it decisively, as hard and as fast as we can.

No More Incrementalism

Under the strategy laid out in these pages, U.S. actions cannot be incremental or proportional. Incrementalism, if you think about it, only helps adversaries be able to dig in. That is never good. Again, consider the specter of Vietnam: "the tempo of the American bombing in North Vietnam was so slow that it allowed the enemy to recover from each operation. There is no case in history of a war won through the piecemeal commitment of resources. Victory comes when the enemy's will to fight is broken by a specific defeat. The whole point of strategy is to figure out what that defeat would be and to inflict it."[21] No less a humanist than Margaret Mead might well have agreed with such a judgment. As she wrote in 1942, "The point of a negotiated peace is so that everybody can stop, have a breathing spell, and fight more efficiently in the future." What she goes on to say may be an even better summation: "War to the finish is never the slogan of people who like war."[22]

This statement, too, is of a piece with traditional American attitudes toward fighting as reflected in Confederate Lt. Gen. Nathan Bedford Forrest's dictum that "war means fighting, and fighting means killing" and Gen. William T. Sherman's famous judgment: "War is cruelty. There is no use trying to reform it. The crueler it is, the sooner it will be over."[23]

By July 1967 former President Eisenhower was so frustrated with President Johnson's course of "gradualism" in Vietnam that he not only urged Congress to declare war against North Vietnam, but by October was saying "the country should 'take any action to win.'"[24] By 1968 others agreed with him that "calibrated pressures as a deterrent obviously had not worked. One reason was a persistent lack of clarity as to who, or what, was being deterred."[25]

According to Richard Betts, it was—ironically enough—the U.S. military that "favored a quick, massive bombing campaign . . . aimed at capitalizing on simultaneity to smash North Vietnamese capabilities. In contrast, it was civilians who favored the 'slow squeeze' approach."[26] Civil-military relations present perennial challenges. The Founding Fathers intentionally designed a system in which neither civilian nor military leaders could do things entirely their way. Nevertheless, it would help to always remember who ultimately has to actually execute policy—those in uniform—and what their preferences might reveal about what they are or are not well suited to do.

▲   ▲   ▲

In terms of proportionality, tit for tat may be useful in situations when both sides genuinely abide by the same ethical and moral standards—and both want to negotiate. Otherwise, that approach, too, prolongs the conflict.[27] As Jeremy Rabkin notes, "if you are in war, you shouldn't be in a war unless you are right. But if you are right, then you have the right to pursue the war effectively."[28] This is why it makes little sense to limit *what* we do. Or, to rephrase this slightly, if we have the ability to knock out our opponent with our first blow, why shouldn't we? Yes, we should always use prudence. But—once war has been declared and destruction of an adversary is under way—either we defeat our enemy or our enemy defeats us. Military objectives have to be set to achieve our strategic end state or else there is no point in proceeding. Simply attempting to do a little bit of something on the cheap almost always guarantees having to do more, harder, later, at greater cost, and with higher risk.[29]

It is important to remember this, too: in a Sovereignty Rules world the United States does not intervene or interfere in another government's affairs. Washington only interferes in another state if its government proves incapable of preventing its citizens from violating our (or an ally's) sovereignty. In that case, we demand that it mend its ways. If it can't, if it doesn't, or if it refuses to, we address the problem ourselves. We then leave it up to those who survive to ameliorate the situation they find themselves in. We will happily educate and train and offer as much advice as anyone cares to solicit. But the United States will no longer dangle carrots; Washington will no longer deal in monetary or material incentives.[30] Nor will we break other governments so that *we* can fix them.[31] When and if we "liberate," it is to leave people to sort out their own future. We monitor in case we have to "liberate" again. But we never occupy. We also do not just hit and run. We hit to destroy those who attacked us, along with their supporters.

Americans' hope should be that, in the wake of such devastation, those most capable of asserting authority and taking control will quickly rise to the occasion and then prevail. Without undue interference they likely will, and order *will* be restored. Anarchy never lasts for long. Even in what appears to us to be chaos there are always strongmen and emergent social structures. If strongmen want to take on the responsibility of governing, so much the better; they will have just seen what will happen to them should they be the next actors to transgress.

If, meanwhile, this smash and "deliver" approach seems a stark and unforgiving use of our military, remember what else the United States would do and what we would do it with. If the public's demand for justice after a future attack will be enormous, the public's desire to help after nature strikes is no less compelling. The same strengths that enable our military to destroy so effectively—speed, agility, and professionalism—are ideal for acute disaster relief. If not exactly flip sides of the same coin, delivering devastation *to* or relieving people *from* devastation are nevertheless two of the things the United States can already do—not just extraordinarily well, but better than anyone else.

As we have tried to remind readers, the strategy presented in these pages is all about aligning ends, ways, and means. This strategy means facing the unvarnished truth about ourselves as well as others. It is no coincidence that we Americans are no better at lengthy military interventions than we are at humanitarian nation building. We are too egalitarian and too impatient to successfully make others over in our image—that takes an imperial ruthlessness we do not possess. Our ruthlessness is far more direct—ideal for getting to the scene quickly and doing immense damage *or* getting to the scene quickly to do immediate good.

In terms of grand strategic "ends, ways, means," what Americans want to have happen needs to fit with what we can do. What we can do has to account for what others might not want us to do. And we need to push this out thirty years. We need to think long term. Or alternatively, we could look to the past, reexamine the Constitution, and reconsider what the Founding Fathers put together and why it has lasted as long as it has. Essentially, their genius yielded a set of fixed values in a flexible format easy to disseminate. That provides us with a tested model for what we need today: a national security strategy with fixed values in a flexible format that is easy to disseminate.

Is the Grand Strategy offered in these pages that strategy?

We Americans today disagree with each other over many issues, including how best to address national security. At one extreme are pacifists: In the pacifist's world, the United States is never justified in the use of military force because "violence never solves anything." Force, if used, should only be applied by an international body and should only be wielded to protect universal human rights. This is the policy proposed by those who favor overarching international governance. Not to stereotype too unfairly, but this stance should bring to mind academics at august institutions and certain "people's republics" on the West and East Coasts.

At the other end of the spectrum are Americans who advocate massive aerial bombardment of any country that disagrees with us. In their view, American military power should be used to turn other countries and all of their inhabitants to dust (or glass). "Just nuke them" is their preferred foreign policy solution. Not to stereotype too unfairly, but strategists of this ilk are often found at backyard barbeques and in the third grade.

Both above sketches are clearly caricatures, but they nonetheless point to the two extremes that do define our strategic personality: liberal idealism and fierce protectionism. Any strategy that promotes one to the complete exclusion of the other is doomed to fail because it will not match who we are. Most of us fall somewhere in between—which is exactly the balance "don't tread on me" married to "to each his own" strives to achieve.

Unlike other grand strategies, this one is not tailored to a specific regime or threat type. Instead, it is designed to handle states as well as non-state actors and to contend with types of rogue behavior we can't foresee today. Rather than assume that a shock *will* occur that causes Washington to have to figure out how to retool national strategy overnight, this book has offered America suggestions for how to retool now.

First, we need to harden the shield. Ergo "Indivisible America." Americans also have to become more willing to wield the sword. That too requires a more Indivisible America. Indivisible America explicitly describes who *we* are. It codifies what is most American—and thus precious—about the American way of life, thereby guaranteeing we understand what we need to do to secure it. It also steels the country to withstand any sort of attack and respond decisively. Perhaps most importantly, it frees others to live as they, not we, prefer.

Recent history has shown that even at the most basic level the United States cannot depend upon fellow democracies to view the world as we do. The failure of the world's "adults" to present a united front against Iraq, North Korea, Sudan, or Iran is sufficient proof that even an improved Security Council or a "Concert of Democracies" is not a practicable concept. The chronic failure of economic sanctions is additional proof that the world is hardly ready for international governance. When the international community can act as a community, *then*, but only then, might we want to consider international "opinion" binding. Until then, we would be far better served by compelling countries to self-police.

ᴧ   ᴧ   ᴧ

The three of us who have written this book believe there are at least six reasons why what we propose is a more viable strategy than any we are familiar with—with the caveat that sovereignty may be only a stopgap as the world shakes out, although it should also prove sufficient to *shake* the world out:

1. The United States will reach the point of having to be decisively destructive on a large scale at some point in the near future. Better to have worked out why and how ahead of time—*before* Chicago is left in ruins.

2. Granting other people the opportunity to remain who they want to be and how they want to be is the principled approach for us to take as twenty-first-century Americans.

3. The only principled way to preserve opportunity, choice, and responsibility for ourselves is to extend this principle to everyone.

4. This is the ultimate liberal agenda—it liberates others to live as they, not we, see fit.

5. This is the ultimate conservative agenda—it conserves our values *un*diluted.

6. This strategy plays to our strengths. In the end, we don't have to be the same, think the same, or practice the same the world over. States just have to accede

to the same set of rules for occupying the planet together. And yes, that then makes this the ultimate states' rights argument.

We can think of two reasonable objections: how does this strategy handle unintended consequences? As history makes clear, there will always be unintended consequences, just as there will always be unforeseen events, and more bad actors *will* pop up. We should count on that. But, if you compare this strategy with other national security strategies, this is the only one that gives us—and the world—a framework for how to respond to bad guys regardless of their degree or brand of badness. Critics might contend that that is no better than saying "if all you have is a hammer, you'll treat everything like a nail." Our rejoinder: when it comes to nails, nothing is more effective *than* a hammer.

The second likeliest objection is that this is not nuanced enough. *Exactly.* This strategy does not pretend that we Americans will always be smarter than our adversaries or that we will be able to accurately prevent second- and third-order effects. What we should want to count on, however, is that we will always be stronger, better armed, and more fiercely determined than anyone who seeks to cause us harm.

▲   ▲   ▲

Are we three authors being unrealistic when we suggest that reinvigorating sovereignty and reviving a more Indivisible America will protect us from twenty-first-century threats? We clearly don't think so, but from time to time we do fear that looking at the world through this lens has predisposed us to think we can solve most of our problems by applying this approach. We certainly do not see anyone offering anything more cogent or anything that better fits with the realities of the day, whether we are talking about the genies of disorder that lurk in the world out there or in the economic and other problems that already trouble most Americans here at home. But it could also be that our professions—being of and around the military—color our view. We know the United States will be confronted by ever more lethal adversaries armed with fewer scruples and ever more diabolical weapons. These and other threats won't just preoccupy the three of us for the remainder of our careers, but will also—literally—consume the lives of too many of those we know in and out of uniform. That fact alone is reason enough for us to want the country to be well prepared in advance.

At the same time, we would also be doing ourselves a disservice if we didn't acknowledge that we do realize, as three high-ranking officials in the Pentagon pointed out to us five years ago, that many Americans may not be ready to enact these changes until, probably, Chicago *is* burning. At the very least, then, we offer this as a contingency for that moment. And we also offer a reminder: the three of us writing this come from significantly different American backgrounds, span two very different generations, did not know each other prior to sharing a classroom in Monterey, and no doubt would have placed slightly different emphases in different places if we had written as three separate individuals. Nonetheless, we have adamantly reached the same conclusion: the conditions of global security need to be reset. The United States *can* do that on its own. But with this strategy it shouldn't have to.

▲ ▲ ▲

In the end, this strategy capitalizes on all the things we Americans are best at. We possess an unparalleled military arsenal and a tried-and-true method of warfare. We should make use of these.

Some other truisms about us as Americans are that we are unbelievably generous as a people. And we are great logisticians. Yet, we do not have a great deal of patience or a very long attention span. Add these together, and we are incomparably good when it comes to rushing aid to distant places in the wake of acute natural disasters. However, we, like almost everyone else, are abysmal at doing much of anything helpful in the face of chronic failure, except to contain it. If, then, our military excels at breaking but not fixing, and if as a people we prefer straight talking *and* straight shooting, why not build a national security strategy around these strengths? Or, to come at this from a slightly different angle: we are the world's dominant power, so why not use that power for the ultimate liberation—"you want to be treated as head of a sovereign state? Fine. We now hold you and your government responsible *and* accountable."

To quickly recap: if ethnographic sensors were augmented by all the other sources of intelligence we currently possess, the United States would be well positioned to ask other governments to deal with problems we believe directly threaten us and our allies. If the response is that our information is incomplete or faulty, the burden would then be on those governments, not us, to prove us wrong. Not only would this encourage far more transparency, but so would what happens to transgressors. Violate U.S. sovereignty and the response will be overwhelming. Washington's aim will be to inflict maximum damage and force surrender. And the United States would not help rebuild afterward.

If this sounds ruthless, it is meant to be. Otherwise, it is hard to imagine how we could keep adversaries from continuing to pop up in locations around the globe. At the same time, no matter how good our sensor net becomes, we have to be prepared for surprises on occasion, particularly in the near term. That is why nothing may be more pressing than building a less divisible America. We need to reprise what has long made us exceptional, and thereby distinct; distinctiveness matters.

The more distinctive we prove ourselves to be in terms of *our* values, the more this frees others to be equally distinctive, but in their own ways.

To the three of us writing this book, the pieces we have presented all hook together conceptually, though they also need to be tied together operationally: who oversees this policy? Who ensures that the information ethnographic sensors collect is transmitted through proper channels? Who explains to the public why indivisibility needs to rest on core Judeo-Christian values?

No doubt what we have presented raises a number of other "what if" questions. Who answers them? Who makes sure they even get posed? Worthy of further consideration as well are the finer points of the capabilities we have sketched. But we would also submit that even if what we have outlined strikes you as impossible or too simplistic for such a complicated world, ask yourself the following questions: why does the world have to be so complicated? Why *can't* we simplify it? Why not take today's constraints and turn them *into* opportunities?

That is what this strategy attempts to do while also providing the means by which to drive transnational terrorists and other violent anti-American actors out of business for good.

If this still seems too radical a lurch, and thus does not seem plausible, here is one final thought exercise: See if, after reading this, you don't find yourself watching, reading, or listening to the news just a bit differently. Or, if you already agree this strategy is worth thinking about, try considering all of its applications. Piracy? This addresses it. Narcotrafficking? This would address that, too. Pollution? The same. Arguably, even world health protocols.

Time Now—Afghanistan

We would be remiss if we didn't try to address how our proposed strategy would tackle current foreign policy, were it implemented today and not at some more ideal Time Zero. Ideally, ethnographic sensors would be grown, and the hardening of "we the people" through civic education would begin. But Iraq and Afghanistan still do loom. Al Qaeda still lurks.

Because this strategy is not one that permits ad hoc responses, some of what needs to be done may seem abrupt. But bear in mind that to do anything requires cleaning up mistakes created through twenty years of strategic drift and ambiguous policy practiced by both political parties and all three branches of government.

So, imagine that the president is sitting with his advisors *after* Chicago has been struck. Or, imagine a daring politician working through an agenda for how to keep America safe in light of our current predicaments. Here would be one potential approach:

1. Call for a Declaration of War against al Qaeda. End the authorizations of force that were used for the initial invasions of both Iraq and Afghanistan and provide a no-nonsense Declaration of War to unify the government and public around a central and clear objective: the destruction of the terrorist organization that murdered close to three thousand Americans in September 2001. Al Qaeda is the organization we are at war with. It is active and thriving in Iraq, Afghanistan, Indonesia, Algeria . . . the list is long.

2. Call for a Standing Declaration of Preemption against Iran. Iranian pursuit of nuclear weapons in violation of the Nuclear Non-Proliferation Treaty, its open support and arming of Hezbollah, and its training, equipping, and assistance of Shi'a insurgents in Iraq all merit putting the regime on notice. The United States needs to give Iran a deadline by which to withdraw support from insurgents in Iraq, while also making it crystal clear that any *further* action taken against us by individual Iranians or non-Iranians receiving Iranian support is grounds for decisive action against both the perpetrators and the government in Tehran.

3. Call for a Standing Declaration of Preemption against Hezbollah. Hezbollah first began attacking the United States in the 1980s. Its rhetoric points to plenty of complicity in transnational terrorism that continues to target Americans.

4. Call for a Standing Declaration of Preemption against North Korea. The international community as a whole needs to see that there will be no remorse from the U.S. government should North Korea push across any of our openly declared "red lines."

5. Publicize the United States' new definition of who we consider to be combatants—and who will bear the responsibility for the deaths of innocents at U.S. hands. Alert all populations about what we will do to organizations that take shelter in their midst, as well as to governments that don't help root them out after an attack.

6. Direct the State Department to discuss with foreign governments the exact nature of the relationship framework and the status of all countries' relations with us. Diplomats need to make clear that we completely eschew the "you break it, you buy it" rule. In the future, we'll break it if others force us to. But once we do, American taxpayers won't fix what our armed forces break. Diplomats will also need to explain U.S. policies toward aid, education, training, and disaster assistance.

▲ ▲ ▲

We acknowledge that in Afghanistan the die has already been cast. The United States has assumed considerable responsibility for trying to fix the Afghanistan we liberated in 2001. For the past ten years we have attempted to do so using American blood, sweat, tears, and dollars. The strategic end state is to now allow the Afghans to take over and "fix" Afghanistan into whatever they want: republic, autocracy, or unending civil war. The Afghans have a constitution, a seated government, and a national defense force. What sovereignty dictates is that they control their own destiny domestically. What we owe the state and the Afghan people is a protected space in which to work this out. Because we demand accountability from Afghanistan for controlling its borders, and currently it cannot, it is incumbent on us to assume responsibility for all borders, mountain passes, and airfields. Only with this protection will we be able to assure the Afghan people that they alone are responsible for shaping their future without armed intervention by their neighbors.

Such a policy fits perfectly within the relationship framework described in chapter 4. As a "struggling state," Afghanistan clearly has a problem, namely al Qaeda and other foreign fighters who have chosen an adversarial relationship with us. Should the government in Kabul accept Afghanistan's status as a struggling state, it will be eligible to receive our help; our commitment to control the borders is not, then, simply a fulfillment of previous "break it/fix it" promises, but is essential to our ability to wage more effective war against *our* adversary al Qaeda.

Bearing in mind our policy of being strategically direct and operationally ambiguous, perhaps Special Operations Forces working with Afghan units are sufficient for this task. Or maybe this is a job better left to NATO forces. Alternatively, Afghanistan might use a little of both with the addition of U.S. airpower and ground reaction forces. Again, whomever and whatever we assign to the problem, U.S. forces would not be concerned with fixing anything organic *to* Afghanistan. Problems endemic to Afghanistan are going to be resolved by Afghans.

Isolating internal violence to Afghanistan in this manner would achieve two things. First, it might well lead to the escalation of violence, but then, the violence should burn itself out. Violence should stop once Kabul establishes the necessary level of control over civil (or, as the case may be, uncivil) behavior—if it can. With *no* material assistance from outside players, civil war, if it comes to that, shouldn't be too prolonged.

How long do we stick with this? For as long as the Afghan government meets our benchmarks for eradicating al Qaeda. If Kabul proves less than serious, then we are back to the business of breaking things ourselves, though we'd likely do this more pitilessly than we have thus far.

Such a set of policies would put the ball squarely in the Afghans' court. Do they have a responsible government? Can the Afghan government credibly demonstrate its responsiveness to its own people so that no non-state actors use Afghanistan as their battleground? Either the current leadership will make their country work or Afghans who can do better will replace them. Or maybe the country will split; after all, if Afghanistan's current borders trap together people who can't or won't get along, then it is not a viable state. Borders have to be congruent with a system of governance that promises and delivers a social contract predicated on responsibility and accountability at all levels, otherwise Afghanistan's sovereignty is only a fig leaf and deserves neither respect nor recognition from Afghans or from us.

Or such would be one sovereignty approach to Afghanistan circa January 2011. Let the quarantine begin.

Note on Sources

No matter how much we have read over the past several years to catch up and keep up with what is being championed in think tanks, the Pentagon, and in the academic literature, we know we will have missed numerous corroborating points of view, as well as arguments that conflict with ours. We can say that with certitude because we also know how many books and articles have appeared since we initially conceptualized *The Sovereignty Solution* in the summer of 2006, a number of which echo some parts of our argument and some of which say some of the very same things we wrote to each other in e-mails, using strikingly similar turns of phrase. These similarities can only reflect that while there may be many different ways to fix a failing foreign policy, unease over the direction in which the United States is headed is still unease; matters for concern *are* matters of concern.

Many of those who offer analyses that jibe with ours, even if their solutions differ, include Leslie Gelb (*Power Rules*), Angelo Codevilla (*Advice to War Presidents*), Christopher Preble (*The Power Problem*), Andrew Bacevich (*The Limits of Power*), Ian Shapiro (*Containment*), Robert Kagan (*The Return of History and the End of Dreams*), Jim Webb (*A Time to Fight*), and Anatol Lieven and John Hulsman (*Ethical Realism*); and all do so from well-established positions that span the political spectrum. Others who offer prescriptive courses of action, like Christopher Layne (*The Peace of Illusions*) or Michael Lind (*The American Way of Strategy*), occupy positions familiar to those well-schooled in theory. We can't claim any such provenance.

We came to *The Sovereignty Solution* by way of a challenge posed by Stephen Peter Rosen (Harvard University) and Andrew W. Marshall, the director of the Office of Net Assessment in the Pentagon: think through what should be put in place today in order to be able to shift national strategy overnight, pending some sort of major shock. They lobbed this at us during a two-day workshop at the Naval Postgraduate School during the summer of 2006. One of the workshop participants helped author the Hart-Rudman Commission Report, so as soon as our guests departed Monterey we began reading that as well as other relevant white papers and articles.

We do not cite everything we looked at—an impossible task given everything that has streamed into our in-boxes over the course of the past four years thanks to "clipping services" run by Naval Postgraduate School librarian Greta Marlatt, Army colonel David Maxwell, and Princeton professor Mike Reynolds, among others.

On the military front alone, there are reams of articles and websites devoted to counter-insurgency. We could have cited, for instance, Brig. Nigel Aylwin-Foster's "Changing the Army for Counterinsurgency Operations" (*Military Review*, November–December 2005) or David Betz's "Redesigning Land Forces for *Wars Amongst the People*" (*Contemporary Security Policy*, August 2007), or the debate between John Nagl and Gian Gentile over just how much emphasis COIN deserves, or almost anything Ralph Peters has written.

Michael Mazarr's "The Folly of 'Asymmetric War'" (*Washington Quarterly*, Summer 2008) and Benjamin Friedman, Harvey Sapolsky, and Christopher Preble's "Learning the Right Lessons from Iraq" (*Policy Analysis*, February 13, 2008) echo a number of our arguments. Bing West, Charles Dunlap, Edward Luttwak, and

Martin Van Creveld have all written things recently with which we agree. Elbridge Colby sent us a copy of his two articles "Restoring Deterrence" (*Orbis*, Summer 2007) and "Making Intelligence Smart" (*Policy Review*, August–September 2007) after reading ours. We read Bill Kauffman's *Ain't My America* only after completing our final draft. The same could be said for a stack of other articles and books. In addition, all three of us have been to Iraq since we spent the summer together in Monterey. In the interim, we have also traveled elsewhere outside the country (Africa, India, Afghanistan) as well as to numerous military installations inside the United States. We draw on that "fieldwork," too.

Acronyms

ACR	Armored Cavalry Regiment
ASEAN	Association of Southeast Asian States
CENTO	Central Treaty Organization
COIN	Counter-insurgency
CSIS	Center for Strategic and International Studies
DOD	Department of Defense
DRC/Zaire	Democratic Republic of Congo
ETA	Euskadi Ta Askatasuna
FARC	Revolutionary Armed Forces of Colombia
FATA	Federally Administered Tribal Areas
FMLN	Farabundo Martí National Liberation Front
FPRI	Foreign Policy Research Institute
IRA	Irish Republican Army
ISAF	International Security Assistance Force
LTTE	Liberation Tigers of Tamil Eelam
NATO	North Atlantic Treaty Organization
NGO	nongovernmental organization
NPS	Naval Postgraduate School
NPT	Nuclear Proliferation Treaty
OLS	Operation Lifeline Sudan
PA	Palestinian Authority
PKK	Kurdistan Workers' Party
PLO	Palestine Liberation Organization
PVO	Private Voluntary Organization
SEATO	Southeast Asia Treaty Organization
SF	Special Forces
SPLA	Sudan People's Liberation Army
UAV	unmanned aerial vehicle
UNAMID	United Nations Mission in Darfur
UNDP	United Nations Development Programme
USAID	United States Agency for International Development
WMD	weapons of mass destruction

Notes

Chapter 1

1. Some would say the George W. Bush administration attempted to do this via Iraq—in the wake of 9/11.

2. Francis Fukuyama and G. John Ikenberry, "Report of the Working Group on Grand Strategic Choices," Princeton Project on National Security, Woodrow Wilson School of Public and International Affairs, 2004, 7.

3. That is Rahm Emanuel, President Obama's chief of staff, talking to *New York Times* economics columnist David Leonhardt, "The *Big* Fix," *The New York Times Magazine* (February 1, 2009).

4. Here is what Anthony Lake (Bill Clinton's first national security advisor and candidate Barack Obama's most senior foreign policy advisor), told Nick Lemann: "traditional statesmen see international relations as a game of chess, and 'post-realists' see it as more like the complicated multidirectional Japanese board game of Go—'but Obama knows you have to play both boards at the same time.'" Nick Lemann, "Worlds Apart: Obama, McCain, and the future of foreign policy," *New Yorker* (October 13, 2008), 115.

   Even Henry Kissinger found that "Obama Is Like a Chess Player"—or so reads the headline of a *Spiegel Online* interview with Kissinger. In the interview Kissinger says, "Obama is like a chess player who is playing simultaneous chess and has opened his game with an unusual opening. Now he's got to play his hand as he plays his various counterparts. We haven't gotten beyond the opening game move yet. I have no quarrel with the opening move." Jan Flieschhauer and Gabor Steingart, "Kissinger: 'Obama Is Like a Chess Player,'" *Spiegel Online International* (July 6, 2009).

5. From remarks Andrew W. Marshall made to participants (Long Term Strategy Seminar, Monterey, CA, June 2006).

6. Christopher Dickey, *Securing the City: Inside America's Best Counterterror Force—The NYPD* (New York: Simon & Schuster, 2009), 23, emphasis ours.

7. This has long been true. Some, like Paul Seabury and Angelo Codevilla, argue that during World War II the United States "chose which political factions to support materially and politically in wartime Europe strictly on the basis

of their ability to fight the current enemy, Germany, without regard to their relationship to the Soviet Union. Thus the United States and Britain are largely responsible for the prominent positions that Yugoslav, Italian, Greek, and French Communists—allied with the Soviet Union—occupied at the end of the war." See *War: Ends & Means* (New York: Basic Books, 1990), 211.

8. Hilton Root, *Alliance Curse: How America Lost the Third World* (Washington, DC: Brookings Institution Press, 2008), 174.

9. Chester Bowles, *Promises to Keep: My Years in Public Life, 1941–1969* (New York: HarperCollins, 1971), 407.

10. Here, for instance, is Ahmed Rashid writing about then-Pakistani president Pervez Musharraf:

> The years of praise by Bush and other world leaders, their unwillingness to impose tougher conditions on Pakistan's military regime, and Musharraf's ability to escape censure on all counts turned Musharraf's head. He became increasingly arrogant and distant, relying on an ever smaller coterie of advisors, listening less and less to anybody. As long as Pakistan remained the center for Talibanization, terrorism, or nuclear proliferation, the world could not ignore the military regime or dispense with Musharraf. (*Descent into Chaos: The United States and the Failure of Nation Building in Pakistan, Afghanistan, and Central Asia* [New York: Viking, 2008], 290–91)

As for anyone who might believe Musharraf's recent ouster is permanent, Pakistan's political history is replete with presidential comebacks.

11. Gwynne Dyer, *Future: Tense: The Coming World Order* (Toronto: McClelland & Stewart, 2004), 93.

12. Done with Saudi and Pakistani assistance—two countries that, more than a decade later, are also a source of worry.

13. As early as the 1970s, traditional Islamic clerics warned Israeli officials about Hamas' founder, Sheikh Yassin. In recalling a 1970s meeting with a traditional Islamic cleric who wanted Israel to stop cooperating with the Muslim Brotherhood followers of Sheikh Yassin, Avner Cohen, a former Israeli religious affairs official who worked in Gaza, recounts how the cleric told him, "You are going to have big regrets in 20 or 30 years." The cleric, Cohen admitted, was right. Andrew Higgins, "How Israel Helped to Spawn Hamas," *Wall Street Journal* (January 24–25, 2009).

Or, to examine a different case, consider Pakistan. In a review of Ahmed Rashid's *Descent into Chaos: The United States and the Failure of Nation Building in Pakistan, Afghanistan, and Central Asia,* William Dalrymple writes: "Ironically, as Rashid makes clear, it was exactly groups such as Lashkar-e-

Taiba, which were originally created by the ISI, that have now turned their guns on their creators, as well as brazenly launching well-equipped and well-trained teams of jihadis into Indian territory. In doing so they are severely damaging Pakistani interests abroad, and bringing Pakistan to the brink of a war it cannot possibly win." See "Pakistan in Peril," *New York Review of Books* 56, February 12, 2009, accessed February 24, 2009, http:www.nybooks.com/articles/22274.

One can find example after example like this.

14. Another example: the Islamic Center of Munich was founded in 1958 and became a hub of radical Islam in Europe. "As Mr. Johnson [author of *A Mosque in Munich*] tells it, American and German governments and several prominent Muslims brought the center to life and competed to control it, playing each off against the other. As Germany and America lost interest, the Muslim Brotherhood emerged triumphant, and Munich turned into a Continental mecca for Muslim activists." Matthew Kaminski, "The German Connection," *Wall Street Journal* (May 6, 2010).

15. Lisa Margonelli, *Oil on the Brain: Adventures from the Pump to the Pipeline* (New York: Nan A. Talese, 2007), 103.

16. Borrowed from John Lewis Gaddis, *Strategies of Containment: A Critical Appraisal of American National Security Policy during the Cold War*, 2nd ed. (New York: Oxford University Press, 2005), viii.

17. John Lewis Gaddis, "What Is Grand Strategy?" (Karl Von Der Heyden Distinguished Lecture, Duke University, Durham, NC, February 26, 2009).

18. Jeremi Suri, "The Promise and Failure of Grand Strategy after the Cold War," *Telegram*, Newsletter of the Hertog Program in Grand Strategy, no. 2, (March 2010).

19. Shawn Brimley, "Crafting Strategy in an Age of Transition," *Parameters* (Winter 2008–9): 28.

20. Andrew Krepinevich, Michael Vickers, and Steven Kosiak, "Hart-Rudman Commission Report—A Critique," April 19, 2000, 1, accessed July 11, 2006, http://www.csbaonline.org/4Publications/Archive/B.20000419.Hart-Rudman_Commis.htm.

21. Or, as Walter McDougall explains, Grand Strategy involves "an equation of ends and means so sturdy that it triumphs despite serial setbacks at the level of strategy, operations, and campaigns" "Can the United States Do Grand Strategy?" *Telegram*, Newsletter of the Hertog Program in Grand Strategy, no. 3 (April 2010).

22. Richard Betts, "Is Strategy an Illusion?" *International Security* 25, issue 2 (Fall 2000): 8.

23. Gaddis, *Strategies of Containment,* 133; also see Robert Bowie and Richard Immerman, *Waging Peace: How Eisenhower Shaped an Enduring Cold War Strategy* (New York: Oxford University Press, 2000), 44.

24. Gaddis, *Strategies of Containment,* 133.

25. As for the importance of the American way of life: "foreign policy thinkers who dismiss the idea of 'the American way of life' and focus on 'vital interests' as the basis of U.S. foreign policy are guilty of a profound philosophical and political error. For there is no interest more vital in American foreign policy and no ideal more important than the preservation of the American way of life." See Michael Lind, *The American Way of Strategy: U.S. Foreign Policy and the American Way of Life* (New York: Oxford University Press, 2006), 7.

26. To quote from Rupert Smith: "it is the appearance of a real enemy that brings the strategic level into play, for whilst it is possible to have a general policy identifying threats in peacetime, it is not possible to have a strategy until there is an opponent," in *The Utility of Force: The Art of War in the Modern World* (London: Penguin, 2006), 210.

In writing about NATO, Lawrence Freedman makes the commonsensical point that "one thing international organizations are not good at is strategy, unless framed in the most vague, platitudinous and cryptic terms." He then makes the extremely interesting observation that "even when individual governments are concocting national strategies, these days there is a general reluctance to talk about other states as potential enemies, now considered tactless, and potentially provocative. So threats tend to be described as themes." Lawrence Freedman, "NATO at Sixty: Power and War," *The World Today* 65, no. 4 (April 2009): 18.

27. For just one example of current thinking about the nature of our future troubles, see *Global Trends 2025: A Transformed World* (The National Intelligence Council, 2008).

28. Remarks, Unrestricted Warfare Symposium Proceedings 2008 (Baltimore, MD: Johns Hopkins University), 41.

29. As seen in the 1999 movie *One Day in September.*

30. Martin Van Creveld, *Defending Israel: A Strategic Plan for Peace and Security* (New York: St Martin's Press, 2004), 149.

31. Number supplied by Gordon H. McCormick, "Suicide Terrorism Data Base (1983–2011)," Department of Defense Analysis, Naval Postgraduate School, Monterey, CA.

32. Some classic examples: the Irish Republican Army (IRA) in Northern Ireland, the Palestine Liberation Organization (PLO), the Euskadi Ta Askatasuna (ETA Basque separatists), Sendero Luminoso (Peru), the Liberation Tamil

Tigers of Eelam (LTTE in Sri Lanka), and the Kurdish Workers' Party (PKK in Turkey).

33. A side note: it seems telling that in very few of the recent accounts written about the wars in Iraq and Afghanistan do reporters or veterans single out the significance of air dominance. The focus is almost always on ground operations. Gunship support, unmanned aerial vehicle (UAV) feeds, etc. are obviously critically important to those operating *on* the ground. The U.S. military's ability to bring these or any air assets to bear appears to be taken for granted—perhaps mistakenly so, especially when one looks beyond Iraq and Afghanistan.

34. Francis Fukuyama, *Blindside: How to Anticipate Forcing Events and Wild Cards in Global Politics* (Washington, DC: Brookings Institution Press, 2007), 172.

In a separate essay on risk management, Paul Bracken writes:

> Prediction—that is, warning—is one way of managing surprise. But it is only one way. Assuredly, if the future could be predicted, then optimized resources could be put in place to deal with the surprise. . . .
>
> Managing surprise through warning is very hard. But this insight is well known. It is difficult to understand why after so many decades of research we still find it advanced as a major insight. ("Intelligence and Risk Management," FPRI [Foreign Policy Research Institute] E-Note, January 9, 2009, http://www.fpri.org/enotes/200812.bracken .intelligenceriskmanagement.html)

35. Andrew Krepinevich, *7 Deadly Scenarios: A Military Futurist Explores War in the 21st Century* (New York: Bantam, 2009), 12.

36. Colin Gray, "The 21st Century Security Environment and the Future of War," *Parameters* (Winter 2008–9): 17.

Probably nothing better illustrates how hard it is to forecast convergences than what happened to the price of oil in 2008. Here is a January 3, 2008, *Wall Street Journal* headline: "Confluence of Events Drove Crude's Ride from $10.72." Here is what the article (by Russell Gold, Neil King Jr., and Ann Davis) reports: "Economists, Wall Street commodity traders and even seasoned energy executives were caught flat-footed by oil's dizzying rise. Looking back, several factors came together at the same time to help oil shoot up roughly tenfold in less than a decade and briefly touch $100."

But then, almost as unexpectedly as prices rose, they fell, thanks again to an unforeseen combination of factors. By November a "combination of conservation and the worst world-wide economic slump in decades" made "a mockery of recent projections that oil would remain expensive and scarce forever. As of late last week, oil prices had fallen below $50 a barrel—compared with more than $140 a barrel this summer." See Joseph White, "Creating a Problem by Driving Less," *Wall Street Journal*, November 24, 2008.

37. The United States does not, for instance, make as much of its military strengths as it could—a topic we return to in chapter 9. But also, as Paul Kennedy, a self-described declinist, writes:

> In this [current] focus upon chronic fiscal deficits and military over-stretch, certain positive measures of American strength tend to get pushed into the shadows (and perhaps should be given more light at another time). This country possesses tremendous advantages compared to other great powers in its demographics, its land-to-people ratio, its raw materials, its research universities and laboratories, its flexible work force, etc. These strengths have been overshadowed during a near-decade of political irresponsibility in Washington, rampant greed on Wall Street and its outliers, and excessive military ventures abroad. ("American Power Is on the Wane," *New York Times*, January 14, 2009)

Kennedy's assessment of our strengths is echoed and amplified by Erik Edelman in "Understanding America's Contested Primacy," CSBA Assessment, 2010.

38. National Intelligence Council, *Global Trends 2025: A Transformed World* (2008): vi.

39. Phil Williams, "From the New Middle Ages to a New Dark Age: The Decline of the State and U.S. Strategy," Strategic Studies Institute paper (Carlisle, PA: U.S. Army War College, 2008), 5.

40. Defense Science Board Task Force Report, "Understanding Human Dynamics," March 2009, 8.

41. David Kilcullen, *The Accidental Guerrilla: Fighting Small Wars in the Midst of a Big One* (New York: Oxford University Press, 2009), 286–87.

42. Ibid., 7.

43. National Intelligence Council, *Global Trends 2025*, 71. Or, for a similar argument see Frank Hoffman, "Conflict in the 21st Century: The Rise of Hybrid Wars," (Arlington, VA: Potomac Institute for Policy Studies, 2007).

44. Paul Bracken, "Technological Innovation and National Security," FPRI E-Note, June 6, 2008, 2, http://www.fpri.org/enotes/200806.bracken.innovationnationalsecurity.html. Of course, the argument that *should* be made is that this is nothing new; when Mao couldn't win conventionally against

Chiang Kai-Shek's forces in China he switched approaches. So did the North Vietnamese and the Farabundo Marti National Liberation Front (FMLN) in El Salvador and so have legions of other rebels and insurgents. It would actually be shocking if they didn't.

45. When it comes to irregular warfare, counterinsurgency, and counterterrorism, even better lessons are likely to be learned from studying non-Western countries' experiences. This is a woefully understudied subject—and the topic for another book.

46. Richard Haass, "The Age of Nonpolarity: What Will Follow U.S. Dominance," *Foreign Affairs* 87 (May/June 2008): 55.

47. Shawn Brimley, "Crafting Strategy in an Age of Transition," *Parameters* (Winter 2008–9): 33.

48. Especially since, as Stephen Biddle and Jeffrey Friedman write in "The 2006 Lebanon Campaign and the Future of Warfare: Implications for Army and Defense Policy," Strategic Studies Institute paper (Carlisle, PA: U.S. Army War College, September 2008), 60:

> Hezbollah is often described as having used civilians as shields in 2006, and, in fact, they made extensive use of civilian homes as direct fire combat positions and to conceal launchers for rocket fire into Israel. Yet the villages Hezbollah used to anchor its defensive system in southern Lebanon were largely *evacuated* by the time Israeli ground forces crossed the border on July 18 (emphasis ours).

49. Martin Van Creveld is no neo-imperialist. Interestingly, he does, however, talk about unleashing artillery barrages and pummeling terrorist strongholds—even when civilians are in the vicinity. For more, see note 18 (in chapter 9). Edward Luttwak invokes North Vietnamese and Viet Cong, German, Ottoman, and Roman methods of relying on deterrence "which was periodically reinforced by exemplary punishments" in Edward Luttwak, "Dead End: Counterinsurgency warfare as military malpractice," *Harper's* magazine, February 2007, 40. And, Paul Seabury and Angelo Codevilla likewise talk about the need for ruthlessness in *War: Ends & Means*.

50. Here is what Yitzhak Rabin (Israeli defense minister at the time of Israel's 1982 invasion of Lebanon) said years later, when he was asked to reflect on the surprises that grew out of the invasion: "the most dangerous is that the war let the Shiites out of the bottle. No one predicted it; I couldn't find it in any intelligence report." See Geoffrey Wheatcroft, "In Search of the Good News," review of *Dreams and Shadows: The Future of the Middle East*, by Robin Wright, *Washington Post National Weekly Edition*, March 31–April 6, 2008.

51. According to Stephen Flynn, "the biggest danger comes not from what terrorists do to us but how we react to what they do to us and the cost associated with that reaction. . . . If we reduce the bang for the buck, we take away the incentive for engaging in catastrophic terror." See Unrestricted Warfare Symposium Proceedings 2008, 76. Elsewhere, Flynn points out that "One defeats terrorist tactics by working to minimize terror, which arises from a feeling of unbounded vulnerability and powerlessness. By empowering people to cope with disasters, they will be less afraid when things do go wrong—which of course will happen from time to time. It really is as simple as that." "Homeland Insecurity: Disaster at DHS," *The American Interest* (May/June 2009), 22.

52. "Perhaps the most important thing a government such as ours can have, as it faces the long-term future of international relations, is the right principles rather than the gift of prophecy"—George Kennan, as quoted in Nicholas Thompson, *The Hawk and the Dove: Paul Nitze, George Kennan, and the History of the Cold War* (New York: Henry Holt, 2009), 204.

Chapter 2

1. For example:

> There persists a very damaging myth in the West, spouted by politicians and the press, that says Russia's assistance is needed with Iran and other rogue states. In fact, the Kremlin has been stirring this pot for years and has a vested interest in further increasing turmoil in the region. The Hamas/Hezbollah rockets, based on the Russian Katyusha and Grad, are not delivered via DHL from Allah. It doesn't require the guile of a KGB man like Mr. Putin to imagine a way to accelerate Iran's nuclear program, which has been aided by Russian technology and protected by the Kremlin from meaningful international action." (Garry Kasparov, "Why Russia Stokes Mideast Mayhem," *Wall Street Journal*, January 12, 2009)

Six months later, in June 2009, and in the wake of Iran's disputed national election, Kasparov further elaborates: "Mr. Putin has a great deal riding on the outcome in Iran. With the Russian economy teetering, he needs a steep increase in oil prices to stave off the collapse of his government. So he has been working to increase tension in the Middle East and now sees the Iranian crisis as potentially helpful—if Ahmadinejad comes out on top." "Iran's Democrats Deserve Full Support," *Wall Street Journal*, June 25, 2009.

2. Stephen Flynn not only focuses on resilience, but also sees the connection between a vulnerable physical infrastructure and increasingly partisan

domestic politics: "Our infrastructure continues to grow frailer while our politics have become more divisive. Neither of these trends bodes well for dealing with the ongoing risk of disaster. We are becoming a less flexible nation just as the likelihood of mass disruptions continues to gather steam." *The Edge of Disaster: Rebuilding a Resilient Nation* (New York: Random House, 2007), xxiv–xxv.

3. Some do recognize how polarization can assist our adversaries. For instance: "A divided America encourages our enemies, disheartens our allies, and saps our resolve—potentially to fatal effect. What General Giap of North Vietnam once said of us is even truer today: America cannot be defeated on the battle-field, but it can be defeated at home. Polarization is a force that can defeat us," in James Q. Wilson, "How Divided Are We?," *Commentary*, February 2006, 21. But no one that we have read focuses on how our adversaries can help such polarization along.

4. At least this was still true as of late 2010. See, for instance, Michael Cox and Richard Alm, *Myths of Rich and Poor: Why We're Better Off Than We Think* (New York: Basic Books, 1999).

5. Exemplified in the title of Ronald Brownstein's 2007 book, *The Second Civil War: How Extreme Partisanship Has Paralyzed Washington and Polarized America* (New York: Penguin Press, 2007).

More recently, Gerald Seib reported:

> Last year [2008], for example, Democrats voted with the majority of their caucus 92% of the time in the House and 87% of the time in the Senate. Republicans voted with the majority of their caucus 87% of the time in the House and 83% of the time in the Senate. In other words, in only a small percentage of cases do either Democrats or Republicans buck the party line. That's a picture of lockstep parti-san voting, and it has been that way since the late 1990s. . . . It hasn't always been this way. . . . In 1969, for example, House Democrats voted with their party's majority just 61% of the time and House Republicans just 62% of the time. ("Enduring Partisan Divide Stokes Skepticism of Washington," *Wall Street Journal*, October 31–November 1, 2009)

6. William Galston and Pietro Nivola, "Vote Like Thy Neighbor: Why the American Electorate Is More Politically Polarized Than Ever," *The New York Times Magazine*, May 11, 2008, 12.

7. This does not mean most former Yugoslavs who fought did so for, or over, religion. But—religion *was* the identifier that most often cost people their lives, property, etc.

8. Samuel Huntington, *Who Are We?* (New York: Simon & Schuster, 2004). As Huntington puts it:

> America's core culture has been and, at the moment, is still primarily the culture of seventeenth- and eighteenth-century settlers who founded American society. Subsequent generations of immigrants were assimilated into the culture of the founding settlers and contributed to and modified it. But they did not change it fundamentally. This is because, at least until the late twentieth century, it was Anglo-Protestant culture and the political liberties and economic opportunities it produced that attracted them to America. (40–41)

9. Allan Bloom, *The Closing of the American Mind* (New York: Simon & Schuster, 1987), 26.

10. Susan Sontag, "What's Wrong with America?," *Partisan Review* (Winter 1967): 57.

11. James Q. Wilson, "How Divided Are We?," 18.

12. Bill Keller, "Editor In Chief," review of *The Publisher*, by Alan Brinkley, *New York Times Book Review*, April 25, 2010.

13. This is hardly confined to television or the Internet. The public library in Monterey has no fewer than five books by the same well-credentialed PhD, David Ray Griffin, Professor (emeritus) of Philosophy and Theology at the Claremont School of Theology. Two of his titles are: *The 9/11 Commission Report: Omissions and Distortions* and *Debunking 9/11 Debunking: An Answer to Popular Mechanics and Other Defenders of the Official Conspiracy Theory.* His coeditor of *9/11 and American Empire: Intellectuals Speak Out*, Peter Dale Scott, is described as a former UC–Berkeley professor.

14. One problem, of course, is that the government has purposely victimized U.S. citizens in the past; for instance, the Tuskegee Airmen as well as those the government knowingly exposed to radiation in Utah during the 1950s, and others to whom it administered drugs.

15. Interestingly it has taken the financial crisis to spark concerns about rightwing American extremism, as evidenced by an assessment released by the Office of Intelligence and Analysis, Department of Homeland Security: "Rightwing Extremism: Current Economic and Political Climate Fueling Resurgence in Radicalization and Recruitment," April 7, 2009.

16. As William Howell and Jon Pevehouse note:

> the making of U.S. foreign policy hinges on how U.S. national interests are defined and the means chosen to achieve them. This process is deeply, and unavoidably, political. Therefore, only in very particular circumstances—a direct attack on U.S. soil or on Americans

abroad—have political parties temporarily united for the sake of protecting the national interest. Even then, partisan politics have flared as the toll of war has become evident. ("When Congress Stops Wars; Partisan Politics and Presidential Power," *Foreign Affairs* 86 [September/October 2007]: 98)

17. J. R. Pole and Jack Greene, *A Companion to the American Revolution* (Oxford: Blackwell Publishers, 2000), 235. According to Pole and Greene:

    Historians estimate that about 15–20% of the population of the thirteen states was Loyalist (or roughly 500,000 people among 3 million residents), but the number was constantly declining as thousands of Loyalists fled the country every year of the war, or changed their affiliation to neutral or Patriot. Due to the highly political nature of the war, a large but unknown proportion of the white population remained neutral. Approximately half the colonists of European ancestry tried to avoid involvement in the struggle—some of them deliberate pacifists, others recent emigrants, and many more simple apolitical folk. The patriots received active support from perhaps 40 to 45% of the white populace, and, at most, no more than a bare majority.

18. Paul Johnson, *A History of the American People* (New York: HarperCollins, 1997), 468. As Johnson elaborates: "The North was divided, bemused, reluctant to go to war; or, rather, composed of large numbers of fanatical antislavers and much larger numbers of unengaged or indifferent voters who had no wish to become involved in a bloody dispute about a problem, slavery, which did not affect them directly."

19. For instance, at one of the most critical points in the war disturbing reports circulated about growing discontent in the Army. Some soldiers reported that "scarcely one of the 200,000 whose term of service is soon to expire will re-enlist." Doris Kearns Goodwin, *Team of Rivals* (New York: Simon & Schuster, 2006), 503.

20. Or, say Filipino insurgents had had this capability at the turn of the nineteenth century. As it is, they attempted to shape the U.S. election in order that William Jennings Bryan rather than William McKinley would become president, Brian Linn, *The Philippine War, 1899–1902* (Lawrence: University Press of Kansas, 2002), 187, 211.

21. Intoned during hearings of the Joint Senate Armed Forces and Foreign Affairs Committee in 1951—cited by Harry Summers, *On Strategy: A Critical Analysis of the Vietnam War* (Novato, CA: Presidio Press, 1982), 35.

    As William Howell and Jon Pevehouse "When Congress Stops Wars," *Foreign Affairs* 86 (September/October 2007) point out:

Although Truman's party narrowly controlled both chambers, Congress hounded him throughout the Korean War, driving his approval ratings down into the 20s and paving the way for a Republican electoral victory in 1952. Railing off a litany of complaints about the president's firing of General Douglas MacArthur and his meager progress toward ending the war, Senator Robert Taft, then a Republican presidential candidate, declared that "the greatest failure of foreign policy is an unnecessary war, and we have been involved in such a war now for more than a year. . . . As a matter of fact, every purpose of the war has now failed. We are exactly where we were three years ago, and where we could have stayed." (100–101)

22. Doris Kearns Goodwin, *Lyndon Johnson and the American Dream* (New York: Harper & Row, 1976), 252.

23. Bui Tin, interview by Stephen Young, "How North Vietnam Won the War," *Wall Street Journal*, August 3, 1995.

   Or, as one former POW held in the "Hanoi Hilton" said of his captors, "They told us all the time how they were going to win the war. . . . Even before Tet, the interrogators always said, 'We can't win on the field of battle. We're going to make friends with dissident groups in your country, and then we're going to force your government out of our country.'" See Jeffrey Goldberg, "The Wars of John McCain," *Atlantic*, October 2008, 50.

24. China and the USSR also paid close attention to domestic divisions in the United States. Hanoi was often in desperate need of supplies. But neither China nor the USSR were willing to fully commit to North Vietnam until they were certain that we Americans were too busy battling each other to effectively pull together to beat the North Vietnamese. As President Nixon later remarked, "after Congress cut off the possibility of future bombing in June 1973, there was no longer any reason for restraint. Moscow and Peking had been willing to help us contain Hanoi—but only if we were determined to do so as well." Richard Nixon, *No More Vietnams* (New York: Arbor House, 1985), 191.

25. In his review of Mike Chinoy's *Meltdown: The Inside Story of the North Korean Nuclear Crisis*, Glenn Kessler writes:

   Chinoy shows that American policy toward North Korea often became incoherent and self-defeating as administration insiders fought desperately to gain the upper hand in internal debates. The North Koreans took advantage of this disarray to build their stockpile of plutonium, believed to total 37 or 38 kilograms, and even to test a nuclear device underground. ("Eyes Off the Ball," *Washington Post National Weekly Edition*, August 14–18, 2008)

This is a passage which points to: (a) how much attention adversaries pay to *all* our fissures, and (b) what can happen domestically when the United States lacks a coherent Grand Strategy to guide policy.

Or, as Andrew Bacevich elaborates:

> ever since Kennedy, presidents themselves and their chief lieutenants have viewed the [national security] apparatus as irredeemably broken. . . . For those who occupy the inner circle of power, the national security state is an obstacle to be evaded rather than an asset to be harnessed. Viewed from the perspective of a defense secretary or national security adviser, professional military officers, career diplomats, or intelligence analysts are not partners but competitors.

Why does a broken national security state endure? According to Bacevich, "It does so not because its activities enhance the security of the American people, but because, by its very existence, it provides a continuing rationale for political arrangements that are a source of status, influence, and considerable wealth." See *The Limits of Power: The End of American Exceptionalism* (New York: Metropolitan Books, 2008), 95.

A grim view, to be sure.

26. According to Rufus Phillips, this was as true of those who opposed the war as of those who waged it: "It was impossible to have a rational discussion with many peace activists. Their issue was never the real country of Vietnam or the real Vietnamese people; it was mainly us, the morality of warfare, the immorality of our government, and the draft." See *Why Vietnam Matters: An Eyewitness Account of Lessons Not Learned* (Annapolis: Naval Institute Press, 2008), footnote on 360.

27. Neil Jamieson, *Understanding Vietnam* (Berkeley: University of California Press, 1995), 346–48.

28. For more, see Anna Simons, *Networks of Dissolution: Somalia Undone* (Boulder, CO: Westview Press, 1995). Nor has this just been true of Somalia:

> As Alex de Waal, Mahmood Mamdani, and others have written, it is hard to resist the conclusion that anti-Arab and US imperial agendas are responsible for a considerable part of the focus on Darfur. Far too much US activism seems to be quite uninterested in the real requirements of peace and development in Darfur, Sudan and the region as a whole.
>
> As far as Chechnya is concerned, while I know deeply moral people working on human rights issues there, I also have to say that as far as most US politicians involved are concerned, their overwhelming motivation is not sympathy for the Chechens, but hostility to Russia. If the Chechen insurgents had been subjects of a pro-western

state, these US figures would have actively supported their ruthless repression. (Anatol Lieven, "Humanitarian Action Can Mask An Imperial Agenda," *Financial Times*, August 21, 2007)

29. Anthony Shadid, *Night Draws Near: Iraq's People in the Shadow of America's War* (New York: Henry Holt, 2005), 321. Or consider Farnaz Fassihi's observation:

> Iraqis think of America as an ultimate superpower, incapable of making mistakes. Iraqis can't comprehend that the reasons behind deteriorating security, the lack of electricity, and the decline in prosperity are largely a result of the incompetence and cluelessness of the Americans rather than any deliberate intention. (*Waiting for an Ordinary Day: The Unraveling of Life in Iraq* [New York: PublicAffairs, 2008], 82)

Meanwhile, one reason electricity was so significant is that "everything followed from electricity, the cornerstone of modern life. With electricity went water, sanitation, air-conditioning, and the security brought by light at night. With electricity went faith in what the Americans, so powerful in war, were prepared to do after" (Shadid, *Night Draws Near*, 134).

30. Here is one example:

> "The key to boosting the image and effectiveness of U.S. military operations around the world involves 'shaping' both the product and the marketplace, and then establishing a brand identity that places what you are selling in a positive light," said clinical psychologist Todd C. Helmus, the author of "Enlisting Madison Avenue: The Marketing Approach to Earning Popular Support in Theaters of Operation." The 211-page study, for which the U.S. Joint Forces Command paid the Rand Corp. $400,000, was released this week. (Karen DeYoung, "The Pentagon Gets a Lesson from Madison Avenue: U.S. Needs to Devise a Different 'Brand' to Win Over the Iraqi People, Study Advises," *Washington Post*, July 21, 2007)

31. Gary Hart, "The Foreign Policy Game," review of *Presidential Command: Power, Leadership, and the Making of Foreign Policy from Richard Nixon to George W. Bush* by Peter Rodman, *New York Times Book Review*, January 18, 2009.

Chapter 3

1. From William Galston and Pietro Nivola's article, "The Great Divide: Polarization in American Politics," *American Interest* (November/December 2006), 9. Galston and Nivola cite Pew Research Center survey data.

2. Charles Kupchan and Peter Trubowitz, "Grand Strategy for a Divided America," *Foreign Affairs* 86 (July/August 2007): 76.

3. According to James Q. Wilson:

   > Since the late 1980s, Republicans have been more willing than Democrats to say that "the best way to ensure peace is through military strength." By the late 1990s and on into 2003, well over two-thirds of all Republicans agreed with this view, but far fewer than half of all Democrats did. In 2005, three-fourths of all Democrats but fewer than a third of all Republicans told pollsters that good diplomacy was the best way to ensure peace. In the same survey, two-thirds of all Republicans but only one fourth of all Democrats said they would fight for this country "whether it is right or wrong." James Q. Wilson, "How Divided Are We?," 19

4. Russ Feingold and Chuck Hagel, "We Need a Better Map of The World," *Miami Herald*, June 16, 2008.

5. One example: "many observers, including in American intelligence, think the Pakistani military and the ISI [Pakistan's intelligence service] play a double game. They make the necessary pledges to secure billions in American aid while keeping ties to Islamists. The calculation, a Pakistani analyst notes, is America will leave sooner or later and the military needs to hedge its strategic bets." Matthew Kaminski, "The Weekend Interview with Richard Holbrooke," *Wall Street Journal* (April 11–12, 2009).

6. For instance, consider Tom Ricks' description of how astutely Ahmed Chalabi "played" us in the run-up to the invasion of Iraq: "The intelligence community . . . had no agents sending reliable reports from inside Iraq. That left a vacuum—and gave Chalabi an opening that he exploited adeptly." Not only did Chalabi know us well, but he was "able to introduce misinformation directly into the system. One senior military intelligence officer recalled being awed by Chalabi's ability to inject himself into the internal deliberations of the U.S. government. "He always got access" during 2002 and 2003. "His views always got where he wanted them to go." Thomas Ricks, *Fiasco: The American Military Adventure in Iraq* (New York: Penguin Press, 2009), 57.

7. Loren Baritz, *Backfire: A History of How American Culture Led Us into Vietnam and Made Us Fight the Way We Did* (New York: Ballantine Books, 1986), 15.

8. As Baritz puts it, "we believe that we can know others reasonably easily because of our assumption that they want to become us," in ibid., 16.

9. Or, as Ali Allawi, one of Saddam Hussein's most ardent critics, writes:

> In official Washington, the ignorance of what was going on inside Iraq before the war was monumental. None of the proponents of the war, including the neo-conservatives, and also no one in the institutes and thank-tanks that provided the intellectual fodder for the war's justification, had the faintest idea of the country that they were to occupy. The academics and researchers who congregated around the Washington think-tanks and the vice-president's office, who had made Iraq their pet project, were blinkered by their dogmatic certainties or their bigotries. There was a fundamental misunderstanding about the nature of Iraqi society and the effects on it of decades of dictatorship. Each strand of American thinking that combined to provide the basis for the invasion was isolated from any direct, even incidental, engagement with Iraq. The State Department, supposedly a citadel of realist thinking, had little first-hand experience of the country, instead relying on inference and analogous reasoning when trying to unravel the possible outcomes in the post-war period. (*The Occupation of Iraq: Winning the War, Losing the Peace* [New Haven: Yale University Press, 2007], 7)

10. Of course, many anthropologists and regional specialists would object that, had policymakers *really* understood the social lay of the land in Iraq, the United States never would have gone in at all, while others of an academic bent would doubtless add that *any* use of force is, by definition, always bad. But that is hardly the argument this book makes. The premise here is actually the opposite: under certain circumstances the use of overwhelming force is the *only* option the United States should consider.

11. For an especially compelling account about how critical it is to know—really know—people, see Rufus Phillips, *Why Vietnam Matters*. He describes the nature of the relations he and Edward Lansdale developed with key South Vietnamese over the course of two decades—and the mistakes made by those who had no such relations.

12. The best of our defense attachés are among the few U.S. government officials to routinely rub shoulders with locals from broadly different backgrounds, in no small measure because most militaries (like ours) draw recruits from a broad cross section of society. Thus, good attachés, if they foster the right sorts of relationships, are plugged into the junior officer and enlisted corps, which is unbelievably useful for getting wind of potential coups. But not even attachés are trained to keep track of who will stay loyal to whom by way of distant kinship ties or sub-sub-sub-clan affiliations once trouble erupts. When attachés do learn about deep local history like this it is usually inciden-

tal to performing their other representational duties; it is not anything they are supposed to concentrate on.

While attachés' duties are in the political-military realm, case officers working for other agencies (like the CIA) typically recruit others to do their sleuthing for them.

13. To again cite Ali Allawi:

> In places such as Sadr City, the giant Shi'a slum of east Baghdad, the dormant Sadrist Movement, about whose existence virtually nothing was known by the west before the war, sprang to life, and within days after the fall of Baghdad it had secured the area. The movement had not been quashed by the former regime, as many had thought, but had simply gone underground. The speed and extent of the Islamist wave that swept over Shi'a Iraq was as if a tsunami had silently and very rapidly spread to cover the South. No one had predicted the strength of this wave and the depth of support that it engendered amongst the poor and deprived population of the area. (*The Occupation of Iraq*, 91)

One can find description after description like this for virtually every social movement that has arisen to surprise those in power. The implication? We shouldn't *be* surprised by the likelihood that trouble can be brewed among the alienated and disenfranchised. Even if we have to pay attention to such communities from neighboring countries or through diaspora rumors, there is no excuse for our not being aware.

14. And the punishment can be horrific—infertility, disease, death, the loss of crops, the loss of herds, the loss of everything.

15. Mark Lowenthal (a former assistant director of central intelligence and vice chairman of the National Intelligence Council) contends that "much attention has been lavished on intelligence analysis" since 9/11, "but the intelligence community's batting average has not gone up. And it won't." He argues that intelligence "tends to do worse on the 'big events' (Pearl Harbor, 9/11, the fall of the Berlin Wall) because these events, by their very nature are counterfactual or surprising." What intelligence is "actually good at" is "keeping policymakers generally well-informed on a recurring basis so that they can make decisions with a reasonable sense of confidence." Mark Lowenthal, "Spooked: The Spineless Spies behind Our Failed Intelligence Community," *Washington Post National Weekly Edition* (June 2–8, 2008).

For this, though, the analysts themselves have to be paying persistent attention.

16. Bob Woodward, *Plan of Attack* (New York: Simon & Schuster, 2004).

17. Gary Schmitt, "'Slam Dunks' & 'Rockstars,'" Memorandum to Opinion Leaders, Project for the New American Century [think tank], April 23, 2004.

18. How might this work? Imagine: you're an ethnographic sensor. Your base: Djibouti. Your job: to spend several years running the local U.S. government–sponsored library service. Since you're in Djibouti with the Djiboutian government's permission, there is nothing covert about your assignment. Nor is there anything sinister about your wanting to learn Somali (the local language). Thanks to your position, you are able to get a feel for both the city and the country, which isn't hard since Djibouti is relatively small. You find that it is especially easy to get to know people in communities outside the capital via a bookmobile that you periodically accompany when it makes its rounds. You also help coordinate local English-language reading groups, work closely with schools and the university to offer otherwise exorbitantly expensive medical and technical textbooks, and provide whatever assistance Djiboutian English teachers might need. This hooks you into all sorts of different communities. Consequently, you learn about Djiboutians' clan structure(s), you familiarize yourself with local (Sufi) religious brotherhoods, and you learn what each different tariqa represents to members (as well as to nonmembers).

But it's not just Djiboutians you get to know. There are numerous non-Djiboutians who use Djibouti as a base or as a point of transit: Somalis from Somalia, Somalis from Somaliland and Puntland, Eritreans, Ethiopians, Yemenis, and Arabs from the Gulf states. At the same time, given Djibouti's small size and dependence on trade, Djiboutians themselves travel to places as far-flung as Malaysia and Pakistan, or the UK and France, where families have long-standing ties.

Basically, plug into Djiboutians and you thereby plug into multiple networks.

Meanwhile, after three or four years in Djibouti, your assignments officer offers you two possibilities: you can stay in the region or return to the United States. Maybe there is a position opening in Nairobi or Addis Ababa; either would permit you to visit Djibouti regularly, while, just as importantly, Djiboutians in Kenya or Ethiopia would be able to visit you. By spending time in another Horn of Africa country you would develop a deeper appreciation for Djibouti's situation and Djiboutians' perspectives; it would also keep you from succumbing to tunnel vision. But even a move back to Washington wouldn't cut you off.

Because virtually all populations have far-flung diasporas these days, by year seven or eight of your career, just as your peers in other professions are starting to chafe at staying in the same job, you've come to appreciate that there's nothing the least bit confining about your long-term assignment of maintaining, broadening, and deepening your Djiboutian ties. In the twenty-first century, there are all sorts of creative ways by which to do this, even from halfway around the world.

Meanwhile, what works for a sensor devoted to Djibouti would need to be tweaked. But, even so, it wouldn't be that different from what could be applied by other sensors in other locales.

In *Securing the City* Christopher Dickey describes just such an "ethnographic sensor" operating in New York City, though neither Dickey nor the NYPD use the term "ethnographic sensor." Nonetheless, Kamil Pasha, a cop, "would live in Bay Ridge, get to know people, and be, as he said later, a kind of walking surveillance camera, never pushing for information, never trying to lead a conversation. The job was to 'observe, be the ears and eyes' of the NYPD inside the community" (187).

Obviously, having people woven into the social fabric in a meaningful and credible, overt way will hardly work in what the military calls denied or inaccessible areas or countries. There the solution would have to be more creative. Anthropologist Ruth Benedict's classic account of World War II–era Japan—in which her aim was to decode Japanese society—was written without Benedict ever setting foot in Japan. She canvassed refugees, expatriates, missionaries, scientists, and anyone else who had spent time in Japan previously.

Where governments remain ruthlessly totalitarian and impenetrable, such as North Korea (or North Vietnam during the Vietnam War), secondary means of collecting sociographic data necessarily become more important. But also, today the Internet yields all sorts of insights into people's interests and inclinations. Given the far-flung nature of so many diasporas, lots of people belong to broad ethnic, religious, and linguistic networks—which is why assigning sensors to pay career-long attention to communities that can stretch from the Hadramaut to Houston is as important as focusing on specific geographic areas.

19. Occasionally individual Americans will admit the obvious: "We wouldn't be here if it wasn't in [American] interests"—so said Commodore John Nowell, commander of the Africa Partnership Station, a two-ship operation in the Gulf of Guinea during 2008. As for America's dual interests of terrorism and oil, as *The Economist* explains, "Despite the talk of soft power and the much-vaunted humanitarian aspect of the naval presence in the Gulf of Guinea, the real emphasis is still on security." "America and Africa: Americans go a-wooing," *The Economist* (April 12, 2008).

Or, as Kishore Mahbubani has written, "the story of Western aid to the developing world is essentially a myth. Western countries have put significant amounts of money into their overseas development assistance budgets, but these funds' *primary purpose is to serve the immediate and short-term security and national interests of the donors* rather than the long-term interests of the recipients." "The Case Against the West: America and Europe in the Asian Century," *Foreign Affairs* 87(May/June 2008): 123, emphasis ours.

20. Or hypothetically, maybe the ethnographic sensor from note 18 above hears from a Djiboutian member of a religious brotherhood that a colleague has just returned from a visit to Indonesia where he heard rumors that some Pakistanis were actively trying to recruit young Indonesian high school students to join the fight against the infidels (meaning Americans). On hearing this, the sensor in Djibouti wouldn't just report it, but would contact counterparts in Indonesia to both alert them and see what they are hearing (because Indonesia is much larger than Djibouti and much more ethnically diverse, there would be multiple sensors there). Again, too, the focus for sensors would be on communities and the seams between communities: across generations, socioeconomic classes, occupations, religions, etc.

21. At least one notable exception is the often cited description of Secretary of State James Baker on the eve of the first Gulf War, when he made it clear to Saddam Hussein via Iraqi foreign minister Tariq Aziz that if Iraq used WMD against U.S. forces, the American people would demand vengeance: "And we have the means to exact it. Let me say with regard to this part of my presentation, this is not a threat, it is a promise. If there is any use of weapons like that, our objective won't just be the liberation of Kuwait, but the elimination of the current Iraqi regime, and anyone responsible for using those weapons would be held accountable." U.S. Department of State Memorandum of Conversation, Secretary James A. Baker III and Foreign Minister Tariq Aziz, Wednesday, January 9, 1991, Geneva, Switzerland, accessed July 10, 2009, http://www.bakerinstitute.org/index.html, 5.

22. Appendix 3, National War Powers Commission Report (Charlottesville, VA: The Miller Center for Public Affairs, The University of Virginia, 2008), 11.

23. Here is George Kennan, expressing

> regret that I in earlier years had had a part, although a very small one, in setting up within our government facilities for the conduct of secret operations. I expressed, as the more mature judgment of later years, the view that all forms of foreign policy that involved secrecy and concealment were neither in keeping with the American tradition nor did they fit naturally with the established modalities for the conduct of American foreign policy. (George Kennan,

Around the Cragged Hill: A Personal and Political Philosophy [New York: W. W. Norton, 1994], 209)

Meanwhile, as of this writing, it is not clear that the 2010 WikiLeaks scandal will do much to alter the nature of diplomacy, although it may change who is granted access to message traffic.

24. It can also increase the likelihood of blackmail, which is the route the next Julian Assange might choose to go.

25. This is also what the African Union (formerly the Organization of African Unity) stipulates. Consequently, Somaliland's stability, tranquility, and prospects for prosperity have led many individuals, but no government thus far, to make the case for recognizing it as a sovereign, independent state (which it was for six days in 1960).

26. Nations numbered 192 by the UN's count in 2010.

27. Robert Jackson, *Sovereignty: The Evolution of an Idea* (Cambridge: Polity Press, 2007), 110.

28. This is a point that even those who would prefer a different system of world governance concede. For example,

> the post-war establishment of new multilateral diplomatic machineries such as the United Nations, NATO and the European Union—while creating new forums for state-to-state interactions—has not altered the fundamental idea that diplomacy is about states identifying their interests and arbitrating them with one another. Indeed, these institutions are premised on the very notion that states can meet there and decide upon their common problems. It is therefore no surprise that diplomats tend to make the world and its myriad problems fall into these shapes. That this process is becoming more and more artificial and disconnected from the reality of the forces at work in the world is not yet evident enough to compel change. (Carne Ross, *Independent Diplomat: Dispatches from an Unaccountable Elite* [Ithaca, NY: Cornell University Press, 2007], 102–3)

29. Garry Kasparov, "Chessboard Endgame," *Wall Street Journal*, December 2–3, 2006.

30. Gerard Prunier, "The Politics of Death in Darfur," *Current History* (May 2006): 198.

A number of prominent Africanists do not consider what has transpired in Darfur to be a genocide. This includes Prunier. Also, not all agree on the causes of the conflict. Some no doubt disagree with Prunier's assessment of various actors in the passage cited. Nevertheless, his larger point is beyond dispute: no one has taken *meaningful* action.

31. Jackson, *Sovereignty*, 123.

32. "The Worst Crimes, the Law and the UN Security Council: Braced for the Aftershock," *The Economist*, March 7, 2009.

33. This is as true of regional organizations as it is of the UN. Consider the case of Myanmar. In October 2007, George Yeo, Singapore's foreign minister, claimed that the Association of Southeast Asian Nations (ASEAN) has

> "very little leverage" over Myanmar's regime, which was admitted to the regional body in 1997 in the hope that constructive engagement might achieve what Western sanctions had not. "We can't do what the big powers can do in terms of trade embargo or freezing bank accounts," said Mr. Yeo. For "can't," read "won't." There is plenty that ASEAN could do. Some regime leaders are thought to have bank accounts in Singapore, which could indeed be frozen. Thailand is by far the largest buyer of Burmese exports (principally gas). Thailand and Singapore are second and third behind China in supplying the country. ("Myanmar: Shouting across the Barbed Wire," *The Economist*, October 6, 2007)

There is often, also, plenty that peacekeepers can—but don't—do. For instance, in September 2009, *The Economist* reported that UNAMID in Darfur

> rarely intervenes to stop the fighting. It has done a bit to boost security in Darfur's towns but has provided almost no protection in rural areas. Even in towns, security has been patchy. On August 29th two UNAMID people were kidnapped in Zalengei. "If they can't handle their own security, how can they protect anyone else?" asked one aid worker. ("The Crisis in Darfur: Neither All-Out War Nor a Proper Peace," *The Economist*, September 5, 2009)

34. In her discussions of the privatization of power in *Territory, Authority, Rights: From Medieval to Global Assemblages* (Princeton: Princeton University Press, 2007), Saskia Sassen suggests, whether she intends to or not, that nothing can compete against the power of the state unless the state refuses to use its power to the fullest extent possible.

Or, as Morton Abramowitz and Thomas Pickering put it in "Making Intervention Work: Improving the UN's Ability to Act," *Foreign Affairs* 87 (September/October 2008): 101: "In an ideal world, noncoercive efforts would produce better behavior. But states persecuting their own people are rarely responsive to peaceful gestures."

35. Or, as Owen Harries notes: "There being no international government, no enforceable law or authority, and hardly any sense of community or common identity, anarchy in the strict sense prevails. That being so, when push comes to shove, as it often does in this game, there is no arbiter, no umpire, except power" ("Power, Morality, and Foreign Policy," *Orbis* [Autumn 2005]: 601). What the next chapter will make clear is how the Sovereignty Solution offers a means for achieving order without anyone needing to exert control.

36. Michael Lind makes much the same point (though he is talking about the "great powers" and not all countries) when he writes: "The paradox of formal collective security organizations like the Council of the League of Nations or the Security Council of the United Nations is this: if the great powers agree, they do not need a formal organization, and if they do not agree, then the formal organization will be paralyzed" (*The American Way of Strategy*, 100).

37. Or, as Rupert Smith notes: "the UN is an organization without a permanent military structure. It therefore has no capacity to create a strategic command, which is why it can never offer a serious option for the use of military force" (*The Utility of Force*, 15).

38. For one history about the evolution of the concept of sovereignty, see Robert Jackson, *Sovereignty*. For another, see Daniel Philpott, "Sovereignty: An Introduction and Brief History," *Journal of International Affairs* 8, no. 2 (Winter 1995). On allegiance, see Saskia Sassen, *Territory, Authority, Rights*, 282–83.

39. See Robert Jackson, *Sovereignty*.

40. Numbers of refugees can be staggering. In February 2007 the *Washington Post* reported that nearly 2 million Iraqis had fled the war, creating the largest refugee crisis in the Middle East in almost sixty years (Sudarsan Raghavan, "A Massive Migration: The War in Iraq Is Propelling a Refugee Crisis in Neighboring Countries," *Washington Post National Weekly Edition*, February 12–18, 2007). In September 2007 *The Economist* reported that up to 2 million migrants from Myanmar were in Thailand ("The Saffron Revolution" [September 29, 2007]: 13).

41. Many, of course, do so for what virtually everyone can agree are purely humanitarian reasons: the eradication of a disease, say. But consider Hezbollah: "There are estimates that Hezbollah provides employment for 40,000 of its wards and schooling for 100,000 children." (Fouad Ajami, "Lebanon's 'Soldiers of Virtue,'" *New York Times*, July 23, 2008). In March 2009 the *Wall Street Journal* reported that a U.S. official responded "with pique" to a British decision to engage in "a direct dialogue with the political arm of Hezbollah. . . . The U.S. official said he wants the British to explain

'the difference between the political, military and social wings of Hezbollah, because we don't see a difference.'" (Jonathan Weisman and Marc Champion, "European Leaders Push Back on Obama's Call for Aid," March 13, 2009).

42. Unfortunately this is as true of gangs *in* the United States as it is of gangs anywhere. There is probably no better depiction than the HBO series *The Wire* of what happens when the state can no longer exert sufficient control, or is itself in bed with "non-state" actors.

   Or consider what William Dalrymple reports from Lahore, Pakistan, when describing "the remarkable human rights campaigner" Asma Jahangir:

   > Asma, who had bravely fought successive military governments, was at a loss about what to do: "Nobody is safe anymore," she told me. "If you are threatened by the government you can take them on legally. But with nonstate actors, when even members of the government are themselves not safe, who do you appeal to? Where do you look for protection?" (William Dalrymple, "Pakistan in Peril," *New York Review of Books*, February 12, 2009).

43. Jakub Grygiel, "The Power of Statelessness," *Policy Review* (April & May 2009): 42.

44. Phil Williams, "From the New Middle Ages to a New Dark Age: The Decline of the State and U.S. Strategy," 3.

45. Richard Haass, "The Age of Nonpolarity: What Will Follow U.S. Dominance, *Foreign Affairs* 87 (May/June 2008): 45.

46. Interestingly *The Economist* reported in late 2007 that "a 1961 convention on reducing statelessness has been signed by just 34 countries," even though the 1948 Universal Declaration of Human Rights "lays down that every human being is entitled to a nationality." "Statelessness: It's Tough to Live in Limbo," *The Economist* (December 1, 2007).

47. Nor does there appear to be a better means of determining citizenship, which defines who belongs to whom (and who can expect what from whom). As Saskia Sassen puts it, "In its narrowest definition citizenship describes the legal relationship between the individual and the polity." As she goes on to note, "the configuration of a polity reached its most developed form with the national state, making it eventually dominant worldwide." See *Territory, Authority, Rights*, 281.

   One can write a whole book—and, indeed, whole books have been written—about the development and evolution of polities. Yet, as Max Weber pointed out early on, for all its flaws, there may be no alternative to the state (with its attendant bureaucracy), given political economies of the type in which we all now live and which we need, given modern modes of production and consumption.

48. Interestingly, Dani Rodrik recently suggested that this same kind of approach be applied to constructing a "new financial order . . . on the back of a minimal set of international guidelines." Essentially, what he advocates is "an architecture that respects national diversity":

> In short, global financial regulation is neither feasible, nor prudent, nor desirable. What finance needs instead are some sensible traffic rules that will allow nations (and in some cases regions) to implement their own regulations while preventing adverse spillovers. If you want an analogy, think of a General Agreement on Tariffs and Trade for world finance rather than a World Trade Organisation. The genius of the GATT regime was that it left room for governments to craft their own social and economic policies as long as they did not follow blatantly protectionist policies and did not discriminate among their trade partners. (Dani Rodrik, "Economics Focus: A Plan B for Global Finance," *The Economist*, March 14, 2009)

49. To include the Vatican, which the United States treats much as a state.

50. Jeffrey Record, "The American Way of War: Cultural Barriers to Successful Counterinsurgency," *Policy Analysis* no. 577 (September 1, 2006): 17.

Chapter 4

1. Another important element to the framework being described is that it is to be applied bilaterally. As a point of contrast, consider Robert Kagan's approach to sovereignty. The example he uses is Pakistan, where "reversing decades-old policies of support" for groups like al Qaeda and the Taliban "may be impossible for any Pakistani leader, especially when the only forces capable of rooting them out are the same forces that created them and sustain them." The question he poses is: "if the world is indeed not to be held hostage by non-state actors operating from Pakistan, what can be done?" His answer: "internationalize the response. Have the international community declare that parts of Pakistan have become ungovernable and a menace to international security. Establish an international force to work with the Pakistanis to root out terrorist camps in Kashmir as well as in the tribal areas."

As Kagan goes on to argue, "nations should not be able to claim sovereign rights when they cannot control territory from which terrorist attacks are launched. If there is such a thing as a 'responsibility to protect,' which justifies international intervention to prevent humanitarian catastrophe either caused or allowed by a nation's government, there must also be a responsibility to protect one's neighbors from attacks from one's own territory, even when the attacks are carried out by non-state actors." Robert Kagan, "The Sovereignty Dodge: What Pakistan Won't Do, the World Should," *Washington Post* (December 2, 2008).

Our argument is somewhat different. In our view it is up to neighbors and/or those attacked to respond. Leaders in those countries have a duty to *their* citizens to protect them from future attacks. The international community does not. Just practically speaking, the "international community" can't manage effective peace enforcement or peacekeeping as it is. It certainly does not respond with counterforce in a timely manner. Nor are there any mechanisms to guarantee that it will "choose" to respond.

This is also why we nodded our heads in agreement when reading Michael Chertoff's "The Responsibility to Contain: Protecting Sovereignty Under International Law," *Foreign Affairs* 88 (January/February 2009). We could have written any one of a number of his sentences. For instance, "This modern international legal order must be predicated on a new principle, under which individual states assume reciprocal obligations to contain transnational threats emerging from within their borders so as to prevent them from infringing on the peace and safety of fellow states around the world" (131–32).

Unfortunately, Chertoff then goes on to write, "Such a set of reciprocal security obligations is unlikely to be crafted in the near future, and the task should not be rushed. In the meantime, the United States and its partners should employ more narrowly sculpted agreements and partnerships to address immediate security challenges." In other words, Chertoff advocates an incrementalist approach to changing the "system." We do not.

2. Here is one approach recommended under President Eisenhower's Solarium Project for handling "trespass" by communists on the Free World:

> Circumstances would dictate the American choice of means. All that would be certain in advance of an incident, which by the definition of armed aggression could not be a "trifling" one is that the United States would respond, and it, as opposed to the communists, would determine how high up the escalatory ladder that response would be. (Robert R. Bowie and Richard H. Immerman, *Waging Peace: How Eisenhower Shaped an Enduring Cold War Strategy* [New York: Oxford University Press, 1998], 132)

Worth noting is that there are at least two differences between Task Force B's approach and ours. Our framework applies to anyone, communist or not. Second, it is others' response to our demands—not the nature of the act itself—that sets the conditions for our subsequent interaction.

3. As an approach, incrementalism "typically offers defeat on the installment plan" (Andrew Krepinevich, "The War in Afghanistan in Strategic Context" testimony before the U.S. House of Representatives Committee on Armed Services, Subcommittee on Oversight and Investigation, November 17, 2009, 6). We'll have more to say about incrementalism in chapter 9.

4. This is somewhat different from other prescriptions. Francis Fukuyama and G. John Ikenberry, for instance, favor a declared doctrine of "attributive deterrence": "if the source state cannot be determined all rogue states with WMD programs will be held responsible" ("Report of the Working Group on Grand Strategic Choices," Princeton Project on National Security, 38). But—what does "will be held responsible" mean?

   Anatol Lieven and John Hulsman want the United States to model itself on Israel:

   > Israel has reportedly made it very clear to Iran in private that if Iran does acquire such weapons and there is a nuclear terrorist attack on Israel that can be even plausibly traced to an Iranian-backed group, then Israel will automatically launch a nuclear strike against Iran. The United States should make the same threat. In the event of a really dreadful terrorist attack on Israel or the United States, the likelihood is therefore that as a result Iran would cease to exist as an organized state and society. (*Ethical Realism: A Vision for America's Role in the World* [New York: Vintage, 2007], 154)

   Barry Posen's notion of obliteration is even starker: "The most important antidote to the risks posed by nuclear proliferation is already in the hands of the U.S.—our own nuclear forces. The U.S. must make it clear that states that deliberately provide nuclear weapons to non state actors will be held similarly accountable." (See "A Grand Strategy of Restraint and Renewal," testimony before the U.S. House Armed Services Committee, Subcommittee on Oversight and Investigations, July 15, 2008, 8.)

   One thing that distinguishes the Sovereignty Solution argument from Posen's is that nowhere do we argue that the United States should respond to nuclear weapons with nuclear weapons.

5. As for the nuclear forensics involved, a "secondary-ion mass spectrometer" should be able to yield "a profile that is often characteristic of a particular type of reactor or centrifuge, and sometimes of an individual machine—and can also indicate how long ago the processing took place." In "A Weighty Matter," *The Economist*, February 27, 2010.

6. As early as 1949 George Kennan worried about Americans' confusion when it came to capabilities and intentions. "His countrymen did not realize, he

wrote in his diary, that what matters are '*intentions*, rather than the *capabilities* of other nations.'" As a result, the United States was "drifting toward a morbid preoccupation with the fact that the Russians conceivably *could* drop atomic bombs on this country." See Nicholas Thompson, *The Hawk and the Dove*, 101. As Thompson goes on to point out, Paul Nitze vehemently disagreed with Kennan and purposely focused on intentions. What the Sovereignty Solution does is split the difference by being totally transparent *about* U.S. intent.

7. Mary Kissel, "The Weekend Interview with Lee Myung-bak," *Wall Street Journal*, June 13–14, 2009.

8. Here, for instance, is Kishore Mahbubani on nuclear non-proliferation and the Nuclear Nonproliferation Treaty (NPT):

> The first problem was that the NPT's principal progenitor, the United States, decided to walk away from the postwar rule-based order it had created, thus eroding the infrastructure on which the NPT's enforcement depends. During the time I was Singapore's ambassador to the UN, between 1984 and 1989, Jeane Kirkpatrick, the U.S. ambassador to the UN, treated the organization with contempt. She infamously said, "What takes place in the Security Council more closely resembles a mugging than either a political debate or an effort at problem-solving." She saw the postwar order as a set of constraints, not as a set of rules that the world should follow and the United States should help preserve. This undermined the NPT, because with no teeth of its own, no self-regulating or sanctioning mechanisms, and a clause allowing signatories to ignore obligations in the name of "supreme national interest," the treaty could only really be enforced by the UN Security Council. And once the United States began tearing holes in the fabric of the overall system, it created openings for violations of the NPT and its principles. ("The Case Against the West: America and Europe in the Asian Century," *Foreign Affairs* 87 [May/June 2008]: 116)

9. Iran, for instance, is a serial offender. The United States has long had plenty of reasons to apply the demand-response-reaction framework to Iran which, had we done so, might then have led to internal changes we (still) don't know how to effect today.

10. For example,

> Mr. Bush signed the Syria Accountability and Lebanese Sovereignty Restoration Act in 2003 but opted to impose only the two weakest sanctions on the list provided by Congress. The U.S. has repeatedly

accused Damascus of providing material support for the insurgency in Iraq, but it has never acted in a way that would show Mr. Assad it is serious about stopping him. Predator strikes against terrorist bases in Syria were ruled out. ("The New Middle East," *Wall Street Journal,* November 27, 2006)

11. As Justin Logan and Christopher Preble put it: "A system of sovereignty grants a kernel of legitimacy to regimes that rule barbarically, it values as equals countries that clearly are not, and it frequently endorses borders that were capriciously drawn by imperial powers. However, it is far from clear that any available alternative is better." See "Failed States and Flawed Logic: The Case against a Standing Nation-Building Office," *Policy Analysis* no. 560 (January 11, 2006): 15.

12. As anthropologists have long noted,

    fragmented systems of authority are found all over the postcolonial world where local strongmen occupy strategic positions between state institutions and the population. . . . In many cases . . . local slumlords, strongmen, and quasi-legal networks have been de facto sovereigns from colonial times. They have at times been tamed and incorporated into governmental structures and have at other times been nodes of opposition to the state. (Thomas Hansen and Finn Stepputat, "Sovereignty Revisited," *Annual Review of Anthropology* 36 [October 2006]: 306)

13. Presumably this will be the role of the newly established Cyber Command, though taxpayers might well wonder how wise it is to make *any* aspect of U.S. national security dependent on systems that can be so readily penetrated and/or attacked from stand-off distances.

14. Not unlike how housing prices reflect how safe certain neighborhoods are.

15. As Mark Bowden notes in his article about the Conficker worm, "In chess, when your opponent checkmates you, you have no recourse. You concede and shake the victor's hand. In the real-world chess match over Conficker, the good guys have another recourse. They can, in effect, upend the board and go after the bad guys physically." See "The Enemy Within," *Atlantic,* June 2010, 83.

16. The United States might need to adopt this approach anyway, just to ensure that potential adversaries understand we won't tolerate cyberterrorism any more readily than we tolerate any other kind of terrorism—*and* to ensure adversaries don't consider this their next venue.

17. Epitomized by international borders—only some of which have ever been fenced.

18. For instance, under the sovereignty rubric no one would have to make the difficult determination of whether a group like Lashkar-e-Taiba, the militant group behind the November 2008 Mumbai attack, is a non-state actor operating from Pakistan or a Pakistani proxy.

19. *Sovereignty*, 16. As Jackson goes on to write, "Ottawa is not answerable to Washington, which has no legal authority over the territory and resident population of Canada. Power has no bearing on sovereignty as such, but the capability and capacity available to a sovereign government can have a profound effect on what it is able to accomplish, and how it relates to foreign governments."

   John Agnew disagrees in *Globalization & Sovereignty* (Lanham, MD: Rowman & Littlefield, 2009). In his view "there is much more to the geography of political power—and thus sovereignty—than is captured by regarding the state territory as the singular unit of political account" (39). Yet as Agnew also has to concede numerous times in his book, "Until sovereignty and territory are symbolically disentangled . . . there is little prospect of seeing the possibility of and realizing a politics more appropriate for such an interdependent and 'fluid' world" (59). Or, even more to the point regarding the indispensability of states, "Today, only states still have the authority under international law to grant or deny the status of citizen" (179).

20. Interestingly, Eugene Goltz, Daryl Press, and Harvey Sapolsky make a somewhat similar point about the muddying effects of U.S. "protection" from a different angle:

   > Many foreign policy analysts believe that the Bosnian crisis was exacerbated by German irresponsibility; the German government recognized the secession of parts of the Yugoslav Republic, despite the risk of inciting civil war. A Germany without the United States to guard its interests would be likely to think harder about the effects of such actions. Japan, too, has ducked its responsibilities under the guardianship of the United States. It has not come to terms with its neighbors for its conduct during World War II. A Japan without U.S. protection would likely discover that reconciliation is cheaper and more effective than confrontation. ("Come Home, America: The Strategy of Restraint in the Face of Temptation," *International Security* 21:4 [Spring 1997], 16)

21. Alex de Waal, *Famine Crimes: Politics & The Disaster Relief Industry in Africa* (Bloomington: Indiana University Press, 1997), 150.

   Numerous countries besides the United States contributed to Operation Lifeline Sudan. Meanwhile, the United States has provided $3.9 billion in humanitarian assistance to Sudan and eastern Chad just since 2004. But—to what exact ends?

> Thirty years into one of the most important bilateral relationships the United States maintains in Africa, Sudan continues down the path of perpetual crisis. The human costs are stunning—the 22-year war between North and South Sudan saw 2 million people die and another 4 million forced from their homes. The genocide in Darfur has led to the deaths of at least 300,000 and the displacement of more than 2.5 million people, with 210,000 persons newly displaced since January 2008. Against this backdrop, some 19 million people—85 percent of Sudan's rural population—live in extreme poverty while oil revenues line the pockets of Khartoum's elite. Meanwhile, the Darfur conflict has spilled over into Chad, triggering war-by-proxy between Khartoum and Ndjamena. ("The Price of Prevention: Getting Ahead of Global Crises," Center for American Progress Report, November 2008, 5)

22. Jok Madut Jok, *Sudan: Race, Religion, and Violence* (Oxford: Oneworld Publications, 2007), 251.

23. Indeed, as Michela Wrong reports,

> If they only set foot on the continent, idealistic Westerners would be astonished to hear how often, and how fiercely, politically engaged Africans . . . call for aid to be cut, conditionalities sharpened. Kenyan journalist Kwamchetsi Makokha is not alone in detecting an incipient racism, rather than altruism, in our lack of discrimination. "Fundamentally the West doesn't care enough about Africa to pay too much attention to how its money is spent. It wants to be seen to do the right thing, and that's as far as the interest goes." (*It's Our Turn to Eat: The Story of a Kenyan Whistle Blower* [New York: *Harper's*, 2009], 326)

24. Venezuela and Colombia, for instance. FARC has long found sanctuary and support in Venezuela. "Mr. Chavez considers the FARC ideological brothers and possible allies against a U.S. invasion he believes might come from Colombia. . . . In Colombia, much of the war against guerrilla groups is fought in places like Arauca . . . which runs along a 185-mile stretch of border between Colombia and Venezuela." See Jose de Cordoba, "Chavez Lets Colombia Rebels Wield Power Inside Venezuela," *Wall Street Journal*, November 25, 2008.

The FARC's disruptive effects in Venezuela likewise fit a broader pattern, in which rulers sometimes cede too much authority to exiles and guerrillas—to their eventual regret.

25. Increasingly, these are being referred to as "forever wars." See, for example, Jeffrey Gettleman, "Africa's Forever Wars: Why the Continent's Conflicts Never End," *Foreign Policy* (March/April 2010).

26. It is actually far worse than this, as the Hollywood movie *Lord of War* suggests. As Douglas Farah reports, "These arms merchants almost always escape international sanctions because they don't work for any one state but have proved useful to many. Worse, much of what they do is not illegal, and the penalties for breaking the few laws that may apply are miniscule and entirely unenforceable." About Viktor Bout, "a Russian air-transport magnate and the world's premier gray-market arms provider," he goes on to note,

> for all his well-documented and unsavory activities, Bout and his cohorts also provide services to the United Nations, as well as governments and militaries around the world. When there was a need to airlift aid to tsunami victims in 2004, Bout's planes were there, flying relief to Indonesia. Need to move U.N. peacekeepers around Africa? Bout can do it—and did, in Rwanda, Congo and elsewhere. Need to move enough weapons, tents, ammunition and food for an invading army in Iraq? . . . In Iraq, his aircraft flew hundreds of flights, delivering ammunition, generators, spare parts and mail.
>
> But the cost is enormous. Over the past year, Bout's aircraft have been discovered delivering weapons to the now ousted radical Islamic regime in Somalia, the Hezbollah militia in Lebanon, pro-Russian factions in Georgia and to many other worrisome players in strategically important hot spots. (Douglas Farah, "War and Terror, Inc.: An Air-Transport Magnate Aids and Abets Our Enemies while Collecting Our Money," *Washington Post National Weekly Edition*, October 1–7, 2007)

27. Which is not to say that people don't attribute the longevity of certain rulers to their use of sorcery, witchcraft, divination, etc.; but convincing people you can tap into supernatural powers is hardly the same as convincing them you should rule because you possess a spark of divinity or are descended from God (or a god).

Chapter 5

1. For more on the differences between Declarations of War and authorizations of force, see David Ackerman and Richard Grimmett, "Declarations of War and Authorizations for the Use of Military Force: Historical Background and Legal Implications," Congressional Research Service Report, 2003.

War was formally declared in 1812; against Mexico (Mexican-American War); Spain (Spanish-American War); Germany and Austria (World War

I); and against six adversaries in World War II. The Congressional Research Service reports that all eight formal Declarations of War in the twentieth century were issued in response to a violation of U.S. territorial sovereignty.

2. Here is one trenchant assessment of our messiest twentieth-century war: "We will never know how North Vietnam's commitment would have fared if the United States had not engaged so many troops but had declared war instead." Paul Seabury and Angelo Codevilla, *War: Ends and Means*, 71.

3. The other problem is that without Declarations of War there are no clear standards for success. Not everyone would agree with the following testimony: "The U.S. has fought five significant military engagements since the collapse of the Soviet Union. Only one of those engagements, the overthrow of the Taliban in Operation Enduring Freedom can reasonably have been considered essential. The two Balkan engagements still have not led to stable political outcomes; U.S. troops remain in Kosovo ten years later." (Barry Posen, "A Grand Strategy of Restraint and Renewal) 2. To some people, Kosovo *does* represent a clear success, and one of the triumphs of Bill Clinton's presidency. The fact that there can be such disagreement isn't good—not unless ambiguity of outcome is the Grand Strategic goal.

4. Or, as Noah Feldman and Samuel Issacharoff put it, "The Constitution should . . . be understood to allow Congress to declare and define the nature of the war while guaranteeing the president's authority to make decisions that are crucial to the tactical conduct of it." See "Declarative Sentences: Congress Has the Power to Make and End War—Not Manage It," *Slate*, March 5, 2007, 2.

5. This turns into a compound problem. When Congress doesn't fulfill its obligations, the media is then granted the opportunity to shirk its duties as the Fourth Estate. Or so one might conclude after reading the following (written by Tom Ricks, who was the *Washington Post's* military correspondent during the period he describes):

> Congress as a whole became unusually important during this period [before the Iraq War], especially the Senate and House Armed Services committees, the two panels that oversee the military establishment and so held the keys to airing Pentagon dissent and other concerns about going to war in Iraq. The Republicans didn't want to question the Bush administration. The Democrats couldn't or wouldn't, so Congress didn't produce the witnesses who in hearings would give voice and structure to opposition. Lacking hearings to write about, and the data such sessions would yield, the media didn't delve deeply enough into the issues surrounding the war, most notably whether the administration was correctly assessing the threat presented by Iraq and the cost of occupying and remaking the country. (*Fiasco*, 88)

This is a point also made by William Howell and Jon Pevehouse:

> The voice of Congress (or lack thereof) has had a profound impact on the media coverage of the current war in Iraq, just as it has colored public perceptions of U.S. foreign policy in the past. . . . Many studies have shown that the media regularly follow official debates about war in Washington, adjusting their coverage to the scope of the discussion among the nation's political elite. And among the elite, members of Congress—through their own independent initiatives and through journalists' propensity to follow them—stand out as the single most potent source of dissent against the president. . . . As Congress speaks, it would seem, the media report, and the public listens. ("When Congress Stops Wars," 105)

6. Not surprisingly, "when Congress has not been consulted or the President acts against Congress's will, courts have been more receptive to challenges to the President's actions" (National War Powers Commission Report, 33).

7. The same goes for electronic (or financial) warfare, should it come to that in the future.

8. The National War Powers Commission (co-chaired by James Baker and Warren Christopher) hoped its report "will persuade the next President and Congress to repeal the War Powers Resolution of 1973 and enact in its place the War Powers Consultation Act of 2009," (4). According to the commissioners, among the things that make their Act noteworthy is that they "seek to clarify what sorts of situations are covered by the statute and which are not." For instance, not only do they replace the term "hostilities" with "significant armed conflict," but they make the following case:

> It is obviously impossible to account for every conceivable armed conflict. But we want to provide more detail and definition in our draft statute than has existed before. *We also want to involve Congress only in conflicts where consultation seems essential.* To use some recent historical examples as a guide, President Reagan's limited air strikes against Libya would not count as a "significant armed conflict." The two Iraq Wars clearly would be considered "significant armed conflicts" (and of course Congress authorized both). The United States' campaign in Bosnia in the 1990s would also count as a significant armed conflict. (36, emphasis ours)

Unfortunately, it is hard to see how the commission's report clarifies anything—since it doesn't offer a method for determining what counts as a "significant armed conflict." Here is where the parsimony of the sovereignty rubric—a violation is a violation and sets the demand-response-reaction sequence in motion—should offer a decisive improvement.

9. In 2005 Leslie Gelb and Anne-Marie Slaughter ("Declare War," *Atlantic Online*, November 2005) proposed "a new law that would restore the Framers' intent by requiring a congressional declaration of war in advance of any commitment of troops that promises *sustained combat*" (2, emphasis ours). While we agree with virtually all Gelb and Slaughter's points, we can't help but wonder about this prescription. Who, for instance, gets to define what sustained combat is: Congress or the executive?

10. Again, ideally an initial strike or sortie might achieve the country's strategic objective. In reality, however, initial setbacks plague all wars. If not, they would be over after the initial counterattack.

11. In describing his recent book coauthored with Christopher Gelpi and Jason Reifler, Peter Feaver writes,

> Our bottom line support for war is a function of two attitudes: the retrospective attitude of whether the war was the right thing in the first place, and the prospective attitude of whether the war will be won. Both affect public willingness to continue the war, but the prospective attitude has a bigger impact. In other words, the long pole in the tent is the public's belief that the war can and will be won. (Peter Feaver, "Is Obama Losing Public Support for Afghanistan," *Foreign Policy [Shadow Government blog] Online*, March 13, 2009)

12. Or, in Angelo Codevilla's words: "no one should declare war without being clear against whom it is being declared: who the enemy is whose demise will give us peace." See "No Victory, No Peace," *Claremont Review of Books*, Winter 2003, 4 (online version).

13. It is worth bearing in mind that Declarations of War do not promise either a nuclear holocaust *or* Armageddon. Ironically, one reason Declarations of War probably sound so belligerent to so many people today is because Congress has not voted for or against a declaration within most people's memory. Therefore, they've been allowed to take on apocalyptic dimensions.

14. William F. Buckley, "George Kennan's Bomb," *National Review*, April 4, 1980, 432.

15. Another reason to flip the switch in this way is that, as Walter Russell Mead puts it, Americans "see war as a switch that is either on or off. They don't like the idea of violence on a dimmer switch." See *Special Providence: American Foreign Policy and How It Changed the World* (New York: Routledge, 2002), 254.

16. There is a precedent for this. President Eisenhower sought a resolution from Congress to allow him to react in defense of Formosa and the Pescadores and "such other territories as may be determined." Here is Stephen Ambrose's account:

The resolution Eisenhower wanted was something new in American history. Never before had Congress given the President a blank check to act as he saw fit in a foreign crisis. On January 28 [1955], by a vote of 83 to 3, the Senate passed the resolution. For the first time in American history, the Congress had authorized the President in advance to engage in a war at a time and under circumstances of his own choosing." (Ambrose, *Eisenhower*, 381–82)

What we are proposing is decidedly *not* a blank check.

17. "Dead End," *Harper's* magazine, 39.

18. Ivan Arreguin-Toft, "How the Weak Win Wars: A Theory of Asymmetric Conflict," *International Security* 26 (Summer 2001): 101–2. Arreguin-Toft cites the Hague Conventions of 1896, 1907, the Geneva Accords of 1946, and the Protocols from 1977 as sources of the "laws of war."

19. In a review of Hugo Slim's book *Killing Civilians: Method, Madness and Morality in War, The Economist's* reviewer answers the "who qualifies as a civilian?" question this way:

    International law provides only a negative description: someone who is not a member of the armed forces, who does not carry a weapon, who does not take part in hostilities. This is clearly inadequate. An estimated 60% of the world's weapons-bearers are civilians (hunters, for example). On the other hand, many of those who do not carry arms (or wear uniforms) may be very much part of the war effort—ammunition workers, porters, victuallers and the like. And what of the ideologues whose hate-filled doctrines fuel the conflict, the newspaper editors who disseminate the propaganda or the taxpayers who pay for the war? Should they be afforded special protection when the unwilling teenage conscript is not? (February 16, 2008)

20. Ironically, but perhaps not surprisingly, rules seem to be much clearer in (and between) small-scale tribal societies than in the industrial/postindustrial settings we're used to.

21. Tellingly, in few if any contemporary exchanges about "Just War," does anyone dare point out that entire communities may be complicit in supporting combatants.

22. Moshe Yaalon, "The Rules of War," *Washington Post National Weekly Edition*, August 7–13, 2006.

23. "What Happened at Haditha," *Wall Street Journal*, October 19, 2007.

24. Hew Strachan, "The Lost Meaning of Strategy," *Survival* 45:3 (Autumn 2005): 48.

25. For one thing, there should be no vacuum—of power, services, justice, etc.—for them to be able to fill.

26. We mean to say: *no* non-state actors deserve to be recognized, regardless of whether they engage in political violence or not. The existence of "non-state" actors defies the point of sovereign control.

    As Roger Scruton writes,

    > Increasingly . . . terrorists use sovereignty purely as a mask, either by imposing themselves as guests on sovereign states to whose future they are more or less indifferent—like al-Qa'eda in Afghanistan—or by establishing global networks that can evade all national jurisdictions while freely operating anywhere. In this they are little different from the multinational corporations which, thanks partly to the World Trade Organization, can ignore or dissolve national sovereignty in their relentless pursuit of markets. ("The United States, the United Nations, and the Future of the Nation-State," Heritage Lectures No. 794, June 5, 2003, 5–6)

27. Only when insurgents seize power with no external support, in which case they are clearly wresting control from an inept and unworthy government, do they deserve recognition (which they will gain as soon as they *become* the state). As for foreign governments that support insurgents, under the sovereignty rubric covert support might as well be overt support. Any government that uses insurgents to wage war by proxy should be assumed to be signaling its willingness to go to war—in which case, why use proxies?

28. This book's argument is that it has also become increasingly difficult to tell the two apart. When media attention is more effective than the enemy's bullets or bombs at getting us to stop a military action, we have entered a looking-glass world in which the power we have amassed becomes utterly useless. Under such circumstances, we are fighting wars we, essentially, no longer want to win. Otherwise, what could explain why we don't finish what we start? Of course, one potential answer to this question is that we have no clear strategy. The Sovereignty Solution is designed to redress both problems.

29. Jakub Grygiel, "The Power of Statelessness," 41.

30. This includes doing things like imposing sanctions on North Korea, but then "allowing" Ethiopia to complete a secret arms purchase from North Korea "in part because Ethiopia was in the midst of a military offensive against Islamic militias inside Somalia, a campaign that aided the American policy of combating religious extremists in the Horn of Africa." See Michael Gordon and Mark Mazzetti, "North Koreans Arm Ethiopians as U.S. Assents: Despite Sanctions, Ally Buys Parts in Secret," *New York Times*, April 8, 2007.

These are the kinds of arrangements the Sovereignty Solution would stop—on all counts. In a Sovereignty Rules world there would be no reason for the United States to permit or prevent other countries from engaging in trade, unless we have declared war against them. We certainly wouldn't agree to any secret arms deals. But we also wouldn't be using Ethiopia as any sort of proxy. This is something we discuss again in chapter 9.

31. Consider the following assessment of the 2009 Gaza conflict and Operation Cast Lead, initiated by Israel to "deter" Hamas:

> The implicit message of the Israeli officials' claim that "regime change" in Gaza is not an objective of Operation Cast Lead is problematic. If sincere, Tel Aviv is wasting lives—Jewish and Palestinian—for very short-term success. If not, the problem is worse, because it only creates confusion—in Israel, among Palestinians, and elsewhere. Ultimately, the only solution—itself limited in time because of dysfunctional Palestinian political culture—is physical destruction of Hamas in Gaza, by killing most of its militants and leaders, be they "political" or "military" (is there a difference, outside Western artificial legalistic and emotional circles?). As it is now, Israel's claim that the goal is not Hamas' removal from power in Gaza is either dishonest, a PR statement, or delusional." (Michael Radu, "Gaza Conflict: Deterrence and Other Missed Points," FPRI E-Note, January 16, 2009)

No matter who one favors in the broader conflict—Hamas or Israel—Michael Radu's "no-holds-barred" argument underscores our point and the clarifying effect sovereignty's approach to transparency would have.

32. See James Johnson, "Maintaining the Protection of Non-Combatants," *Journal of Peace Research* 37, no. 4 (July 2000): 421–48.

33. So are perspectives like the following:

> It is not the intention of the civilian label to air-brush civilians out of war as innocent or un-threatening bystanders, but to find a super-ordinate identity which asks war-makers to respect an essentially forgiving umbrella identity for the majority of their ambiguous but unarmed enemies in order to limit the killing in war. (Hugo Slim, *Killing Civilians: Method, Madness, and Morality in War* [New York: Columbia University Press, 2008], 273–74)

Unfortunately, no soldier we know would know how to translate this into plain enough English to help make a judgment call in the field. To his credit, the author of this passage does offer that "those who covertly militarize civilian status . . . are responsible for a breach of trust. In the old language of the laws of war, they are guilty of perfidy" (267). Even so, he still doesn't explain how anyone is supposed to "distinguish between tolerable ambiguity in civilian identity and actual abuse of civilian status" (267).

Our point is that this is precisely why the rules need to be readjusted. Or, to cut to the chase, civilians and communities can no longer be afforded the opportunity to play it all ways. Choice they deserve. Responsibility we may have to force them to accept.

34. Hollywood special effects only compound this. But it was the military that made this "real" during briefings during the first Gulf War.

35. This is why Martin Van Creveld advises "Let there be no apologies, no kvetching about collateral damage caused by mistake, innocent lives regrettably lost, 'excesses' that will be investigated and brought to trial and similar signs of weakness." See *The Changing Face of War: Lessons of Combat, from the Marne to Iraq* (New York: Ballantine Books, 2006), 245.

36. Consider, for instance, the following analysis:

> [Prior to the invasion] certain operations directed against Saddam Hussein's regime were deemed off-limits because they targeted civilians or risked producing disproportionate damage to civilians and civilian infrastructure. Starting in late 2002, the Pentagon also enlisted UN agencies and nongovernmental organizations to help draw up a "no-strike" list including thousands of schools, mosques, sensitive cultural sites, hospitals, water-treatment facilities, power plants, and other elements of civilian infrastructure. *The list placed significant constraints on air and land operations.* (Colin Kahl, "How We Fight," *Foreign Affairs* 86 [November/December 2006]: 89, emphasis ours)

Rules of engagement have likewise gotten much stricter in Afghanistan.

37. To quote one self-described human rights activist and specialist in international law,

> Guerillas [sic] and terrorists have always existed and never fit neatly into the Geneva Conventions framework, but they operated on the margins until globalization scattered the tools of mass destruction around the world. . . . Even in powerful states, intelligence services, militaries and laws all evolved to handle "traditional" conflicts and traditional threats from belligerent foreign states. Yet terrorists—like other non-state actors—are, by definition, not party to the Geneva Convention. They play by a different set of rules—if indeed there is any set of rules they follow. (Rosa Brooks, "The Politics of the Geneva Conventions: Avoiding Formalist Traps," *Virginia Journal of International Law* (Fall 2005): 2 [online])

As Jeremy Rabkin concurs, "even Geneva has specifications: it applies to the treatment of people who subscribe to the Convention and live up to its terms" (Orin Judd et al., "Redefining Sovereignty," Heritage Lecture #1007, July 20, 2006).

38. *Jus in bello* refers to conduct in a war; *jus ad bellum* refers to the lawfulness of going to war.

39. As Michael Walzer has recently written,

> People get killed in wars; soldiers get killed, civilians too, and we need to understand who is responsible for those deaths. If we are able to accomplish that, and if we assign responsibility clearly and firmly, so our judgments have political consequences (in pub-lic opinion, United Nations resolutions, intellectual debates, and ultimately in diplomatic initiatives and policy decisions), we will have done as much as we can to minimize the number of civilian deaths. We will also have confronted and acknowledged the pain-ful truth that many of those deaths, terrible as each one may be, have been brought about by soldiers fighting justly. ("Responsibility and Proportionality in State and Nonstate Wars," *Parameters* [Spring 2009]: 52)

40. The Taliban, for instance, have "taken advantage of changes in U.S. air and artillery tactics, adopted to decrease civilian casualties that have alienated the population." Once the United States began to limit air strikes and cultur-ally offensive night ground raids in late 2009, the Taliban "adjusted its own tactics, gathering in populated areas and increasing its night operations, and 'the playing field is leveled.'" Karen DeYoung, "'A Game of Will': U.S. Forces in Afghanistan Are Getting Slammed by an Evolved Taliban," *Washington Post National Weekly Edition* (September 7–13, 2009).

41. This certainly seems to be Anthony Cordesman's assessment in "The 'Gaza War': A Strategic Analysis" (final review draft, CSIS [Center for Strategic and International Studies], February 2, 2009). See, especially, the section titled "Technology versus 'Human Shields.'" Cordesman, meanwhile, concludes "it is far from certain that Israel's tactical successes achieved significant strategic and grand strategic benefits" (ii). Indeed, the entire operation may have sim-ply complicated Israel's long-term problems.

42. Populations understand imminent danger. Refugees are proof of this. What the United States achieved prior to the second battle of Fallujah in Iraq is exactly what the demand-response-react sequence should trigger as soon as a state refuses our demands: "The new battle followed months of military planning and political measures . . . a concerted effort was made to encourage civilians to leave the city—the U.S. count was that by the time the offensive was launched, only 400 civilians remained, out of a city of perhaps 250,000."

Ricks, *Fiasco*, 399. According to Colin Kahl, "How We Fight," *Foreign Affairs* 86 (November/December 2006):94, "military and media estimates suggest that at least 250,000 of Fallujah's 280,000 inhabitants fled in advance of the onslaught" thanks to "an extensive information campaign urging residents to leave."

43. While this would be the step when adversaries might think they can run out the clock, everything done to reinvigorate sovereignty would have prepared the public to hold Congress to account for time-sensitive Declarations of War. This also falls under creating a more Indivisible America.

44. Of course, if we'd really been in a Sovereignty Rules world, students and activists would have had no reason to seize the embassy—but that doesn't help with the counterfactual.

45. Hague Convention III, Relative to the Opening of Hostilities, 1907, Article 1. The convention had forty-two signatories including the United States. It remains in effect.

46. Rupert Smith, *The Utility of Force*, 376.

47. To invoke Rupert Smith, "one of the endemic problems of our modern conflicts is the lack of political will to employ force rather than deploy forces—meaning will is close to zero—which is why many military interventions fail: the force capability is voided." *The Utility of Force*, 118.

Chapter 6

1. Whatever hardware we don't have, we could manufacture—this has always been an American strong suit.

2. Samuel Huntington, *American Politics: The Promise of Disharmony* (Cambridge: Harvard University Press, 1981), 15.

3. Parag Khanna, "Waving Goodbye to Hegemony," *New York Times*, January 27, 2008.

4. For one explanation of why they don't agree, see Carl Bialik, "In Counting Illegal Immigrants, Certain Assumptions Apply," *Wall Street Journal*, May 8–9, 2010.

5. "We return always to the question of numbers. Although it is true that no one knows exactly how many are here illegally from Mexico and Latin America, both sides in the debate often accept as reasonable estimates of 11 to 12 million—with an additional 500,000 to 1 million arriving every year. Given porous borders, such guesses are outdated almost as soon as they are published." Victor Davis Hanson, "Immigration: Discomfort in 'Mexifornia,'" accessed August 29, 2007, http://www.hoover.org/publications/digest/7467722.html, 2.

On March 19, 2009, the *New York Times* reported that "about a third of the country's foreign-born residents, an estimated 11.9 million people, are here illegally, testing traditions of assimilation and stirring frustration and political opposition. Never before have so many of America's immigrants come here unlawfully."

The Economist one month later (April 18, 2009) cited the same figure for 2008 (not 2009), adding that this was "up 42% since 2000" (27).

Nor is it just the United States that has problems counting and tracking illegal immigrants. In May 2008 it was reported "Canadian authorities can't find 41,000 people who were classified as security risks or illegal immigrants and ordered to leave the country." *Monterey County Herald* (May 5, 2008).

6. Cited in John Fonte, "To Possess the National Consciousness of an American," *Hudson Institute*, 2000, accessed January 12, 2007, www.jillnicholson.com/johnfont.htm.

7. Cited in Patrick Buchanan, *State of Emergency* (New York: St. Martin's Press, 2006), xiv.

8. "Remade in America: The Newest Immigrants and Their Impact," *New York Times* (March 15, 2009).

9. This leads to all sorts of problems for elected officials, as a long April 5, 2009, *New York Times* story titled "Deportation Furor Catches Texas Mayor in Middle" makes clear. In an accompanying sidebar, the *New York Times* explains, "State and local authorities have responded in different ways to the influx of Hispanic immigrants. Some law enforcement agencies have joined Immigration and Customs Enforcement (I.C.E) in identifying and arresting immigration law violators. Others have been expressly forbidden from enforcing immigration laws."

10. To illustrate the ways in which (legal) immigrants can be a national security asset, consider former New York Police Commissioner Raymond Kelly's approach:

> He took what many in Washington and other parts of the country might have seen as New York City's greatest weakness, the presence of millions of people born outside the United States—that foreign 40 percent of the population—and recognized that those immigrants would be the core of its defense. They provided the key linguistic skills and the invaluable human intelligence; they literally talked the talk and walked the walk of cultures everywhere on earth. They were what gave the NYPD "the reach that you potentially can have throughout the world," Kelly said. But more than that, *they shared a notion of freedom and security, opportunity and prosperity.*

It sometimes seems a delicate thing, the American dream, but those who believe in it are amazingly resistant to those who would attack it, and when law enforcement understands that, then the city—and the nation—can remain secure. (Christopher Dickey, *Securing the City*, 272, emphasis ours)

11. This is nothing new. When Dwight Eisenhower was president of Columbia University (before he was president of the United States) his attitude was that "every student who came to Columbia must leave it first a better citizen and only secondarily a better scholar. To the faculty, that attitude was embarrassing—Eisenhower made Columbia sound like a high school civics class. When Eisenhower raised nearly a half million dollars for Teachers College to carry out a Citizenship Education Project, and another huge sum for a Chair of Competitive Enterprise, the embarrassment deepened." Stephen Ambrose, *Eisenhower*, 242.

12. Or, as Diane Ravitch says, "What we need is not a marketplace, but a coherent curriculum that prepares all students." As she notes of today's choices and "standards," "we are not producing a generation of students who are more knowledgeable, and better prepared for the responsibilities of citizenship." "Why I Changed My Mind about School Reform," *Wall Street Journal* (March 9, 2010).

13. As Jonathan Yardley writes in a review of Margaret MacMillan's *Dangerous Games: The Uses and Abuses of History*, "If the American public knew history better than it does, it would be harder to pull off these [political] deceptions, but unfortunately most Americans have been taught history badly and prefer not to think about it at all. That makes us suckers for warped history that gets us into trouble overseas, and at home as well." "Getting History Right," *Washington Post National Weekly Edition*, July 27–August 2, 2009.

14. Arthur Herman, "The Lies of Tet," *Wall Street Journal* (February 6, 2008).

15. For instance, "Media misreporting of Tet passed into our collective memory. That picture gave antiwar activism an unwarranted credibility that persists today in Congress, and in the media reaction to the war in Iraq." Herman goes on to note that "the war in Vietnam was lost on the propaganda front, in great measure due to the press's pervasive misreporting of the clear U.S. victory at Tet as a defeat" (ibid).

16. As with everything related to Vietnam, one can find many different interpretations of Tet's impact. Paul Seabury and Angelo Codevilla's assessment strongly suggests the North Vietnamese purposely took aim at Americans' divisibility:

    Because of the Americans' overwhelming firepower, the attack (since known as the Tet Offensive) was doomed to fail, and Communist forces in South Vietnam never recovered from the losses sustained in that attack. Had North Vietnam's leaders been mistaken in their assessment that the shock of the Tet offensive would have a decisive effect on America's "effete elite," the casualties they suffered would have meant losing the war. But their assessment of the U.S. government's domestic vulnerability proved correct. (*War: Ends & Means*, 187)

17. Those in decision-making circles claim they pointed this out to no effect and that the president wouldn't accept the need to clarify why he went to war. Douglas Feith quotes a memo he wrote prior to one of the president's "major speeches" about Iraq in May 2004:

> There is a widespread misconception that the war's rationale was the existence of Iraqi WMD stockpiles. This allows critics to say that our failure to find such stockpiles undermines that rationale. If the President ignores this altogether and then implies that the war's rationale was not the terrorism/state sponsorship/WMD nexus but rather democracy for Iraqis, the critics may say that he is changing the subject or rewriting history. ("How Bush Sold the War," *Wall Street Journal*, May 27, 2008)

18. In the same op-ed, Feith goes on to write, "Before the war, administration officials said that success would mean an Iraq that no longer threatened important U.S. interests—that did not support terrorism, aspire to WMD, threaten its neighbors, or conduct mass murder. But from the fall of 2003 on, the president defined success as stable democracy in Iraq."

One of the Sovereignty Solution's many advantages is that there can be no such "rationale creep."

19. Under the Sovereignty Solution, the nature of the relationship framework and the openness of the demand-response-reaction sequence would also render moot another of the problems currently plaguing our counterterrorism operations against the Taliban which, according to Graham Allison and John Deutch, require "light U.S. footprints backed by drones and other technology that allows missile attacks on identified targets. The problem is that the U.S. government no longer seems to be capable of conducting covert operations without having them reported in the press." "The Real Afghan Issue Is Pakistan," *Wall Street Journal* (March 30, 2009).

20. Richard Betts, "Is Strategy an Illusion?, 49.

21. Kathy Roth-Douquet and Frank Schaeffer in *AWOL: The Unexcused Absence of America's Upper Classes from Military Service—and How It Hurts Our Country* (New York: Collins, 2006) offer an interesting liberal-meets-conservative discussion about the significance of military service.

William F. Buckley Jr. tilts at conservatives and liberals alike in *Gratitude: Reflections on What We Owe to Our Country* (New York: Random House, 1990).

Recently *The American Interest* published "A Call to National Service," penned by Michael Brown, City Year CEO; AnnMaura Connolly, City Year senior vice president; Alan Khazei, Be The Change CEO; Wendy Kopp, Teach for America, founder and CEO; Michelle Nunn, Points of Light Foundation/Hands on Network CEO; Gregg Petersmeyer, director of the White House Office of National Service, 1989–92; Shirley Sagawa, former deputy chief of staff to [First Lady] Hillary Clinton; and Harris Wofford, former Senator from Pennsylvania (January/February 2008).

22. Margaret Mead, "A National Service System as a Solution to a Variety of National Problems" in Sol Tax, ed., *The Draft: A Handbook of Facts and Alternatives* (Chicago: University of Chicago Press, 1967), 105.

23. Carol Armistead Grigsby, "Binding the Nation: National Service in America," *Parameters* (Winter 2008–9): 120.

24. Mead, " A National Service System," 109.

25. President Truman tried. In 1946 he formed an Advisory Commission on Universal Training:

> The purpose of such a program, Truman told his commissioners, was to give "our young people a background in the disciplinary approach of getting along with one another, informing them of their physical make-up, and what it means to take care of this temple which God gave us. If we get that instilled into them, and then instill into them a responsibility which begins in the township, in the city ward, the first thing you know we will have sold our Republic to the coming generations as Madison and Hamilton and Jefferson sold it in the first place." (Aaron Friedberg, *In the Shadow of the Garrison State* [Princeton, NJ: Princeton University Press, 2000], 166)

26. On pandering:

> Raising and spending large quantities of money for campaigns not only distinguishes the modern era from all previous periods of American history, it also gets in the way of governing. "It's now basically all money," Sen. Christopher J. Dodd of Connecticut told me. He had just come from the weekly luncheon meeting of the Senate Democratic caucus. "Almost the entire luncheon was devoted to money" and how to raise it, he said. "When I first came [to the Senate in 1981], these lunches were a place for great debates and discussions. . . . They were wonderful moments. I don't want to sound

melodramatic, but the republic's at risk—truly at risk because of this." (Robert Kaiser, "Special Interests: Obama's Most Ambitious Promise May Be the One to Curb K Street Lobbyists," *Washington Post National Weekly Edition*, February 9–15, 2009)

27. Stephen Flynn, "Homeland Insecurity: Disaster at DHS," 26.

28. A term borrowed from James Kurth, "What Are We Fighting For? Western Civilization, American Identity, and U.S. Foreign Policy," Foreign Policy Research Institute monograph, January 2009. It is also used by G. John Ikenberry and Anne-Marie Slaughter in *Forging a World of Liberty Under Law* (Woodrow Wilson School of Public and International Affairs: Princeton University, 2006).

29. Kurth, "What Are We Fighting For?", 5.

30. "For more than half a century, far-sighted people in many countries have been working on a project for international law and order, that is our best and perhaps our only chance of avoiding global disaster on an unprecedented scale. It is obviously a hundred-year project at the very least, for it flies in the face of history and of traditional ideas about human nature." Gwynne Dyer, *Future: Tense*, 240.

The Sovereignty Solution premise: shouldn't we try something that better fits with history *and* with human nature?

31. Which is not to be confused with questioning government.

32. It has been suggested that the idea of indivisibility itself might be divisive. Perhaps. But our premise is that it won't be if the American people fully understand how vulnerable certain kinds of divisibility make us.

33. "Nigerians have a strong sense of being Nigerian, but they do not share with each other the same concept of what that means. . . . Nigerians have never agreed—or been given the chance to agree—what Nigeria is." Richard Dowden, *Africa: Altered States, Ordinary Miracles* (New York: PublicAffairs, 2009), 451.

34. Again, by putting the burden of responsibility back on the shoulders of those who want to be heads of state, sovereignty promises to do a better job of correcting the imbalance between corrupt, inept, and/or repressive regimes and the populations they abuse or marginalize than anything activists have tried thus far. For instance, have sanctions had any impact on the junta's behavior in Myanmar? Did they have any impact on Saddam Hussein? Did they ever, really, chasten Fidel Castro?

35. Where the marriage between nation and state is not as firm as it could or should be, sovereignty should help. Where it is already strong, nothing but sovereignty is likely to be acceptable—at least to most people. Ironically,

members of the elite *might* be willing to trade away certain sovereign prerogatives for what they regard as greater collective security or because they
believe this is the morally preferable thing to do. But we would wager *most*
Americans aren't the least bit interested in becoming less American—any
more than most Russians, Chinese, or Indians, etc. are interested in becoming less themselves.

36. This is something that no less a Democrat than President John F. Kennedy
    both recognized and intoned. In *Counselor*, Ted Sorenson writes,

    > JFK and I had agreed that Woodrow Wilson's call "to make the world
    > safe for democracy"—which sounded like imposing our system on
    > mankind, exactly what he did not want the Communists to do with
    > their system—should be changed to "making the world safe for
    > diversity," thereby envisioning the day when each country, includ-
    > ing those within the Communist orbit, would be free to choose its
    > own system. (*Counselor: A Life at the Edge of History* [New York:
    > HarperCollins, 2008], 327)

37. Perhaps not surprisingly, Margaret Mead also makes much of diversity in
    her 1942 book, *And Keep Your Powder Dry* (New York: William Morrow and
    Company). She likewise argues for Americans to be far more realistic about
    their national character. But the goal she has in mind is 180 degrees different
    from that presented in this book. Here is what she writes in the "Preface from
    England—1943" to explain why she wrote her book: "It was written with a
    profound faith in the strengths of my own people and in a belief—a belief
    which will find an echo, if I am not mistaken, in every British mind—that
    every nation does best to cultivate its strengths and watch warily over its
    weaknesses, denying neither, accepting both."

    So far, so good—she could join us as a coauthor. But then, she goes on:

    > It was written in the belief that only by each people develop-
    > ing their separate genius to the full as they cooperate more and
    > more with each other can a culture develop which will take all
    > these themes, not only those from Britain, the United States and the
    > Dominions, but from China and Russia, from France and Burma,
    > from India and Italy, from Yugoslavia and Japan and Germany, from
    > the glory that was Greece and the future dream of an ordered world
    > society of peoples, in which each may stand in his own appointed
    > place and find it good. (xxiii–xxiv)

    By an "ordered world society," Mead envisions "the organization of the
    whole human family into one orderly unit" (234). The Sovereignty Solution
    takes the opposite view. We believe order is far easier to achieve by using the
    diversity Mead identifies "to each his own" ends instead. For an argument

that accords with ours and implicitly tilts at Mead's, see Jeremy Rabkin, *Law Without Nations? Why Constitutional Government Requires Sovereign States* (Princeton, NJ: Princeton University Press, 2005).

Chapter 7

1. Eugene Goltz, Daryl Press, and Harvey Sapolsky, "Come Home, America," 5. For more on this theme:

   > Aside from the disaster in Vietnam, the United States has been a reasonably good Asian cop. But how long can it continue to play that role? The longer this postwar arrangement goes on, the longer it will take the East Asian powers to manage their own security responsibly. The same can be said of the Europeans, as became painfully clear in the Balkan conflicts. (Ian Buruma, "After America: Is the West Being Overtaken by the Rest?" *New Yorker*, April 21, 2008, 130)

2. Stephen Ambrose, *Eisenhower*, 495.

3. Chester Bowles, *Promises to Keep*, 580. Bowles was twice ambassador to India, a former New Dealer, and governor of Connecticut.

4. Owen Harries, "Power, Morality, and Foreign Policy," 611.

5. For further corroboration here is something else the British realized (by way of India):

   > A Resident was posted to advise the various Hindu maharajahs or Muslim nawabs, but as the Oxford scholar Sidney Owens found in the 1850s, "the native Prince, being guaranteed in the possession of his dominion but deprived of so many attributes of sovereignty, sinks in his own esteem, and loses that stimulus to good government which is supplied by the fear of rebellion and deposition. He becomes a *soi fainéant*, a sensualist, an extortionist miser, or a careless and lax ruler." Karl Meyer and Shareen Blair Brysac, *Kingmakers: The Invention of the Middle East* (W. W. Norton, 2008), 415.

6. Interestingly enough, Eisenhower was a major advocate of foreign aid. According to Stephen Ambrose,

   > foreign aid represented America's "best investment." It helped keep down the cost of the American military establishment and provided consuming power in recipient nations. . . . It was a program that, to the President, was so obviously good for America that he could not understand how anyone could be opposed. But opposed Congress was, and his virtual one-man attempt to push through an adequate foreign-aid program failed. (*Eisenhower*, 438)

No doubt Eisenhower's instincts were correct for the 1950s, when countries throughout Africa, Asia, and the Middle East were receiving their independence. Indeed, Paul Collier's argument in *The Bottom Billion: Why the Poorest Countries Are Failing and What Can Be Done About It* (New York: Oxford University Press, 2007) is almost Eisenhoweresque. Unfortunately, in the fifty plus years since Eisenhower was president and most developing countries earned their independence, corruption has become so entrenched that it *is* the circuitry. There are no viable workarounds aid can assist.

7. Bob Davis, "World Bank, UN Set Plan for Poor Nations," *Wall Street Journal*, September 18, 2007.

8. Bambang Harymurti, "Corruption Fighter," *Wall Street Journal*, May 14, 2007.

9. Arvind Sumbramanian, "A Farewell to Alms," *Wall Street Journal*, August 22, 2007.

10. Worth noting are how many of the arguments used to achieve welfare reform in this country apply to foreign aid (read: foreign aid welfare) abroad.

11. James Traub, "Can Pakistan Be Governed?", *The New York Times Magazine* (April 5, 2009), 48.

12. "Somalia: The World's Most Utterly Failed State," *The Economist*, October 4, 2008.

13. Here is the March 20, 2010, *The Economist* describing a World Food Program report: "The report says that systematic collusion between local WFP staffers, Islamist militants and food transporters has led to the diversion of up to half of the food it ships to Somalia, with some of it going to jihadists" (52).

14. Dambisa Moyo, "Why Foreign Aid Is Hurting Africa," *Wall Street Journal*, March 21–22, 2009.

15. We can't say it any better than this:

> With intellectual humility, Mr. [Simon] Johnson, a professor of Massachusetts Institute of Technology's Sloan School of Management, faced a roomful of peers at the annual meeting of the American Economics Association last weekend and said, "Public health had the germ theory of disease. Economics has made great progress, but it's still waiting for its 'germ theory of disease.'" That probably overstates the challenges remaining to public-health warriors—avian flu, AIDS/HIV, malaria and all—but not the shortcomings of economic understanding of what poor countries should do to achieve sustained growth. (David Wessel, "Why Economists Are Still Grasping for Cure to Global Poverty," *Wall Street Journal*, January 11, 2007)

16. Here, for instance, is the mayor of Tal Afar (Iraq) regarding the prospect of the 3rd ACR rotating out and being replaced by a new unit: "'When you leave, I will leave too,' the mayor threatened. 'What you are doing is an experiment, and it isn't right to experiment on people.'" Ricks, *Fiasco*, 424.

17. Iqbal Quadir, "Foreign Aid and Bad Government," *Wall Street Journal*, January 30, 2009.

18. "Rebuilding Haiti: Weighed Down by Disasters," *The Economist*, February 14, 2009.

19. Whether NGOs staying was a good thing is debatable: "By building a parallel state that is more powerful than Haiti's own government aid groups are ensuring Haiti never develops and remains dependent on charities." Jose De Cordoba, "Aid Spawns Backlash in Haiti," *Wall Street Journal* (November 13–14, 2010). Alternatively, "NGOs are like one-night stands. They will romance the country to get their fix right up until a more interesting disaster comes along." That is *The Economist* quoting Patrick Moynihan, the president of the Haitian Project (May 22, 2010).

20. Michael Oren, "Fatah Isn't the Answer," *Wall Street Journal*, June 20, 2007.

21. Hilton Root, *Alliance Curse: How America Lost the Third World*, 28.

22. As Leslie Gelb has said: "Power is power. It is neither hard nor soft nor smart nor dumb" (*Power Rules: How Common Sense Can Rescue American Foreign Policy* [New York: *Harper's*, 2009], xi). Thus, if you're going to wield it—wield it. Why disguise it?

23. Worth noting is that it wasn't a U.S. government-orchestrated or international embargo that weakened South Africa's economy and helped end apartheid, but a boycott. Boycotts have always been extremely useful instruments—as much for the spotlight they cast as the costs they exact. They would be perfectly allowable under the sovereignty rubric, and would likely be a decisive improvement over the mixed signals Washington sends.

24. To quote from Kuperman directly,

    the emerging norm of humanitarian military intervention, which is intended to prevent genocide and ethnic cleansing, perversely causes such violence through the dynamic of moral hazard. The norm, intended as a type of insurance policy against genocidal violence, unintentionally encourages disgruntled sub-state groups to rebel because they expect intervention to protect them from retaliation by the state. Actual intervention, however, is often too late or too feeble to prevent such retaliation. Thus, the norm causes some genocidal violence that otherwise would not occur. (Alan Kuperman, "Suicidal

Rebellions and the Moral Hazard of Humanitarian Intervention," *Ethnopolitics* 4, no. 2 [June 2005]: 149)

25. Michael Abramowitz, "Unfulfilled Promises: U.S. Action on the Darfur Crisis Has Not Matched Bush's Impassioned Rhetoric," *Washington Post National Weekly Edition*, November 5–11, 2007.

26. Here is what Alan Kuperman wrote about Darfur in 2006: "The rebels, much weaker than the government, would logically have sued for peace long ago. Because of the Save Darfur movement, however, the rebels believe that the longer they *provoke* genocidal retaliation the more the West will pressure Sudan to hand them control of the region." "Strategic Victimhood in Sudan," *New York Times*, (May 31, 2006) emphasis ours.

27. In many African countries, most expatriates traveling on behalf of businesses, churches, or NGOs are likewise met by expediters. It is usually only errant graduate students and world travelers who have to pass through airport gauntlets on their own.

28. This is not to suggest that corporations or private ventures should not, or could not, invest in building infrastructure—railroads, port facilities, etc. But, as will be made clear in the next few pages, businesses and shareholders would assume all the risk—not the U.S. government or taxpayers.

29. While it may have been true in the 1960s that countries like Zambia and Zaire had fewer than two dozen university graduates at independence, this is hardly true any more. Consider, for instance, this anecdote from the oil fields of Chad:

> "People hide their degrees out of fear the bosses would be afraid of your level," says a Chadian Exxon radio operator who has a master's degree in English and French literature. "When they saw the guys had master's degrees, they felt they couldn't talk like before." Of the sixteen hundred Chadians who are employed as guards in the oil fields, many are former students or teachers, though they're treated like foot soldiers by the former French paratroopers who run the guards. "We're the best-educated security force in the world," crows a former law student as he complains about working conditions. (Lisa Margonelli, *Oil on the Brain*, 189)

30. Or, for a slightly different variation on this theme, consider the following:

> Since 2003, about two-thirds of the nearly $30 billion in international aid to Afghanistan has been routed through foreign consultants, companies, and organizations hired by the US government and its allies to help Afghan officials write laws, set up banks, and other-

wise help run the country. The foreign advisers became so powerful and numerous that they constituted a de facto shadow government. . . . But Afghan officials have begun to push back, complaining the Americans are often overpaid, underqualified, and unfamiliar with the culture of the country. Even the best, most qualified advisers can sow mistrust because they answer to the US government or firms rather than to Afghan officials. The American practice of hiring its own as consultants also risks undercutting the Obama administration's message that Afghan president Hamid Karzai must root out corruption, some analysts say, because many Afghans view it as cronyism. (Farah Stockman, "Afghanistan Wary of US Plan to Send More Advisers," *Boston Globe*, November 12, 2009)

31. "Dancing with Despots: When Bankers Are Pimps," *The Economist*, March 14, 2009. According to the article,

Despite all the aid, investment and remittances that flow from richer economies to poorer ones, too much capital sloshes right back. That is one big reason why parts of Africa and Central Asia, for example, remain chronically poor, even—indeed, especially—where abundant natural resources could in theory be used to finance roads, schools and local enterprise.

The Economist goes on to note that in much of Asia "also blighted by graft, leaders more often keep ill-gotten gains in local accounts"—unlike in Africa and Central Asia.

"In 2003, the World Bank estimated that some 60 per cent of privately owned wealth, around $40 billion, was held outside the continent—double what Africa was receiving in aid at the time. Others put the figure as high as $150 billion." Richard Dowden, *Africa: Altered States*, 80.

32. In September 2005.

33. Consider the "true" costs of oil today. They can't be calculated.

In the years since 1988, the U.S. military presence in the Gulf has grown from nothing, to $50 billion a year for the 1990s, to a full-scale occupation costing more than $132 billion a year in 2005. By one estimate, the hidden costs of defense and import spending are the equivalent of an extra $5 for every gallon of imported gasoline, a cost that doesn't show up at American gas pumps. (Lisa Margonelli, *Oil on the Brain*, 203)

One can be certain that not even these figures take into account costs to, of, and for veterans' benefits related to service in the Middle East, never mind costs run up by other government agencies (e.g., the CIA, NSA, State Department, etc.).

34. "The locals say the oil companies do not repair them [the pipes], the oil companies say the locals cut the pipes to create a spill then claim compensation. It is more profitable than farming, say the oil companies." Richard Dowden, *Africa: Altered States*, 458–59.

35. Or, as Gerard Prunier comments, "In thirty-seven years of studying Africa I have seen more whites manipulated by blacks than the other way around" (138). He is especially cynical about the Kagame administration in Kigali: "Washington's game plan . . . has always been considered more of a resource to be tapped than an obligation to be obeyed." *Africa's World War: Congo, the Rwandan Genocide, and the Making of a Continental Catastrophe* (New York: Oxford University Press, 2009), 139.

36. In October 2010 there were violent clashes between Zambians and Chinese mine supervisors: "Like other impoverished governments in sub-Saharan Africa, Zambian officials have welcomed Chinese companies and their foreign currency. But local miners have for years protested what they say are insufficient wages and unsafe working conditions at Chinese-run mines. That has led to clashes between miners and their supervisors. Zambia's lead opposition party, the Patriotic Front, has charged the government with allowing Chinese investors to operate above the law." Nicholas Bariyo and Sarah Childress, "Zambians Riot After Miners Are Shot," *Wall Street Journal* (October 18, 2010). Substitute other commodities for copper, and other countries for Zambia, and one finds similar tensions.

37. Of course, as we pointed out earlier, church and state are not exactly separate in the United States; our orientation remains very Protestant. But—no single denomination is allowed to dominate. Along these lines, imagine if no economic interest were considered more dominant than another, which none should be since we are a country full of competing business interests.

38. "Since 2002, the dollar has lost about a third of its value compared with other currencies. That doesn't sound good—and it's not, if you're a Japanese exporter or an American tourist. But it is potentially great news for American workers." Who gains from a falling dollar? According to the *New York Times* Investors, nations rich with resources, American industry, and Chinese industry. Who loses from a falling dollar? China's central bank, other foreign industry, and other central banks. Bill Marsh, "Winners and Losers as the Dollar Falls," *New York Times* (December 6, 2009).

Or, as the *Wall Street Journal* notes, "By making U.S. exports cheaper, a weaker dollar could help the U.S. trade deficit continue to shrink. But at the same time, it contributes to the rise in commodities prices, which are often priced in U.S. dollars." Jon Hilsenrath and Mark Gongloff, "U.S. Stands By as Dollar Falls: Traders Question Commitment to Strong Greenback; Asian Central Banks Intervene," *Wall Street Journal,* October 9, 2009.

39. Worth noting too is that even when the aim is to protect Americans from foreign competition,

> international trade today is no longer a competition between our producers and their producers. It is more appropriately characterized as a competition between entities that increasingly defy national identification. Dramatic increases in cross-border investment and the proliferation of transnational production and supply chains have blurred any meaningful distinctions between our producers and their [foreign] producers. Very often, they are we and we are they, working collaboratively toward the same objectives. Daniel Ikenson, "Made on Earth: How Global Economic Integration Renders Trade Policy Obsolete," Trade Policy Analysis No. 42, Cato Institute (December 2, 2009) 14.

40. If all Americans signed waivers acknowledging this *before* they traveled, then all Americans would be living up to those twin principles of choice and responsibility, the very same principles we expect everyone else in a Sovereignty Rules world to adhere to.

Canada has apparently enacted a blanket variant of this: "in the future, if Canadians are convicted by due process in a democratic country, the government won't request their repatriation." "Canada: Prisoners of Ambiguity," *The Economist* (May 24, 2008).

Unfortunately, to our sovereignty way of thinking, Canada's approach may create more problems than it solves. For instance, what counts as a "democratic" country and who gets to determine this? As Amanda Cumberland, of Fair Trials International told *The Economist,* Canada is not alone in picking and choosing which of its citizens to help. More to the point, "unless governments explain their policy clearly, they raise suspicions that their actions are determined by media interest, politics or ideology."

This is why requiring all Americans to sign waivers before traveling abroad would underscore the overarching sovereignty message: break the law somewhere else at your own risk.

41. This is also why we agree with the initial part of Christopher Layne's analysis that "there is no single, objectively 'true' national interest." What Layne goes on to say, however, is just what the Sovereignty Solution tilts against—

> Thinking in terms of national interest improves the quality of statecraft by forcing decision makers to ask the right questions—about the relations of ends to means, about what is necessary versus what

merely is desirable—when they formulate grand strategy. Applied to grand strategy, the concept of national interest reminds policy-makers . . . that they must "be calculators instead of crusaders." (*The Peace of Illusions: American Grand Strategy from 1940 to the Present* [Ithaca, NY: Cornell University Press, 2007], 203)

The Sovereignty argument is that policymakers need not be calculators and should *not* be crusaders. By applying sovereignty principles—and the demand-response-reaction framework to international relations—the only calculations needed to match ways and means to literal (and therefore known) ends is the "end" of those who attacked us.

42. Certain governments might initially *want* to refuse the no-strings delivery of American assistance. But, over time, the no-strings nature of our assistance would make it extremely difficult for them to afford to reject it.

43. For example, see the 1999 WGBH *Frontline* episode "Triumph of Evil."

44. Which is not to suggest that India didn't also have other reasons for wanting to see Pakistan divided in two.

45. Celia Dugger, "Ending Famine, Simply by Ignoring the Experts," *New York Times*, December 2, 2007.

46. Of course, every country would have had multiple agendas. For some heads of state, the free-for-all in DRC/Zaire enabled them to stamp out opponents who had long used DRC/Zaire as a sanctuary. But, by way of illustrating the broader point,

> Three states involved in the war—Namibia, Chad, and Zimbabwe—had few reasons to feel directly threatened by the situation in Congo. Yet all three sent troops to back Kabila's regime, despite not sharing borders with Congo. Their motives for intervening, therefore, must have laid [*sic*] elsewhere. Namibia's motivations are unclear. While the government claimed to be enraged by Rwanda's and Uganda's violation of DRC sovereignty, the political opposition accused the Namibian president of sending troops into Congo to defend his family's mining interests there. The case of Chad is also ambiguous, but there are two possible explanations for its troop deployments. First, Chad supposedly received financial assistance from Libyan President Muammar Gaddhafi, who was eager to exert his influence in sub-Saharan Africa. Second, Chad might have been interested in the gold mines of northern Congo. Zimbabwe, on the other hand, had three explicit reasons for intervening in the DRC, all having to do with opportunism. (Boaz Atzili, "When Good Fences Make Bad Neighbors: Fixed Borders, State Weakness, and International Conflict," *International Security* 31, no. 3 [Winter 2006/07]: 165)

Or, as Gayle Smith, David Sullivan, and Andrew Sweet note, "These countries' involvement, motivated in large measure by a desire to profit from Congo's natural resources, has had ripple effects across the continent. Zimbabwe's intervention, for example, allowed Robert Mugabe's government to stay afloat when the state coffers were empty" ("The Price of Prevention: Getting Ahead of Crises," The Sustainable Security Series from the Center for American Progress, November 2008, http://www.americanprogress.org/issues/2008/11/pdf/sustainable_security4.pdf, 8).

47. Mukoma Wa Ngugi, "Troubled African Democracies," April 19, 2008, accessed May 1, 2008, http://www.zcommunications.org/znet/viewArticlePrint/17190.

Chapter 8

1. Another point worth keeping in mind is that despite the catchiness of the terms "de-territorialized" or "addressless terrorism," all humans reside and sleep somewhere, even if they change their location every night.

2. "Cluster Weapons: Collateral Damage," *The Economist* (December 13, 2008(. It seems odd that anything so toothless should be considered a model, but nonetheless, "the 'Ottawa process' that recently produced effective international bans on antipersonnel land mines and cluster munitions may be the future model. That process involves like-minded NGOs banding together to create single-issue treaties to be joined by any interested state, thereby avoiding parliamentary and diplomatic logjams too often seen in Geneva-based negotiations. The Ottawa process also subverts the objections of militarily powerful Western nations that may have reason to cling to the jus in bello status quo. We are likely to see its more frequent use." Or so predicts Gary Solis in Scott Horton, *The Law of Armed Conflict: Six Questions for Gary Solis*, accessed April 27, 2010, http://harpers.org/archive/2010/04/hbc-900006912.

3. Some might argue that broad participation paves the way to greater interoperability across militaries. But surely a better time and place for attempting enhanced interoperability is via joint exercises—not in real world wars.

4. Thomas Wright, "On Reforming the International Order," *Policy Analysis Brief* (The Stanley Foundation, February 2009), 4.

5. There is, of course, another problem with coalitions of the willing: "Coalitions of the willing tend to leave the unwilling bristling." Roger Cohen, "For Europe, a Moment to Ponder," *New York Times* (March 25, 2007).

6. Tad Galen Carpenter, "NATO at 60: A Hollow Alliance," *Policy Analysis*, no. 635 (March 30, 2009): 2.

7. Craig Nelson, *Thomas Paine: Enlightenment, Revolution, and the Birth of Modern Nations* (New York: Penguin, 2007), 112.

8. John Lewis Gaddis, *Surprise, Security, and the American Experience* (Cambridge: Harvard University Press, 2004), 23.

9. Department of Defense, *Joint Publication 1-02, DOD Dictionary of Military and Associated Terms (2006)*, accessed December 18, 2006, http://www.dtic. mil/doctrine/jel/doddict/data/a/index.html.

10. Lawrence Freedman, "NATO at Sixty: Power and War," *World Today* 65, no. 4 (April 2009): 16.

11. "Political honor society" is Ted Galen Carpenter's term. See "NATO at 60: A Hollow Alliance," CATO Institute's *Policy Analysis* no. 635 (March 30, 2009): 1.

    As Richard Betts puts it,

    > The organization has always been, and continues to be, both a political and military organization, but the priorities are now reversed. NATO has become a political club more than the military alliance it was originally designed to be. The difference between a club and an alliance is that a club is inward-looking, oriented to enjoying association and common bonds, while an alliance is outward-looking, subordinating internal relationships to the business of confronting common threats. ("U.S. National Security Strategy: Lenses and Landmarks," 28)

12. David Barno, Lt. Gen. (ret.), Senate Armed Services Committee Testimony, February 26, 2009, 2.

13. For instance Pakistani prime minister Yousuf Raza Gilani, whose first White House visit since winning office in February 2008 inspired President Bush to describe Pakistan as "a strong ally and a vibrant democracy." AP, "Bush Proclaims Pakistan a Strong Ally," *Monterey County Herald* (July 29, 2008).

14. Of course, it didn't hurt to have Anglophile Americans, like FDR, or Anglo-Americans like Winston Churchill.

15. Interestingly, "When America was attacked in September 2001, NATO formally invoked Article 5 for the first time. But the Bush administration did not want to be encumbered by a formal alliance. Instead it cherry-picked the allied assets it needed to help topple the Taliban." *The Economist* (March 28, 2009). This is one reason that Norwegian SEALs, among others, serve in land-locked Afghanistan.

16. According to Akhil Reed Amar, it was to be the Senate because "composed of statesmen chosen for their wisdom by state legislatures, the Senate could check a hasty or corrupt president and guard against proposals that might result in the imprudent creation of international obligations or the needless displacement of state law." *America's Constitution: A Biography* (New York: Random House, 2006), 190.

17. Some are already suggesting this, though for a slightly different set of reasons than we do:

    > Thanks to decades of global efforts, the international system has most of the rules it needs in the areas of human rights, terrorism, crime and nonproliferation. What's more important is for individual governments to muster the will to enforce them. Treaties still have their uses, but they should be reserved for rare cases, like the creation of a mutual defense pact or perhaps President Obama's vision for the elimination of nuclear weapons. In most circumstances, the bright light of national laws will work just fine. (James Rubin, "Farewell to the Age of the Treaty," *New York Times*, November 21, 2010)

18. Leslie Gelb, *Power Rules*, 162.

19. G. John Ikenberry and Anne-Marie Slaughter, *Forging a World*, 10.

20. Anatol Lieven and John Hulsman, *Ethical Realism*, 122.

21. Fukuyama and Ikenberry, "Report of the Working Group on Grand Strategic Choices," Princeton Project, 5.

22. One could write reams about all the various proposals. Better still would be to map the various propositions—for G-20s, concerts of democracies, Global Freedom Coalitions, etc.—as a set of Venn diagrams and then superimpose these on a world map to determine how they might actually work, either geopolitically or logistically.

    Meanwhile, here may be the ultimate "all things to all multilateralists" formulation:

    > Should all institutions be open to all states, should states be forced to choose between competing models, or should the United States oppose multilateralism and focus solely on strengthening bilateral alliances? The answer probably lies in a combination of bilateral, mini-lateral, and multi-lateral structures that preserves the key US role in the region but also builds confidence between China and its neighbors [for example]. In order to adhere to the principle articulated above [that no action be taken that may detrimentally affect the interests of other states] it is important that this institution building not lead to the emergence of competing cooperative blocs; therefore it would help if the institutions overlapped, with all major countries cooperating with every one of their neighbors in at least one forum on one issue even if they are excluded from other forums on different issues. As long as the overall structure is inclusive, major powers should not fear not being a part of every organization. Thomas Wright, "On Reforming the International Order," Policy Analysis Brief, The Stanley Foundation (February 2009), 7.

What is neat about this—beyond what it suggests in terms of Venn diagrams—is that it is much more egalitarian than most other propositions we have reviewed. In effect, every country would become a Gulliver in Lilliput. Unfortunately, in practice it is hard to imagine that such webs won't then feel like Lilliputian constraints.

23. Clearly there are some people who don't take quite as dim a view as we do of what such groups have accomplished.

24. Of course, under the current dispensation policymakers sometimes turn to multilateral negotiations and collective deliberation on purpose, so that they don't *have* to act. The UN Security Council debated an intervention in Rwanda until 800,000 people were dead. The Sovereignty Solution would do away with charades like this, too.

25. Christopher Hemmer, "Grand Strategy for the Next Administration," *Orbis* (Summer 2007): 457.

26. "The European Union and Georgia: Treaty Gamesmanship," *The Economist*, August 23, 2008.

27. Or, as Shannon O'Neil writes, "When it comes to the gun trade, U.S. law prohibits the sale of weapons to foreign nationals or 'straw buyers,' who use their clean criminal records to buys [*sic*] arms for others. It also forbids the unlicensed export of guns to Mexico. Nevertheless, over 90 percent of the guns seized in Mexico and traced are found to have come from the United States.... Reducing the tools of violence in Mexico is a first step in addressing U.S. responsibility." "The Real War in Mexico: How Democracy Can Defeat the Drug Cartels," *Foreign Affairs*, 88 (July/August 2009): 70.

28. Ironically, if any country should be making demands under the Sovereignty Solution, it is Mexico—making demands of us. For economic reasons the Mexican government cannot say to the United States right now, "enforce your border, stop the demand for drugs, stop the free flow of automatic weapons." Nor, under sovereignty, could it do so unless—like us—it made a good-faith effort to rein in its own citizens first. Even then, it is unlikely Mexico would ever say to the United States "do these things, or else." Mexico can't militarily afford the "or else." Though also, under sovereignty, Mexico shouldn't have to make demands we won't meet since we, for our part, would already be enforcing our southern border—ideally, in tandem *with* Mexico. Or, if Mexico views its sovereign obligations differently than we do and *doesn't* enforce its northern border to our satisfaction, then that would be all the more reason for us to be more (rather than less) vigilant about both sides of the border from our side of the Rio Grande.

29. Tighter professional linkages among police departments, intelligence services, militaries, treasury ministries, etc. are absolutely essential to cutting

"trans" from "national" when it comes to transnational threats. Investigative work done to track, monitor, and chase down leads, paper trails, electronic transfers, and so on is clearly essential both to preserve accountability and to prove to others that your government is either not guilty—or *is* being framed.

30. Ties between our respective security professionals may well be extremely close. This was certainly the case among French and American counterterrorism specialists even when French and American politicians were trading jibes prior to the Iraq War. However if no one knows about these professional linkages except those "in the know," politicians, pundits, and others can continue to hurl insults—with cumulatively ill effects.

31. Or, will Georgians. Tellingly, in the case of U.S.-Georgian relations there appear to have been crossed signals leading to exactly the kind of moral hazard Alan Kuperman identifies (see previous chapter)—something that an actual alliance could have mitigated. Or, better yet, if we had a system in which alliances clearly meant certain things and "no alliance" meant equally clear things, no such misunderstandings would have occurred.

Unfortunately, in the case of the United States not coming to Georgia's assistance,

> President Bush lionized Mr. Saakahsvili as a model for democracy in the region to a point that the Georgian leader may have held unrealistic expectations about the amount of support he might receive from the U.S. and the West. These officials also point to a lack of clarity governing the U.S.-Georgia military relationship, which was increasingly close but not yet a formal alliance. About 130 American military trainers have been stationed in Georgia to train local troops, and Tbilisi deployed 2,000 soldiers in Iraq before this month's fighting with Russia forced them home. But the U.S. wasn't formally committed to protecting Georgia against outside aggression." (Jay Solomon and Mary Jacoby, "U.S. Criticized on Strategic Ties to Georgia: American Officials Asked Saakashvili to Avoid Conflict," *Wall Street Journal,* August 12, 2008)

It is actually worth quoting from the next paragraph of the *Wall Street Journal* story as well, in which the reporters' sources say that "Secretary of State Condoleezza Rice seemed so preoccupied with Iraq, Iran and the Arab-Israeli conflict that she didn't have time to fashion an effective response to Russia's muscle-flexing on its borders"—just to remind readers that in a Sovereignty Rules world Georgia would not be an issue to which the United States should have responded unless we already had a treaty with Georgia or Russia, or unless we were attacked. The same would hold for our relations with countries in the Middle East, so Secretary of State Rice would not have been distracted by them in the same ways or for the same reasons the story suggests she was.

32. Here is one of Pakistan's former defense secretaries talking (in late 2007 or early 2008) about "the undercurrents of mistrust" among the governments of Pakistan, Afghanistan, and the United States: "I think we did not have a common plan because we did not have common objectives. You can't have partners who are suspicious of each other. The Americans are suspicious of us. We are suspicious of the Americans. The Afghans are suspicious of us. We are suspicious of the Afghans," quoted by Steve Coll in "Letter from Pakistan: Time Bomb," *New Yorker*, January 28, 2008.

    Or, as Ryan Crocker, former ambassador to Pakistan (2004–7) and Iraq (2007–9) has written, "Never in Pakistan's six decades of existence has the U.S. sustained a long-term, strategic commitment to the country." "Pakistan is Not America's Enemy," *Wall Street Journal* (October 12, 2010).

33. Another problem with being at cross-purposes internally is that shrewd foreign governments can work our seams. This has been a real problem in a number of embassies since the advent of the war on terrorism. The number of U.S. agencies and operatives working abroad has not only exploded, but (for security reasons) not all of them always let each other know what they are doing. In contrast, countries with good internal intelligence agencies (e.g., most one-party states) often do know what Americans in their country are up to.

34. Frank Gardner, *Blood & Sand: Life, Death and Survival in an Age of Global Terror* (London: Bantam Press, 2006), 281.

35. Craig Whitlock, "The Collapse of the Cole Case: U.S. Efforts Are Frustrated by the Release of Bombing Plotters in Yemen," *Washington Post National Weekly Edition*, May 12–18, 2008.

36. As of this writing, the United States is expanding its presence in Yemen (again).

37. Edward Lansdale, *In the Midst of Wars: An American's Mission to Southeast Asia*, 2nd ed. (New York: Fordham University Press, 1991).

Chapter 9

1. This is an argument made by Martin Van Creveld in *The Rise and Decline of the State* (Cambridge: Cambridge University Press, 1999); by Anna Simons, "The Death of Conquest," *National Interest* (Spring 2003); and by Richard Betts, "The Trouble with Strategy: Bridging Policy and Operations," *Joint Forces Quarterly* (Autumn 2001–Winter 2002). Here is Betts: "Unless one

completely conquers an enemy's territory, extinguishes its government, and rules directly as an occupying power, it is not a straightforward matter to translate operational success into desired enemy behavior in the postwar world" (25).

2. Kishore Mahubani minces no words: "the twentieth century showed that no country welcomes foreign invaders. The notion that any Islamic nation would approve of Western military boots on its soil was ridiculous." "The Case against the West," 112.

3. Of course much of the resistance also had to do with Iraqis jockeying against each other, using us as their tool or foil.

4. "The goal should be to isolate extremists from the communities in which they live." David Kilcullen and Andrew Exum, "Death From Above, Outrage Down Below," *New York Times*, May 17, 2009.

5. One can go back in history and find numerous striking examples of prisoner abuse leading to public outrage once it has been exposed. For instance abuse at Hola prison in Kenya shocked the British public during Mau Mau. Or, for the effect graphic images and accounts have had, consider the My Lai massacre. In terms of the radicalizing effect recent images and accounts have had in this country, the "ambush at Ruby Ridge" and Waco come to mind. And both continue to be used to draw recruits into the militia movement in the United States.

6. One can't help but wonder how much sense it makes, and what (or whose) purposes it serves for us to disperse our detainees from Guantanamo to places like Palau and Bermuda.

7. Interestingly we did something like this during the second Battle of Fallujah. "The battle to retake that city . . . was a once-and-for-all attack to send a message to the rest of the cities in the Sunni Triangle: You don't have to like the Americans, but if you tolerate the presence of the insurgents, this will be your fate." Ricks, *Fiasco*, 398. Among the arguments this book is making is that the United States should have done this with the First Battle of Fallujah. The United States should always apply overwhelming force the first time—so that there is no desire among people on the ground for a second time.

8. One premise behind the sovereignty argument is that while hollow threats and insincere gestures may have been useful for purposes of diplomacy in the past, both smack too much of hypocrisy today.

9. "Is Strategy an Illusion?," 29.

10. Ambrose, *Eisenhower*, 145.

11. Taken from the course syllabus for "Wicked Problems," taught by Professor Nancy Roberts, Naval Postgraduate School (2008).

12. Rupert Smith, *The Utility of Force*, 292.

For a different description of the conundrum, consider the following:

> Escalation management is inherently difficult with nonstate actors and is even more so with global jihadists. There are several reasons for this, not the least of which is that escalation management depends largely on deterrence. Jihadists are difficult to deter because it is difficult to make threats of punishment credible against elusive individuals and groups that reject the established order. Consequently, traditional two-player escalation management is disabled in the struggle with radical Islam, and limiting costs in this long-term conflict will require constraining and, ideally, eliminating the jihadists' ability to escalate the fight but doing so in ways that minimize the escalatory effects that U.S. and jihadist actions have on other actors in the environment. (Forrest Morgan et al., "Dangerous Thresholds: Managing Escalation in the 21st Century," RAND Project Air Force, 2008, xix).

In other words, do harm but don't do harm; accept the environment as it is even though this permits the jihadists to be elusive. . . . One can go through this or any one of a number of other reports sentence by sentence and, in trying to figure out how to apply what is being recommended, conclude that the advice is to play by the jihadists' rules because . . . Because why? Unfortunately, no one asks "why?"

Meanwhile, there can be no escalation risks or escalation management to have to worry about if you go all out from the outset.

13. In assessing the Gaza War fought between Hamas and Israel (in late 2008– early 2009), Anthony Cordesman points out that

> both sides suffered by prolonging the war, which became steadily more political with time. Both faced the problem that civilians were a weapon of war that they could potentially exploit but simultaneously threatened their position. Both were locked into a position very similar to the one they faced before Hamas began its rocket attacks and Israel began to retaliate. "Victory" of any kind was victory in winning the ceasefire and its aftermath; not the tactical or military outcomes that would not fundamentally change the military position and capabilities of either side. ("The 'Gaza War': A Strategic Analysis," 33–34)

Such inconclusiveness is among the things that lead others to conclude that "there is no such thing as winning in this new kind of war." Ariel Siegelman, "From Lebanon to Gaza: A New Kind of War," U.S. Army and Marine Corps Counterinsurgency Center COIN Colloquium (2009), 8.

14. When Special Forces (SF) officers say they have no interest in going back to Afghanistan to "eat more moon dust" that is symptomatic of a major problem. Some might dismiss this attitude as a leadership issue, which is often how officers respond to anything having to do with morale. But, Afghanistan—initially—represented every SF solder's ideal: a just war in a rugged environment in which the forces of good (us) would fight alongside brave locals against a determined foe. It is viewed as anything but that by many now.

15. This is drawn from a speech given by Michele Flournoy, the under secretary for policy for the Department of Defense, "Rebalancing the Force: Major Issues for QDR 2010," delivered April 29, 2009, at CSIS.

16. Not surprisingly this was also the criticism leveled at new doctrine the Israeli Defense Forces employed against Hezbollah in 2006. As Matt Matthews reports, "the language and style incorporated in the doctrine proved nearly incomprehensible to many officers within the IDF." "We Were Caught Unprepared: The 2006 Hezbollah-Israeli War," The Long War Series Occasional Paper 26 (Leavenworth, KS: Combat Studies Institute Press, 2008), 64. Consequently, they couldn't carry it out.

17. Whether Leslie Gelb exaggerates or not, his assessment is certainly in line with ours:

   > No other country can move fully modernized strike aircraft carriers to a region and threaten mayhem. The three U.S. carrier strike groups at one point deployed near the Gulf could alone destroy every significant military and economic target in Iran. The United States alone can find enemies almost anywhere, when they get careless, with drones or spy satellites, and can fire missiles to destroy them in their cars or hideouts, as they watch reruns of *Seinfeld*. We alone can destroy almost any country's capital and drive its leaders from power with conventional firepower in weeks. (*Power Rules*, 166)

   Martin Van Creveld says something similar regarding Israel's capabilities:

   > Israel's neighbors are centralized both demographically and politically . . . they tend to contain one or two cities which are far larger and symbolically more important than the rest. The destruction of these cities would be tantamount to the annihilation of their societies. . . . The experience of other countries since 1945 also shows that, to prevent the outbreak of war, the damage on both sides does not have to be symmetrical. (*Defending Israel*, 135)

18. In his questioning of conventional wisdom about "lessons learned" in the wake of Iraq—many of which, he argues, are based on misreadings of the facts—Charles Dunlap writes,

In order to work, a "shock and awe" strategy, whether it is air- or ground-centric, must impose real shock and awe. The truncated air attack and relatively quick land force capture of Baghdad imposed little of either. . . . While Iraq's armed forces may have been overcome, the Iraqi people felt no such effect. The rampant looting and theft that followed regime collapse demonstrated that many Iraqis, perhaps most, were in no way awed by the ground forces of the invading coalition. The aggressive energy of a society raised on totalitarianism had not yet been sapped. As a result, the malleability of a truly defeated nation ready for productive change did not exist in Iraq as it did in postwar Germany and Japan.

As he goes on to note,

exposing the repressed people to the spectacle of relentless disintegration of a feared totalitarian regime over an extended period can imprint observers with a profound appreciation of the power of the invader. What is more, enemy efforts to maintain the cohesion of regime forces—not to mention leadership cadres—become increasingly difficult amid the destruction. Collapsing dictatorships can begin to cannibalize their own leaders—at every level—and this may serve to decimate the ranks of those who otherwise may become key insurgents over the longer term. (Charles Dunlap, "Can Another 'Iraq' Be Prevented?," FPRI E-Notes, September 25, 2007)

Dunlap provocatively suggests that airpower may be a far more useful tool than critics are willing to admit—when used against combatants. He does not make quite the same argument Martin Van Creveld does about the deterrent value that inheres in applying decisive overwhelming force:

To put Mao on his head: You must refuse to admit a distinction between "active" fish and the "passive" sea in which they swim.

In other words, the true objective of your strike is not to kill people per se. Rather, it is to display your ruthlessness and your willingness to go to any lengths to achieve your objective—a war for hearts and minds, only by different means. Clausewitz once wrote that war is a moral and physical contest by means of the latter. The same is even more true of the massacre that accompanies a war: If you do it right, it may even prevent a war that has not yet broken out. It is therefore essential that careful consideration should be given to the means.

Forget about infantry, it is too slow; especially when it operates in urban terrain . . .

Airpower and missiles are much better and will save you from suffering casualties. In their case, the problem is that they are deployed from a distance; the victims, unable to see who is massacring them, will not be properly impressed by your determination. . . . If inflicting real damage is your objective, as it should be, then old-fashioned, heavy "dumb" iron bombs are much superior.

Everything considered . . . the weapon of choice should be artillery. . . . Unlike aircraft, they can fire nonstop for hours, even days, giving the target population no peace, shattering their nerves, and reducing their world to screaming chaos. (Martin Van Creveld, *The Changing Face of War*, 242–43)

Where we differ from Van Creveld is in the military aim. While we agree with him that deterrence is critical, we don't believe the point should ever be to purposely make an object lesson of another group of people. Under the sovereignty rubric, war would not be used to posture or to transmit signals. The United States would engage in it only after an attack and after another government (or local source of authority) refused to ensure that we cannot be attacked again. Whatever additional messages our actions might convey would be collateral; they should never be the purpose. Trying to fulfill multiple agendas, or killing multiple birds with one stone, takes us into the realm of trying to be clever. Trying to be clever flies in the face of needing to be clear.

19. Rupert Smith, *The Utility of Force*, 274.

20. This is also critically important to do to avoid falling into the trap George Kennan identifies:

I sometimes wonder whether in this respect a democracy is not uncomfortably similar to one of those prehistoric monsters with a body as long as this room and a brain the size of a pin: he lies there in his comfortable primeval mud and pays little attention to his environment. He is slow to wrath—in fact, you practically have to whack his tail off to make him aware that his interests are being disturbed; but, once he grasps this, he lays about him with such blind determination that he not only destroys his adversary but largely wrecks his native habitat. (Thompson, *The Hawk and the Dove*, 133)

21. As Paul Seabury and Angelo Codevilla, *War: Ends & Means*, go on to write: "the United States could choose to bomb any place in the country at any time. This was a potentially decisive advantage. . . . Nevertheless, the United States never even tried to use this superiority as part of a plan to defeat North Vietnam" (139).

22. Margaret Mead, *And Keep Your Powder Dry*, 215.

23. As noted by John Shelton Reed, "From Atlanta to the Sea," review of *Southern Storm* by Noah Andre Trudeau, *Wall Street Journal*, August 4, 2008.

24. Stephen Ambrose, *Eisenhower*, 562.

25. John Lewis Gaddis, *Strategies of Containment*, 247.

26. "Is Strategy an Illusion?," 30–31. Perhaps this shouldn't be so surprising since, as Strategic Air Force Com. Gen. Thomas S. Power is said to have told a Pentagon audience in 1964, "the task of the military in war was to kill human beings and destroy man-made objects," and to do it "in the quickest way possible." Gaddis goes on to describe Power saying, "It had been 'the moralists who don't want to kill'" that had given "Hitler his start and got us into the mess in Cuba and Vietnam." John Lewis Gaddis, *Strategies of Containment*, 249.

27. One Israeli's assessment of Israeli leaders' "lack of determination to win" seems instructive: "Many in Israel's top political and military echelons have convinced themselves that terrorism cannot be defeated by force, that to stop it one must compromise and accept some of its demands. But how do you 'compromise' with a terrorist organization sworn to destroy you?"

    As Daniel Doron goes on to argue,

    > Israel could achieve military victory by eliminating or incarcerating Hamas's leadership, not two or three a month (so that they are replaceable) but a few hundred at once. By breaking its command structure and its logistical apparatus, Hamas can be rendered inoperative.
    >
    > But for this to happen, Israel and Western democracies must treat the terrorists' mortal challenge as a war for survival, not as a series of skirmishes. And in war, you must fight to win, by all traditional means. ("Israel's No-Win Strategy," *Wall Street Journal*, March 8–9, 2008)

28. Jeremy Rabkin in Orin Judd et al., "Redefining Sovereignty," 8.

29. "In Lebanon, both the Israelis and the Syrians tried half-measures—arming proxies, mounting limited interventions, striking at selected targets—to no avail. America's own determination to stabilize Iraq on the cheap and postpone making hard decisions have made major elements of the disasters that have unfolded there since 2003." Daniel Byman and Kenneth Pollack, "Things Fall Apart: Containing the Spillover from an Iraqi Civil War," Analysis Paper Number 11 (The Brookings Institution, January 2007, xx).

30. Again, it is vital that countries align their own ends, ways, and means. That means no welfare from us—and military, education, and training assistance only if a struggling state agrees to our benchmarks.

31. This, in no small measure, is just one of the things that distinguishes the sovereignty approach from recent (or current) U.S. policy. According to Tom Ricks, "In the feel-good days after the fall of the Berlin Wall and before 9/11, and even for some time after, when the U.S. military was the armed wing of 'the sole superpower,' Pentagon officials liked to talk about 'rapid decisive operations.'" Apparently even Secretary of Defense Rumsfeld bought into such an approach. Through "the devastating cumulative effect of 'dominant maneuver, precision engagement and information operations' . . . we would possess [and here Ricks quotes Secretary Rumsfeld] the option for one massive counteroffensive to occupy an aggressor's capital and replace the regime." Ricks, *The Gamble: General David Petraeus and the American Military Adventure in Iraq, 2006–2008* (New York: Penguin Press, 2009), 160–61.

Worth reiterating: in a Sovereignty Rules world the United States does not replace regimes. Nor does it occupy.

Acknowledgments

This argument wouldn't exist without our fellow members from the 2006 Long Term Strategy seminar in Monterey: Joe Benson, Mark Davey, Eddie Kostelnik, Ned Mason, Scott (Joe) Peterson, Don Redd, Fred Renzi, and Cameron Sellers. All were instrumental. Don Redd was especially vital to the cause throughout. We happily share credit with them, while all blame—for errors, faulty thinking, political insensitivity—belongs to us.

This argument wouldn't exist had Andrew W. Marshall not offered his support for the idea of such a seminar in the first place.

We owe a particular debt to Bob Andrews who reacted so positively to our earliest briefing that this book is as much his doing as anyone's. Thanks to Patrick Parker for trying to help us push the argument in Washington, to Adam Garfinkle for publishing the earliest version, and to Chip Franck for overseeing Joe, Don, and Duane's master's degree thesis at NPS. Andrew May, Steve Rosen, Samantha Ravich, Jackie Newmyer, and Adam Garfinkle helped us kick start the project. All were gracious whenever we bombarded them with crude early versions of the manuscript. Other people we pestered with not-ready-for-primetime drafts, who nonetheless responded with critical advice, include Michael Noonan, Jim Schlesinger, and Adam Bellow.

We met Jakub Grygiel through the pages of *The American Interest*. His comments and support throughout have been invaluable. Michael Freeman, Brent Lindeman, and Brad Burris likewise made it through early drafts, for which we are grateful. Randy Burkett graciously read a final draft in record time.

We benefited from being able to "test" the argument at SAIS thanks to Jakub; at Claremont McKenna thanks to Jenny Taw; and at the Australian Strategic Policy Institute in Canberra.

As for all Anna's students who didn't realize when they signed up for classes that they might have to hear about sovereignty—here's the book we promised years ago.

If only we had gone to Adam Kane at NIP at the outset; Adam never hesitated. Jeanette Nakada deftly edited the text.

Finally, we come to those who have had to put up with us and our obsession from the outset: John Jordan, Leigh McGraw, Tom McGraw, and Pamela Lauchengco. We think it's fair to say that all our family members have wanted this book out as long as we have. As for the next generation who we hope will be the real beneficiaries: Katie, Tommy, and Sydney McGraw and Christian, Connor, Heather, and Ethan Lauchengco remind us daily of what is truly important—and that sometimes bedtime stories do indeed deserve precedence over national security strategy.

Index

adversaries and rivals: divisible America, benefits of divisiveness to, 19–20, 136; divisible America, exploitation of by, 4, 20–21, 27, 30–31, 155n3, 158–59nn23–25; Grand Strategy development, 11–13, 150n26; learning lessons from, 16, 153n45; nuclear devices and programs of, 52–53, 173–74nn4–6; preparations for attacks by, 18, 154nn51–52; shaping of environment by, 13–17; state-on-state warfare, 50–51; undermining of U.S. by, 19–20. *See also* non-state actors and groups

Afghanistan: air operations in, 141, 151n33; authorizations of force and declarations of war, 61–62; challenges faced by military in, 125; as flashpoint, 124; intelligence and cross-cultural awareness about, 35; international aid to, 197–98n30; Iran and U.S. operations in, 19–20; learning lessons from, 16; morale of soldiers serving in, 210n14; mujahidin, support for, 9–10, 148n10; NATO forces in, 108; Operation Enduring Freedom, 179n3; rules of engagement in, 185n36; Sovereignty Solution, use of in, 139–41; suicide bombings in, 13; U.S., relationship with, 207n32; violence in, 141

Africa, 14–15, 45, 92–93, 97–99, 198n31, 199n34. *See also specific countries*

agreements. *See* treaties, conventions, and agreements

al Qaeda. *See* Qaeda, al

alliances: coalitions of the willing, 106–7, 202n5; concept and definition of, 107–9; entanglements and disentanglements, 20, 95, 98–99, 107;

multilateral alliances, 110–14, 204–5nn22–24; relevance of, 105–6; security personnel, working relationships between, 114, 205–6nn29–30; treaties, conventions, and agreements, 105–6, 108–9, 139, 202n2, 204n17; twenty-first century alliances, 109–10, 204n17; U.S. commitments to, 106–7, 202n3

allies: commitment trap and U.S. vulnerability, 9; dependability of, 134; dependence on U.S. by, 89–90, 194n1; nation-building and stabilization operations, 18; protection with and from, 73; proxies and proxy heads of state, use of, 9–10, 68, 147–48n7, 148n10, 148–49nn13–14, 183–84n30, 213n29; relationships and agreements with, 108–9, 203nn13–16

arms merchants and trade, 58, 178n26, 183–84n30

Association of Southeast Asian Nations (ASEAN), 168n33

attachés, local knowledge of, 162–62n12

attributive deterrence, 173n4

authorizations of force and declarations of war, 61–62, 178–79n1

barbarianism, 66–67

Bosnia, 124, 176n20

Bout, Viktor, 178n26

Brzezinski, Zbigniew, 9–10

Bush, George W., 29, 42, 99, 147n1, 148n10, 174–75n10, 179–80n5, 203n15, 206–7n31

Chad, 42, 103–4, 176–77n21, 197n29, 201–2n46

Chechnya, 159–60n28

About the Authors

Anna Simons is a Professor of Defense Analysis at the Naval Postgraduate School. She previously taught anthropology at UCLA. She graduated from Harvard College, and earned her PhD in social anthropology from Harvard University. She is the author of *Networks of Dissolution: Somalia Undone* and *The Company They Keep: Life Inside the U.S. Army Special Forces.*

Joe McGraw is an active duty Special Forces officer with over 17 years in the US Army. He is married to Lt. Col. Leigh McGraw and father of three small children. He has served in combat with his Special Forces A-Team and his Special Forces Company, and has spent over 12 years with US Army Special Forces.

Duane Lauchengco received his commission into the Infantry from West Point and followed Airborne, Ranger, and Special Forces training with deployments to overseas combat zones as a Special Forces officer. Army life has kept him busy for the last 17 years, and his wife even busier with their four children.